Working with Domestic Violence and Abuse Across the Lifecourse

also in the Knowledge in Practice series

Safeguarding Adults Under the Care Act 2014
Understanding Good Practice
Edited by Adi Cooper OBE and Emily White
Foreword by Lyn Romeo
ISBN 978 1 78592 094 3
eISBN 978 1 78450 358 1

Safeguarding Adolescents
Risk, Resilience, Rights and Relationships
Edited by Dez Holmes
ISBN 978 1 78775 359 4
eISBN 978 1 78775 360 0

Working with Domestic Violence and Abuse Across the Lifecourse

Understanding Good Practice

Edited by
Ravi K. Thiara and **Lorraine Radford**

Foreword by Dez Holmes

Jessica Kingsley Publishers
London and Philadelphia

First published in Great Britain in 2021 by Jessica Kingsley Publishers
An Hachette Company

2

Copyright © Jessica Kingsley Publishers 2021
Foreword copyright © Dez Holmes 2021

Practice tip 3 on pp.214–215 reproduced with kind permission of Kate Iwi.

Front cover image sources: Tom Ham and Graham Morgan. The cover image
is for illustrative purposes only, and any person featuring is a model.

A CIP catalogue record for this title is available from the
British Library and the Library of Congress

ISBN 978 1 78592 404 0
eISBN 978 1 78450 758 9

Printed and bound by CPI Group (UK) Ltd, Croydon, CR0 4YY

Jessica Kingsley Publishers' policy is to use papers that are natural,
renewable and recyclable products and made from wood grown in
sustainable forests. The logging and manufacturing processes are expected
to conform to the environmental regulations of the country of origin.

Jessica Kingsley Publishers
Carmelite House
50 Victoria Embankment
London EC4Y 0DZ

www.jkp.com

Dedication

To Dr Gurdev Singh Purewal (Dev mammaji) for always being such an inspiration to me – your warmth, your love, your humility and your positivity will stay with us always.

To Emma, Abi and Jasmine.

Contents

Foreword

Dez Holmes, Director of Research in Practice

Despite significant progress in policy and practice, domestic violence and abuse continues to bring pain and trauma to the lives of too many people.

Advances in research and practice have enabled the evidence base to develop, and our understanding of domestic violence and abuse is ever evolving. We know that people of all ages and backgrounds can experience this pernicious form of harm, but we are paying closer attention to the complex interplay between domestic abuse, poverty and disadvantage. We know that domestic violence and abuse can manifest in a multitude of ways, and this varies according to our circumstances and our life stage, but we have much learning yet to do about how to develop a systemic response to people across their lifecourse.

At the time of writing, the nation is still coming to terms with the impact of COVID-19. There are serious concerns that domestic violence and abuse may have increased, particularly during lockdown, and may have been exacerbated by structural and financial inequalities, and mental health pressures. Against this backdrop, the Domestic Abuse Bill is soon to receive royal assent and be passed into law.

This book, therefore, offers a timely and pertinent contribution to national discourse. By adopting a lifecourse perspective, it challenges us to think deeply about the need for a whole-person response to domestic violence and abuse. Each chapter focuses on a different aspect or life stage, with attention given to the impact of domestic abuse on children, intimate partner violence between young people, and the experiences of older people. It also offers an intersectional perspective, focusing in on the experiences of victims/survivors with disabilities and those from Black and minority ethnic backgrounds, and considers the interplay between domestic abuse, mental ill health and substance misuse. Importantly, it does not shy away from exploring some of the most complex aspects of this field: working with perpetrators and understanding child-to-parent abuse.

This book challenges us to reflect critically on the siloed, fragmented way in which our response to domestic violence and abuse has evolved. It encourages us to reconsider established wisdom and inspires us to push for a more holistic, person-centred, boundary-spanning approach. An approach that reflects the complexity of human experience; an approach where professionals' efforts are shaped not by arbitrary service boundaries, but are instead fuelled by a common purpose and shared commitment to help people of all ages, from all walks of life, to be safe and supported.

While this book is richly evidence-informed, it is not intended just for research-minded readers. Any practitioner, manager or strategic leader looking to advance their knowledge will find something thought-provoking in this book. Any policy-maker will find constructive challenge and a call to take a lifecourse perspective. Any activists fighting for a more holistic approach will find affirmation and inspiration.

That many victims/survivors are able to speak out and even recover from the trauma of domestic abuse is a testament to their extraordinary courage. This book invites us to be almost as brave.

Chapter 1

Introduction

Lorraine Radford and Ravi K. Thiara

This book is about domestic violence and abuse (DVA) and safeguarding, and brings together up-to-date knowledge and current practice on protecting adults, children and young people. We include working with diverse victims/survivors with varied needs across the lifecourse and responses to perpetrators.

There has been huge progress in awareness about violence against women and violence against children as well as in policy responses to reduce these abuses of human rights globally, regionally and nationally across the nations in the UK. Through partnerships, cross-national collaborations, sharing knowledge and improved multi-sector working we have started to break down the specialisms and fragmented silo thinking that has blighted research, policy and practice on violence prevention.

At the global level commitments made in international conventions and treaties to reduce levels of violence against women and children have been formalized in the Sustainable Development Agenda and the goals and targets for 2030 adopted by all United Nations (UN) member states (especially the goals on gender equality and peaceful communities and the associated targets 5.2, 16.1 and 16.2) (UN 2015). Work is currently underway in many countries to implement and monitor the evidence-based strategies, developed and agreed by international organizations and partnerships, to reduce levels of violence against children (INSPIRE, WHO 2016) and violence against women (RESPECT Women, WHO 2019).

Similar commitments and actions have been taken at the regional level. In Europe, the *Council of Europe Convention on Preventing and Combating Violence against Women and Domestic Violence* (Istanbul

Convention) (CoE 2016) provides a comprehensive blueprint for action, and has led to the implementation of national strategies in many countries. The Council of Europe *Gender Equality Strategy 2018–2023* (CoE 2018) reaffirms commitment to the UN Sustainable Development Goals, the Istanbul Convention and implementing children's rights in six strategic actions, including preventing and tackling violence against women and domestic violence. Recognition of the gendered impact of DVA, its unequal impact on minorities and socially excluded groups, and disadvantages over the lifecourse underpin these European strategies.

These are welcome changes, but many gaps persist in our knowledge and practice about preventing and responding to DVA. This book aims to address some of these by focusing on safeguarding practice across the lifecourse, recognizing the diverse experiences and needs of adults and children in contemporary Britain.

We both began writing about domestic violence and children in the 1990s, and the inequalities and different experiences that mothers and children face have always been part of this work (Hester and Radford 1992; Hester *et al.* 1994; Rai and Thiara 1996). Since the mid-1990s, working in a multi-agency context and in child protection with children living with domestic violence has become standard practice (NICE 2016; Stanley and Humphreys 2015). The shifting research and policy landscape provided one motivation for developing this book.

A large body of research has addressed the cross-cutting and interconnected aspects of the abuse of children and adults, experiences of DVA and other forms of victimization such as sexual violence and the compounding, and sometimes lifelong, impact that living with DVA can have on wellbeing. Since 2010, the national strategies in England and Wales on violence against women and girls have included earlier intervention and prevention to address the intergenerational consequences of DVA (HM Government 2016).

Developments in research, policy and practice have brought increased recognition of the value of 'differential responses' where services are tuned to match different levels of need and risk, to meet 'complex' needs, or to provide earlier help and work preventively to make ending violence 'everybody's business' (HM Government 2016). While several texts have addressed specific aspects of the diversity of DVA experiences across the lifecourse, by focusing on children and domestic violence for example, or mental health and abuse, there is as yet no text that concisely brings together the key issues for practitioners in an accessible and evidence-informed manner.

This edited volume aims to recognize the importance of evidence-informed practice when working with DVA. By 'evidence-informed practice' we mean bringing together research evidence, practice experience and the views of people who use services and their families, to inform and strengthen decision-making and professional judgement. Bringing together content relevant to both adults and children's services, contributors to this book give an accessible overview of what good social work and social care practice looks like when working with children and adults experiencing DVA. The importance of recognizing family dynamics and using whole-family approaches in work with adult victims, children and perpetrators to address the diverse range of needs and circumstances is also underlined.

This book is timely for numerous reasons, not least the policy and practice changes recently introduced:

- The introduction of an offence of controlling and coercive behaviour under the Serious Crime Act 2015.

- The inclusion of DVA as a circumstance for which safeguarding adults may be enlisted under the Care Act 2014, which brings DVA firmly into the adult social work arena.

- Growing recognition that DVA affects all groups of people and, although a gendered crime, is not just limited to younger women.

- A focus in the Care Act on asset-based and whole-family approaches, as well as an emphasis on social work skills and approaches.

- Recognition of the tensions associated with addressing DVA involving children, and a need for a new approach that navigates the need to protect children with the need to effectively support survivors.

- The mainstreaming of a Making Safeguarding Personal (MSP) approach to safeguarding adults.

- Increased understanding of how intimate partner violence (IPV) is a risk for many young people, and how it interacts with other forms of adolescent harm.

- Increased recognition and concern about adolescent-to-parent abuse.

- The impact of economic adversity and the COVID-19 pandemic on health and social care services.

Themes and terminology

Three themes in our thinking about a lifecourse perspective on DVA underlie the structure and organization of the book. These three interrelated themes of *coercive control* (Radford and Hester 2006; Stark 2007), *developmental experiences of violence* (Radford *et al.* 2011; Radford 2012) and *intersectionality* (Hester and Radford 1996; Thiara and Gill 2010) have rippled through our work over several years of research and writing, and are brought together in this volume. Where possible, the terminology used in this book will be based on the definitions used in current law and policy. There are no official or government definitions of a lifecourse perspective, of intersectionality, or of developmental experiences of violence, and we have drawn our definitions of these terms from research and scholarly publications.

Domestic violence and coercive control: It has long been recognized within specialist services that DVA is not only physical violence and its threat, but also a range of sexual, psychological, financial and other manipulating and controlling behaviours that trap a victim within an abusive relationship and reduce her[1] options for a safe and independent life.

The UK government defines DVA as being:

> Any incident or pattern of incidents of controlling, coercive or threatening behaviour, violence or abuse between those aged 16 or over who are or have been intimate partners or family members, regardless of gender or sexuality. This can encompass, but is not limited to, the following types of abuse: psychological, physical, sexual, financial and emotional. (CPS 2015)

This includes so-called 'honour'-based violence, female genital mutilation

---

1   We use 'her' to reflect the gendered nature of DVA. We acknowledge that men are also sometimes victims/survivors and that violence occurs to men and to women in same-sex relationships and in transgender relationships.

(FGM) and forced marriage, and victims are not confined to one gender or ethnic group.

'Coercive control' refers to the abuser's use of tactics, other than direct physical violence (such as isolation, monitoring, emotional manipulation, humiliation) to maintain dominance over a partner and the gendered nature of DVA (Crossman and Hardesty 2018; Stark 2007). Examples of coercive control include the enforcement of rigid or petty household rules, gaslighting behaviours, isolation from family and friends, immigration status-based abuse and, quite commonly for women with children, an undermining of their mothering and emotional manipulation of and threats to harm or abduct the children (Thiara and Humphreys 2017; Thiara and Roy 2020).

The government definition of DVA also includes coercive and controlling behaviours that are defined as follows:

- Coercive behaviour is an act or a pattern of acts of assault, threats, humiliation and intimidation or other abuse that is used to harm, punish, or frighten their victim.

- Controlling behaviour is a range of acts designed to make a person subordinate and/or dependent by isolating them from sources of support, exploiting their resources and capacities for personal gain, depriving them of the means needed for independence, resistance and escape and regulating their everyday behaviour. (CPS 2015[2])

Section 76 of the Serious Crime Act 2015 created a new offence of controlling or coercive behaviour in an intimate or family relationship. For the purposes of this offence, behaviour must be engaged in 'repeatedly' or 'continuously'. Another, separate, element of the offence is that it must have a 'serious effect' on someone, and one way of proving this is that it causes someone to fear, on at least two occasions, that violence will be used against them. There is no specific requirement in the Serious Crime Act that the activity should be of the same nature. The prosecution should be able to show that there was intent to control or coerce someone (CPS 2015).

One aspect of coercive control highlighted from our own research is the persistence of these behaviours after separation, often via women's

---

2   Public sector information licensed under the Open Government Licence v2.0, www.nationalarchives.gov.uk/doc/open-government-licence/version/2

relationships with their children. This issue is explored further in several of the chapters in this book, particularly in Chapter 2 (the impact of DVA on children and young people by Lorraine Radford, Nicky Stanley and Amanda Elwen) and Chapter 8 (working with perpetrators by Chris Newman).

Developmental experiences of violence: A second theme from our own research, which also runs throughout the chapters in this book, is the understanding that experiences of violence, abuse and victimization and their impact vary across the lifecourse. Research on violence in childhood (Finkelhor 2008; Know Violence in Childhood 2017) highlights in particular the differential risks and vulnerabilities of infants, children and young people to different types of violence, abuse and victimization across the lifecourse, with infants and teenagers worldwide being those most at risk of homicide.

Children and infants, as well as adults in need of extensive personal care, have physical and developmental vulnerabilities that expose them uniquely to the risk of dependency-related forms of violence, abuse or neglect from caregivers. Indeed, neglect is a specific form of abuse limited to children and adults who are dependent on others for personal care, such as the elderly, ill, disabled or incarcerated.

A wide-ranging review of the research on violence in childhood, covering all forms of physical, sexual and psychological abuse, as well as exposure to DVA, affirms other research that shows that for child protection it is important to recognize that the types of victimization experienced and the perpetrators responsible change over childhood (Know Violence in Childhood 2017; see Figure 1.1). Early victimization experiences tend to be associated with younger children's dependency and the settings in which they live. Younger children are most likely to be physically or sexually abused by a family member or caregiver as they spend more time in the home with the family. Older children and young people spend more of their time outside the immediate family or home environment, and are likely to be exposed to a wider range of perpetrators (in addition to the risks within the family): adults in positions of trust or authority, peers, employers, neighbours and intimate partners (Finkelhor 2008; Know Violence in Childhood 2017; Kumar *et al.* 2017).

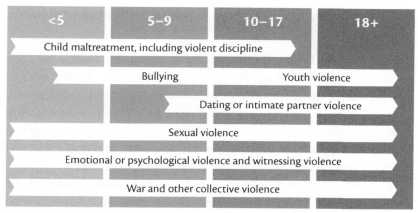

Figure 1.1 Adapted from selected forms of violence according to the most likely age of occurrence (UNICEF 2017, p.9), adapted from 'RESPECT Women: Preventing Violence Against Women' (WHO 2019).

The impact will vary in relation to the nature, severity and duration of the abuse, and developmentally in relation to the child or young person's ability to understand the abuse, their coping strategies and responses from family, friends, the wider community and services (Kendall-Tackett 2008). A lifecourse perspective on DVA recognizes that there is no single lifecourse trajectory for impact, and not everybody will have the same outcomes. Experiences of different types of violence, such as childhood exposure to domestic violence and direct experiences of child abuse and neglect, or living with DVA and being bullied at school, often coexist and accumulate over the lifecourse. A child who lives with DVA is also at greater risk of experiencing other types of violence or abuse from adults or peers in a range of settings (Elloneni and Salmi 2011; Finkelhor, Ormrod and Turner 2007; Fisher *et al.* 2015). Children who experience multiple victimizations (polyvictimization) tend to have the poorest outcomes (Radford *et al.* 2013).

The impact of violence is not fixed and static, but is also subject to change over time and across the lifecourse and through periods of transition. These issues are addressed in several chapters of this book, particularly in Chapter 2 (safeguarding children from domestic violence by Lorraine Radford, Nicky Stanley and Amanda Elwen), Chapter 5 (relationship abuse and older people by John Devaney and

Elizabeth Martin) and in Chapter 9 (adolescent-to-parent abuse by Victoria Baker).

Intersectionality: DVA does not happen in an isolated bubble between individuals unaffected by the wider social context. Most forms of interpersonal violence disproportionately affect groups in a community or population which are disadvantaged as a result of interacting structural inequalities such as poverty, gender inequity, racism, ageism and sexual orientation, together with institutional and organizational practices that do little to challenge or even reinforce them.

The term 'intersectionality' is used in this book to refer to the interconnected nature of social inequalities based on categories such as gender, age, class, 'race', immigration and sexual orientation, as they apply to a given individual or a group. Intersectionality considers all the factors that underlie systems of discrimination and disadvantage together, focusing on the overlapping and interdependent systems of inequalities based on gender, 'race' and class, for example (Chantler and Thiara 2017; Crenshaw 1989; Thiara and Gill 2010). Chapters 6 and 7 (intersectionality and abuse by Aisha K. Gill and Gurpreet Virdee and disabled women and DVA by Ravi K. Thiara and Ruth Bashall) look in detail at how intersectional location shapes and differentiates the experiences of DVA, the former using anonymized case studies to illustrate the intersectional experiences of violence and abuse among black and minority ethnic (BME) girls and women.

Intersectionality is important to understanding and working with the different experiences of DVA that adults and children may have. Gender inequalities are key risks for women and girls, but this has a differential impact on experiences of violence across the lifecourse and varies according to social location. The DVA research literature has been historically divided over a debate about the 'equality of violence' that proposes gender is largely irrelevant as both men and women are equally victims and perpetrators of partner abuse (Dobash and Dobash 1992). We maintain that gender is highly significant as a driver for DVA and for most forms of violence, whether males or females are victims or perpetrators, and there is no 'equality' in violence regarding the influence of gender and age, although the influence of these intersects in different ways over the lifecourse.

The research literature on DVA has prioritized gender as a driver of violence, whereas in the child protection literature gender neutrality is reflected widely in the language used to refer generically to 'children' and their 'parents' (most often mothers in social work practice). Victimizations are less gender-specific for younger children, as boys and girls are similarly at risk of abuse and neglect in the family. However, as the child grows older, more gendered, adult patterns of victimization emerge, with teenage boys suffering more overall victimizations than girls, but girls experiencing much more DVA, gender-based violence and sexual abuse (Finkelhor 2008; Ligiero *et al.* 2019; Radford *et al.* 2011, 2013).

A lifecourse perspective on violence looks at experiences of violence over the lifetime, from infancy to later life, and how this shapes people's lives. This developmental perspective recognizes that processes from early life onwards can influence and shape health and wellbeing across a lifetime and potentially across generations. It takes into account the individual twists and turns that can occur on the way, looking at the context – social, environmental and physical – in which individuals are born and in which their lives unfold over time (Olofsson 2014).

A lifecourse perspective requires a holistic approach to violence that considers how different experiences of violence over different stages of the lifecourse can accumulate and influence wellbeing. It looks at the timing of violent experiences and how an individual copes at different ages (for example, in infancy and early childhood, adolescence and growing older), through major life events (significant and abrupt changes, for example, bereavement, pregnancy and divorce) and common periods of transition (involving changes in status, such as migration or leaving the parental home). It aims to take into account intersectional factors, considering different individual pathways to surviving violence in the context of intersectional structural and environmental inequalities and drivers of violence in a particular society.

Structure and organization of the book

Each of the chapters that follows examines a different area of DVA research and practice considering DVA at different stages of the life cycle, from childhood to adolescence (Chapters 2, 3, 8 and 9), to later life (Chapter 5), to the different intersectional experiences and challenges for practice for BME and migrant women and girls and for disabled women (Chapters 6 and 7), and for adults affected by problematic substance use and/or mental health problems (Chapter 4). Some of the issues and approaches covered in this book are relatively new, and we cannot promise to have brought together all the answers to questions readers may have about best practice and the best evidence. In some cases these do not exist. Many of the chapters have been written through a partnership between researchers and practitioners. In each chapter we have tried to keep a focus on succinctly presenting the research, policy and practice challenges, focusing on turning the tide of attention away from individual failings and responsibilities towards more trauma-informed, strengths-based and empowering methods of working with victims/survivors.

References

Chantler, K. and Thiara, R.K. (2017) '"We are still here": Re-centering the quintessential subject of intersectionality.' Special Issue: 'What is intersectional about intersectionality now?' *Atlantis: Critical Studies in Gender, Culture & Social Justice 38*, 1, 82–94.

CoE (Council of Europe) (2016) *Council of Europe Convention on Preventing and Combating Violence against Women and Domestic Violence* (Istanbul Convention). Istanbul: CoE.

CoE (2018) *Council of Europe Gender Equality Strategy 2018–2023*. Strasbourg: CoE.

CPS (Crown Prosecution Service) (2015) *Domestic Violence and Abuse Guidelines for Crown Prosecutors*. Legal Guidance, Domestic Abuse. Available at: https://www.cps.gov.uk/legal-guidance/domestic-abuse-guidelines-prosecutors

Crenshaw, K. (1989) 'Demarginalising the intersection of race and sex: A Black feminist critique of antidiscrimination doctrine, feminist theory and antiracist politics.' *The University of Chicago Legal Forum*, 139–167.

Crossman, K. and Hardesty, J. (2018) 'Placing coercive control at the center: What are the processes of coercive control and what makes control coercive?' *Psychology of Violence 8*, 2, 196–206.

Dobash, R. and Dobash, R. (1992) *Women, Violence and Social Change*. London: Routledge.

Elloneni, N. and Salmi, V. (2011) 'Polyvictimization as a life condition: Correlates of polyvictimization among Finnish children.' *Journal of Scandinavian Studies in Criminology and Crime Prevention 12*, 1, 20–44.

Finkelhor, D. (2008) *Childhood Victimization: Violence, Crime, and Abuse in the Lives of Young People*. Oxford: Oxford University Press.

Finkelhor, D., Ormrod, R. and Turner, H. (2007) 'Polyvictimization and trauma in a national longitudinal cohort.' *Development and Psychopathology 19*, 1, 149–166.

Fisher, H., Caspi, A., Moffitt, T. and Wertz, J. (2015) 'Measuring adolescents' exposure to victimization: The Environmental Risk (E-Risk) Longitudinal Twin Study.' *Development and Psychopathology 27*, 1399–1416.

Hester, M. and Radford, L. (1992) 'Domestic violence and access arrangements for children in Denmark and Britain.' *Journal of Social Welfare and Family Law 1*, 57–70.

Hester, M. and Radford, L. (1996) *Domestic Violence and Child Contact Arrangements in England and Denmark*. Bristol: Policy Press.

Hester, M., Humphries, J., Qaiser, K., Radford, L. and Woodfield, K. (1994) 'Domestic Violence and Child Contact.' In A. Mullender and R. Morley (eds) *Children Living with Domestic Violence: Putting Men's Abuse of Women on the Child Care Agenda* (pp.102–121). London: Whiting & Birch.

HM Government (2016) *Ending Violence against Women and Girls: 2016 to 2020*. London: Home Office. Available at www.gov.uk/government/publications/strategy-to-end-violence-against-women-and-girls-2016-to-2020 [updated March 2019].

Kendall-Tackett, K. (2008) 'Developmental Impact.' In D. Finkelhor (ed) *Childhood Victimization* (pp.65–101). Oxford: Oxford University Press.

Know Violence in Childhood (2017) *Ending Violence in Childhood, Global Report*. New Delhi, India: Know Violence in Childhood.

Kumar, S., Stern, V., Subrahmanian, R., Sherr, L., *et al.* (2017) 'Ending violence in childhood: A global imperative.' *Psychology, Health & Medicine 22*, Suppl. 1, 1–16.

Ligiero, D., Hart, C., Fulu, E., Thomas, A. and Radford, L. (2019) *What Works to Prevent Sexual Violence Against Children: Evidence Review*. Together for Girls. Available at: www.togetherforgirls.org/svsolutions

NICE (National Institute for Health and Care Excellence) (2016) *Recognising and Responding to Domestic Violence and Abuse*. Available at: www.nice.org.uk/about/nice-communities/social-care/quick-guides/recognising-and-responding-to-domestic-violence-and-abuse

Olofsson, N. (2014) 'A life course model of self-reported violence exposure and ill-health with a public health problem perspective.' *AIMS Public Health 1*, 1, 9–24.

Radford, L. (2012) *Re-Thinking Children, Violence and Safeguarding*. London: Bloomsbury.

Radford, L. and Hester, M. (2006) *Mothering through Domestic Violence*. London: Jessica Kingsley Publishers.

Radford, L., Corral, S., Bradley, C. and Fisher, H. (2011) *Child Abuse and Neglect in the UK Today*. London: NSPCC.

Radford, L., Corral, S., Bradley, C. and Fisher, H. (2013) 'The prevalence and impact of child maltreatment and other types of victimization in the UK: Findings from a population survey of caregivers, children and young people and young adults.' *Child Abuse & Neglect 37*, 10, 801–813.

Rai, D. and Thiara, R.K. (1996) *Redefining Spaces: The Needs of Black Women and Children and Black Workers in Women's Aid*. Bristol: Women's Aid Federation England.

Stanley, N. and Humphreys, C. (eds) (2015) *Domestic Violence and Protecting Children: New Thinking and Approaches*. London: Jessica Kingsley Publishers.

Stark, E. (2007) *Coercive Control*. Oxford: Oxford University Press.

Thiara, R.K. and Gill, A.K. (eds) (2010) *Violence Against Women in South Asian Communities: Issues for Policy and Practice*. London: Jessica Kingsley Publishers.

Thiara, R.K. and Humphreys, C. (2017) 'Absent presence: The ongoing impact of men's violence on the mother–child relationship.' *Child & Family Social Work 22*, 1, 137–145.

Thiara, R.K. and Roy, S. (2020) *Reclaiming Voice: Minoritised Women and Sexual Violence. Key Findings*. London: Imkaan.

UN (United Nations) (2015) *Transforming Our World: The 2030 Agenda for Sustainable Development*. A/Res/70/1. New York: United Nations General Assembly. Available at: www.un.org/ga/search/view_doc.asp?symbol=A/RES/70/1&Lang=E

UNICEF (2017) *Preventing and Responding to Violence Against Children and Adolescents: Theory of Change*. New York: UNICEF.

WHO (World Health Organization) (2016) *INSPIRE: Seven Strategies for Ending Violence Against Children*. Geneva: WHO. Available at: www.who.int/publications/i/item/inspire-seven-strategies-for-ending-violence-against-children

WHO (2019) *RESPECT Women: Preventing Violence Against Women*. Geneva: WHO. Available at: www.who.int/reproductivehealth/publications/preventing-vaw-framework-policymakers/en

Chapter 2

Safeguarding Children and Young People Exposed to Domestic Violence and Abuse

Lorraine Radford, Nicky Stanley and Amanda Elwen

Introduction

In this chapter we look at the impact living with domestic violence and abuse (DVA) has on children and young people, and what we know about effective interventions. In the UK, one in every six children between the ages of 11 to 17 report living with domestic violence at some time during childhood (Radford *et al.* 2013). There has been an increased awareness of the consequences for child health and wellbeing in recent years, and a steady development of new interventions and practice approaches. The purpose of this chapter is to give an up-to-date overview of what we know about working with children and young people affected by DVA today, taking into account the changing landscape of policy, practice and research. At the end of this chapter you should be aware of how children of different ages and with different vulnerabilities are affected, and what this means for assessment and for providing support across the spectrum of needs.

Throughout this chapter we use the term 'mothers' to refer to the primary caregiver and victim/survivor of DVA. This approach is taken to reflect the gendered nature of DVA. We acknowledge that men are also sometimes victims/survivors and that violence occurs to men and to women in same-sex relationships and in transgender relationships. We highlight these diversities and key points for practice where relevant.

Children's experiences of living with domestic violence and abuse

Women with children living in single-parent households are up to three times more likely to experience domestic violence than childless women (ONS 2019), and risk of DVA may increase for some women during pregnancy or shortly after the birth of a child (Stanley 2011). Only a few research papers were published on children's and young people's experiences of domestic violence before the late 1980s. Since then, many studies based on direct research with children have shown there are at least five ways children and young people may be harmed by living with DVA.

Overlapping of violence to parent and to child

A UK-wide community survey of children's experiences of violence found that those exposed to domestic violence were over eight times more likely than children not so exposed to have experienced physical violence from a caregiver (Radford *et al.* 2011a).

In England and Wales, over one in three (35.7 per cent) adults aged 18–74 report witnessing domestic violence as children prior to the age of 16; 25.4 per cent of adults report witnessing DVA and also experiencing at least one other form of child abuse (emotional, physical or sexual) (ONS 2020a).

A global review and meta-analysis of research studies found that, in population-based studies, where DVA is reported, there is a 3.64 times greater likelihood of there also being child abuse and neglect at a later stage (Chan, Chen and Chen 2019).

Children may also be hurt directly by being 'caught in the crossfire' or if trying to protect the mother. Mothers may be hurt when trying to protect a child (Stanley 2011).

'Witnessing'

Research on children 'witnessing' or being 'exposed' to DVA (Graham-Bermann and Edleson 2001; Jaffe, Wolfe and Wilson 1990) goes beyond the focus on physical violence to assess the harm that can be caused if children are present, or if they see or overhear DVA. Children may witness a violent event, or afterwards see injuries to a parent, damage to the home or harm to a family pet. They may experience fear when they hear violence in another room. They may blame themselves for the abuse happening if the violent parent begins an attack with an argument about the child or something the child has done (McGee 2000; Mullender *et al.* 2002).

Being drawn into the abuse by the perpetrator

Perpetrators may target coercive and controlling behaviours at the mother's relationship with the child, or try to draw the child into a pattern of undermining the mother (Katz 2015a; Stark 2007). This can persist post separation as controlling behaviour during an abusive relationship often continues after parents part (Birchall and Choudhry 2018; Radford and Hester 2015). Examples of coercive control targeted at mothering include: threats to harm or abduct a child or to 'tell social services you are an unfit mother' to prevent a woman leaving the relationship; involving the child in the denigration and constant criticism ('your mother is useless'); forced witnessing of the violence ('teaching mummy a lesson'); physically or emotionally isolating the mother from the child; or undermining the mother's parental authority (Radford and Hester 2006).

Harm to the primary caregiver

DVA can have a harmful impact on a victim/survivor's physical and mental health and her capacity to parent (Hooker *et al.* 2016). While it is recognized that experiences of DVA vary, and many victims/survivors make great efforts to counteract and compensate for the adverse impact of DVA on their children (Letourneau, Fedick and Willms 2007), harmful health impacts, ranging from homicide to physical disability and chronic ill health, or drug or alcohol dependency, combined with financial abuse and impoverishment, can severely undermine the resources needed for parenting. Children may need to take on caring tasks and, while some may be proud of the support they are able to give, others may feel isolated, crave a 'normal' life and suffer lost opportunities from missing school (Stanley 2011).

Living with the 'fall out'

Children living with DVA are at greater risk of experiencing additional adversities and further violence in childhood, and these tend to accumulate over time (ONS 2020a; Radford *et al.* 2011a; Stanley 2011). Families living with DVA are likely to experience more isolation from sources of social support such as family and friends, more poverty (Mullender *et al.* 2002), greater transience due to separations, homelessness or frequent moves to find a safe family home (Bowstead 2017) and disrupted schooling (Radford *et al.* 2011b).

Women often leave or remain in an abusive relationship 'for the sake of the children' (Secco, Letourneau and Collins 2016). 'Helping' professions – such as the police, child protection services, healthcare and the family courts – may inadvertently become enlisted in a violent father's efforts to maintain coercive control over a partner or ex-partner and the child. The mother-blaming verdict of an abused woman as 'not coping' is likely to be heightened in situations where she has a disability or where the violence has had a detrimental impact on a woman's physical or mental health (see Chapters 4 and 7 in this volume). The individual efforts of violent men to isolate, marginalize, disempower and highlight the 'failure' of abused women as mothers can be reinforced and magnified by the disjointed and poorly coordinated practices of professionals in law enforcement, the courts and child protection services (Radford and Hester 2015).

Good safeguarding practice recognizes that it is important to take into account the specific experiences adults and children have of DVA, how they have responded, tried to cope and support one another, and to build on their strengths in trying to end the abuse (Aria *et al.* 2019; Katz 2015b; Laing and Humphreys 2013).

Developmental impacts

All children who live with DVA are at risk of having poor outcomes, and for some, the consequences can be lifelong:

> Constantly on edge. Never free, never safe. It was like, there was no safe [place]…being at home wasn't safe at all…you're constantly alert. You don't sleep properly, you just sit there and wait for something to happen. (Mona, aged 17, quoted in McGee 2000, p.72)

The impact can include a range of physical, emotional and behavioural consequences – low birth weight, low self-esteem, depression, post-traumatic stress reactions, aggression, running away from home and risk-taking behaviour in adolescence (Bair-Merritt, Blackstone and

Feudtner 2006). Children are at increased risk of experiencing other forms of violence and abuse, of developing emotional and behavioural problems and experiencing other adversities in childhood (Holt, Buckley and Whelan 2008; Schechter *et al.* 2011). Emotional and behavioural problems have been found to be significantly associated with the mental health of the mother who has experienced domestic violence (McFarlane *et al.* 2014). While over a third of children who have lived with DVA appear to be no worse off than children living in the community without this experience (Kitzmann *et al.* 2003), children who have had chronic exposure to DVA over time appear to have the poorest outcomes (Stanley 2011).

Even when living in the same family, different children may be affected differently. As with all forms of child maltreatment, the impact for children manifests in different ways at different developmental stages. Figure 2.1 summarizes commonly observed effects of DVA on children at different developmental stages.

Birth and infancy
- Low birth weight; premature birth; impact of violence on foetal health
- Higher risk of homicide; delayed language development and toilet training; sleep disturbance; crying and fretfulness; fear of separation

Preschool (1–4 years)
- Bedwetting; asthma; headaches; stomach aches; nightmares
- Emotional dysregulation; behaviour problems; social problems
- Low self-esteem; post-traumatic stress disorder; poor empathy; tantrums; aggression; being anxious

School-aged (5–12 years)
- Post-traumatic stress disorder; conduct disorders; depression; low self-esteem
- Aggression; trouble at school; being withdrawn
- Intervening to protect; blaming themselves for the violence

Adolescence (13–17 years)
- Internalizing and externalizing symptoms
- Self-harm and suicidal thoughts; withdrawal from friends
- Use of drugs or alcohol to cope; gangs; running away
- Withdrawal or exclusion from school
- Impact on romantic relationships

Figure 2.1 The developmental impact of domestic violence and abuse on children and young people.

Infants and very young children are especially vulnerable because of their dependence on adults for all aspects of their care and healthy development. A child's health and development may be affected by abuse towards the mother during pregnancy, which can result in miscarriage, premature birth, low birth weight or birth defects (Boy and Salihu 2004). Stress and stress-related behaviour, such as smoking and alcohol use during pregnancy, can affect the foetus (Coker, Sanderson and Dong 2004). The foetus may also be harmed by a woman's inability to attend health checks in pregnancy if her partner prevents her from doing this (Lipsky *et al.* 2003). Infants may be at risk of being hurt if the mother is assaulted while holding a child. Children under the age of one year are at greatest risk of homicide (ONS 2020b).

Studies, mostly completed in the USA, have identified delayed language and toilet training, sleep disturbance, emotional distress and fear of being left alone in infants and toddlers (Lundy and Grossman 2005). The first three years of a child's life are important for creating secure attachments with caregivers, and living with DVA or neglect can create attachment problems for a parent and child and influence the child's subsequent ability to form secure relationships (Howe 2005). The psychological state of the mother can also have an effect on an unborn child or an infant, so that the mother feels insecure or ambiguous about her attachment and feelings towards the child, or lacks confidence in her capabilities as a parent (Jaffe, Wolfe and Campbell 2012).

Some studies suggest that *preschool-aged children* exposed to DVA are at greater risk of having behaviour problems, social problems, symptoms of post-traumatic stress disorder (PTSD), difficulty developing empathy and self-esteem (Holt *et al.* 2008). They may have temper tantrums, be aggressive, anxious, despondent, irritable, cry and have sleep disturbances or show physical symptoms of their emotional distress in bedwetting, nightmares, asthma, headaches or stomach aches (Jaffe *et al.* 2012).

Most of the research on children and DVA has looked at older children and adolescents. *School-aged children* between the ages of 5 and 12 will have increased cognitive and social skills, and will begin to try to understand the family circumstances and the violence. They may have fears, anxieties and show internalizing symptoms (such as PTSD, depression and low self-esteem), adjust their behaviour or attempt to manage the conflict, try to intervene to protect a parent or sibling, or to avoid it by hiding and being withdrawn. It is fairly common for children to blame themselves for the violence happening and to be unwilling to talk about the abuse for a range of reasons, such as not wanting to cause trouble, or fearing being bullied at school (Lloyd 2018; Stanley 2015). Children may find it difficult to talk to the mother about the violence, worrying that it may cause upset (Nixon *et al.* 2017). They may show externalizing symptoms such as aggression and behavioural problems – getting into trouble at school, for example (Jaffe *et al.* 2012).

Adolescents may suffer from the same problems as younger children in terms of internalizing and externalizing symptoms, although the consequences for their behaviour may be greater. Common problems observed in adolescents living with DVA include self-harm and suicidal thoughts, use of drugs or alcohol to cope, withdrawal from friends or getting involved with gangs or crime, running away from home, and withdrawing or being excluded from school. Living with violence may also have an impact on their own romantic relationships (Jaffe *et al.* 2012).

A note about the 'cycle of violence'

Although cross-sectional (a one-off survey) research has found that there is an association between childhood exposure to DVA and increased risk of victimization or perpetration of intimate partner violence (IPV) in adulthood, the strength of this link is weak (Radford *et al.* 2019), and many children and young people who grow up in violent homes do not reproduce their parent's abusive behaviour in their own relationships. Rather than assuming a direct causal relationship between childhood exposure to DVA and reproducing this behaviour in adult life, the research suggests interactions between different individual, family, peer and community-related factors may influence vulnerabilities for girls and boys. For example, the impact of living with DVA in early childhood may affect a child more if the child is also directly physically abused by a parent and lives in a community where during adolescence they mix with peers involved in violent crime (Radford *et al.* 2019). While the impact on some children may be significant, substantial numbers of maltreated children show no apparent adverse consequences in adulthood (Kitzmann *et al.* 2003). Research further suggests that the adverse consequences for children decline if they are safe and free from fear of further violence (Finkelhor and Turner 2015; Jaffe *et al.* 2012). A lifecourse perspective can be helpful in debunking unhelpful thinking about the inevitability of a 'cycle of violence' and redirecting efforts onto opportunities for change for children, young people and their caregivers at different points in their development.

Resilience and protective factors

There is a growing research literature on protective factors and resilience to child maltreatment, including living with DVA. Resilience is defined as:

> ...a process of navigating through adversity, using internal and external resources (personal qualities, relationships, and environmental and contextual factors) to support healthy adaptation, recovery and successful outcomes over the life course. (Alaggia and Donohue 2017, p.23)

There are two aspects to this process: healthy functioning after having a substantial experience of adversity, including violence, and the adaptability necessary to overcome an experience of adversity. In a review of 19 studies on childhood exposure to DVA and resilience, Alaggia and Donohue (2017) identified individual, interpersonal and contextual factors of resilience in children.

Resilience factors in children exposed to domestic violence and abuse

Individual

Self-confidence, greater self-worth, ability to regulate emotions, spirituality or faith, commitment to breaking the cycle of violence, being motivated or having goals, academic success, internal locus of control, and an easy temperament.

Interpersonal

One secure attachment; access to one safe adult; a protective mother; maternal warmth, sensitivity and good mental health; an in-home social network (that is, a social network that includes trusted adults such as relatives who come into the home); peer and social support.

Contextual

Safe haven and accessible community resources; exit options such as leaving home for university or further study; having an educated mother with her own stable employment; connection to spirituality or faith; bicultural influence.

Alaggia and Donohue (2017) suggest that practitioners could play an important role in supporting children and young people by: (a) identifying and promoting existing protective factors to foster the resilience process; and (b) seeking opportunities to foster resilience processes through positive adaptation. Having a good, emotionally supportive relationship with an adult caregiver, most often the mother, contributes significantly to a child's ability to overcome the consequences of living with domestic violence (Mullender *et al.* 2002). Providing support for the mother, rather than undermining her, is now widely seen to be effective child protection practice (Stanley 2011). Peer support has been found to moderate the adverse impact of DVA on older children and help prevent school drop out (Tajima *et al.* 2011).

Developments in policy and practice

It is increasingly recognized that safeguarding children includes preventing abuse from happening in the first place ('primary prevention') as well as responding to ensure the health and wellbeing of those who have lived with abuse. Current policy and practice responses to children and domestic violence (see the 'Policy and guidance' box below) emphasize the importance of coordinated multi-agency working for children and their families across a continuum of different levels of assessed need. 'Differential responses', in theory, are based on the understanding that not all children will be affected in the same way, and some may require different types of help at different levels of specialism or intensity. The types of support children may need and their ability to access services will also be influenced by their age, whether or not the DVA is ongoing and the parents are living together, wanting to separate or are living apart (Laing and Humphreys 2013).

Policy and guidance

The *Children Act 1989* sets out statutory responsibilities for promoting child welfare and taking action to protect children from significant harm.

Section 120 of the *Adoption and Children Act 2002* (in force in 2005) states that 'seeing or hearing the ill-treatment of another person' is a form of harm to a child.

Section 11 of the *Children Act 2004* places a statutory duty on certain agencies to cooperate to safeguard and promote the welfare of children. This includes: local authorities, NHS services and trusts, the police, probation services and young offender institutions. People who work in these agencies and who do not report suspected cases of abuse or neglect may be subject to disciplinary proceedings, but do not currently face criminal penalties.

What to Do If You're Worried a Child Is Being Abused[1] was published by the government in 2015 as a resource for all people working with children (HM Government 2015). This gives advice on recognizing the signs of abuse and what to do if it is suspected.

Working Together to Safeguard Children[2] is statutory guidance that sets out the responsibility of those in the education, community and care sectors to safeguard children from all forms of abuse and neglect, including living with domestic violence. This states that: everyone who works with children has a responsibility for keeping them safe; and everyone who comes into contact with children and families has a role to play in sharing information and identifying concerns. Domestic abuse is mentioned as a particular issue where practitioners should consider the child's need for early help services such as family and parenting programmes, assistance with health and mental health issues and emerging problems related to living with the abuse (HM Government 2018, p.13).

Statutory Framework for the Early Years Foundation Stage (DfE 2017)[3] sets out safeguarding and welfare responsibilities covered by the Regulations under Section 39(1)(b) of the Childcare

---

1   See https://assets.publishing.service.gov.uk/government/uploads/system/uploads/
    attachment_data/file/419604/What_to_do_if_you_re_worried_a_child_is_being_abused.pdf
2   See https://assets.publishing.service.gov.uk/government/uploads/system/uploads/
    attachment_data/file/779401/Working_Together_to_Safeguard-Children.pdf
3   See https://assets.publishing.service.gov.uk/government/uploads/system/uploads/
    attachment_data/file/596629/EYFS_STATUTORY_FRAMEWORK_2017.pdf

Act 2006 for all providers in the early years sector, including childminders.

Section 34 of the *Children and Social Work Act 2017* provides for primary prevention work in schools (after 2020) against DVA, stating that relationships education will be provided to primary school children and relationships and sex education will be provided (instead of sex education) in secondary schools.

The National Institute for Health and Care Excellence (NICE) guideline *Child Abuse and Neglect* (2017)[4] provides evidence-based (non-mandatory) guidance on identification and responses to child abuse and neglect, including exposure to DVA, for all practitioners in contact with children and young people and commissioners and managers of services.

Child Abuse and Neglect, Quality Standard 179 (NICE 2019)[5] provides expected standards within organizations for identification and response to child abuse and neglect.

Keeping Children Safe in Education: Statutory Guidance for Schools and Colleges (DfE 2020)[6] came into force in September 2020. This makes it clear that keeping a child safe is everybody's responsibility, and sets out requirements for governing bodies and for staff working in schools and colleges.

Ending Violence against Women and Girls: 2016 to 2020 (HM Government 2016)[7] for England and Wales focuses on early intervention and prevention responses including support for children.

The reality of service provision is challenging, varies from area to area and is far away from fulfilling this ideal of a range of services to meet the different needs of children who have lived with DVA (House of

---

4   See www.nice.org.uk/guidance/ng76/resources/child-abuse-and-neglect-pdf-1837637587141
5   See www.nice.org.uk/guidance/qs179/resources/child-abuse-and-neglect-pdf-755456
     69305285
6   See https://assets.publishing.service.gov.uk/government/uploads/system/uploads/
     attachment_data/file/835733/Keeping_children_safe_in_education_2019.pdf
7   See https://assets.publishing.service.gov.uk/government/uploads/system/uploads/attachment_
     data/file/522166/VAWG_Strategy_FINAL_PUBLICATION_MASTER_vRB.PDF

Commons 2018, 2020; Radford *et al.* 2011b). While the policy scope to respond to children affected by domestic violence has expanded to include provisions for prevention and *earlier* help, resources in statutory and voluntary services, especially within specialist domestic violence services, have declined. For many countries the COVID-19 pandemic has increased the risk for adults and children living with DVA and brought additional resource challenges (Bradbury-Jones and Isham 2020; Sacco *et al.* 2020; Usher *et al.* 2020). In this climate of competition and resource squeeze it is increasingly important that services demonstrate the effectiveness and impact of their work.

Effective safeguarding

Research reviews (Austin *et al.* 2019; Howarth *et al.* 2016; Radford *et al.* 2019; Rizo *et al.* 2011; Trevillion *et al.* 2020) have found a diverse range of interventions for children and families living with DVA. There are three main programme groups with some evaluation evidence: primary prevention programmes mostly delivered in schools; parenting interventions; and therapeutic work for the parent and child to repair harm caused. (Interventions for perpetrators as fathers/parents are discussed later, in Chapter 8.) Some programmes are also multi-component, bringing in different approaches such as individual therapy and group work, for example. Although there is no space in this brief chapter to review all the research on different types of interventions, key points from the review studies of effective responses are as follows:

- To make an impact on the extent of DVA we need both primary prevention and protective responses, stopping DVA occurring in the first place as well as providing protection for children and caregivers experiencing abuse.

- Responses should address the whole child and family situation, DVA and its impact on the child and the victimized parent, other forms of violence and abuse and other adversities (such as mental health, poverty) that may coexist.

- A 'one size fits all' approach, reliant on a single agency or single intervention, will not adequately address the varying needs of individual children and their families. Coordinated multi-agency working is essential across the different levels of need of individual children, ranging from the support needed for all children to thrive (healthcare, education, etc.) to more specialist intervention as in child protection and therapeutic care for children with behavioural or emotional problems.

- Not all families living with DVA will need a child protection response, especially if the abused parent and child can be helped to be safe.

- Supporting a non-abusive caregiver and her or his relationship with the child is effective child protection.

- Earlier identification and earlier assistance may help prevent the escalation in the severity and impact of DVA.

- Most evaluated interventions have focused on children after separation from the violent adult, but children and mothers may need help and support while living with the perpetrator. Whole-family, strengths-based and resilience building and empowerment approaches aim to address the needs of families, whether living with or apart from the perpetrator.

- Responses should be holistic and relevant to the family's specific needs, and these change with time.

In what follows we briefly review research findings and messages for practice when working with parents, babies and preschool-aged children, children aged 5–11, and children and young people aged 12–17.

Supporting children in infancy and the early years

Reviews have found a clear gap in research on the effectiveness of interventions with this younger age group of children and their families as most studies have focused on older children able to take part in group work or 'talking therapies' (Howarth *et al.* 2016; Radford *et al.* 2019; Rizo *et al.* 2011).

Parenting support and home visitation for children in infancy and the early years: Parenting support and home visitation programmes are recommended by the World Health Organization (WHO) as effective strategies to prevent violence against children (WHO 2016). There is substantial research on home visitation and parenting support (Mejdoubi *et al.* 2015; Olds *et al.* 1986, 1997), although most studies look at the impact of prevention on child abuse and neglect in general rather than addressing DVA specifically (Radford *et al.* 2019). Parenting programmes appear to have a positive effect on risk factors or proxy measures associated with child maltreatment, such as maternal psychosocial health and parental perceptions about harsh parenting practices, and may thus contribute indirectly to preventing child abuse associated with DVA. These programmes tend to work predominantly with mothers, however, and show little evidence of engaging with or facilitating change in perpetrators of DVA or fathers at risk of perpetrating DVA.

Programmes such as the *Nurse–Family Partnership* in the USA (Eckenrode *et al.* 2017), the *Family Nurse Partnership* programme in the UK (Robling *et al.* 2016) and *VoorZorg* in the Netherlands (Medjoubi *et al.* 2015) all include DVA towards the mother as a vulnerability factor for child maltreatment. However, the programmes tend to be health and parenting-focused, and do not necessarily address directly reducing the domestic violence or reporting on changes in domestic violence incidence. In the UK the *Family Nurse Partnership* is offered to mothers on the basis of age, targeting those aged 19, and not necessarily women assessed as vulnerable to DVA. The Building Blocks evaluation of the *Family Nurse Partnership* found no impact on short-term primary health outcomes, and further research is needed to show the impact on child maltreatment and DVA in the longer term (Robling *et al.* 2016). In Hawaii the *Healthy Start* home visitation programme evaluation collected data on domestic violence and abuse as an outcome measure alongside data on child maltreatment for 643 families (Bair-Merritt *et al.* 2010). Compared with mothers in the control group who had not received the programme, those in the intervention group reported lower rates of DVA victimization and lower rates of perpetration of violence towards their partner when the child was aged three. No differences were found, however, between the two groups at the longer-term follow-up.

The *Domestic Violence Enhanced Home Visitation Program* (DOVE) in the USA is a six-session, brochure-based empowerment programme that gives pregnant mothers affected by DVA information on the cycle of violence, safety planning and local DVA support services. An experimental study (randomized control trial, RCT) compared outcomes for 124 pregnant mothers on DOVE embedded within a routine home visitation parent support programme with outcomes for 115 mothers on a standard home visitation programme. Mothers in both groups reported less DVA in the postnatal period, but mothers who had received the DOVE programme showed significantly greater reductions in DVA experiences (Sharps *et al.* 2016).

Whole-family approaches for children in infancy and the early years: Children's social care has increased its capacity to identify DVA but still struggles to find appropriate ways of achieving change in families where children experience DVA. Many social workers acknowledge that failing to work with perpetrators places responsibility on women for men's violence and results in 'mother blaming'. Moreover, there is recognition that separation is not always the answer to DVA: some families do not want to separate, and DVA often continues beyond the point of separation. Whole-family approaches that directly address DVA are increasingly popular, although much more needs to be known about father engagement, how the violence is addressed, and what interventions are promising for families where the perpetrator is still involved because the victim is not in a position to separate or the children have continued post-separation contact. While some promising evidence is emerging, there remain considerable gaps in knowledge about effective responses for children in these different circumstances where different responses may be needed.

Three main whole-family DVA models can be identified:

- One organization works with all family members. They are usually seen separately and individually, perhaps with different workers for the victim, perpetrator and children; sometimes they are seen together.

- Different organizations or professionals work with different members of the same family, but coordinate their work – in this case, much depends on the quality of the collaboration and coordination.

- Interventions are delivered to the family as a group – the family is always seen together. This approach draws on the family group conference model.

Whole-family interventions need to address some key concerns:

- Whole-family approaches may fail to recognize the gendered power dynamics that underpin DVA – DVA affects different family members differently.

- The safety of women and children may be compromised.

- Fathers may resist or evade whole-family interventions and women and children become the focus of services' scrutiny by default.

- Social workers and other practitioners lack confidence and skills in working with abusive men (Stanley and Humphreys 2017).

Evaluation findings in the UK of programmes such as *For Baby's Sake* (Domoney *et al.* 2019; Trevillion *et al.* 2020) indicate some promising feedback from parents for whole-family approaches that combine domestic violence treatment and trauma-informed approaches, to address adult mental health, with parenting and infant mental health-focused support. *For Baby's Sake* was developed by the UK charity The Stefanou Foundation, and it works with both expectant parents, whether living together or apart, from pre-birth up until the child reaches the age of two. There are different modules for mothers and fathers, focusing on safety, reducing stress and supporting parenting, building attachment and improving knowledge of healthy child development. Mothers' sessions address trauma, safety and DVA impact, while fathers' sessions include anger, masculinity, sexual respect and the impact of DVA on children, and draw on methods of work with perpetrators. The evaluation found some success of the programme in involving parents; only 11 to 18 per cent of parents disengaged from the programme after signing up. However, over a four-year period of research the data that could be collected on outcomes regarding mothers' safety and mental health was rather limited (only nine parents had before-and-after programme data on levels of DVA experiences), partly due to lack of practitioner time and difficulty in follow-up (Trevillion *et al.* 2020). The researchers propose that better outcome measures should be developed to assess the impact of whole-family approaches in future studies.

Therapeutic support for children in infancy and the early years: For younger children below the age of four there are some limited but promising findings on using play therapies to support attachment, interaction and boundary setting (Waldman-Levi and Weintraub 2015). There are also evaluations of counselling and child and parent psychotherapy programmes delivered to mothers and preschool-aged children that focus on improving child and parent interactions and activities (Lieberman, Ippen and van Horn 2006; Lieberman, van Horn and Ippen 2005; Timmer *et al.* 2010). Reduced maternal distress or PTSD symptoms and fewer behavioural problems have been found in families completing these programmes. However, the outcomes for comparison groups who did not receive the programmes are not clear, as comparative data was unavailable or difficult to collect.

Supporting children aged 5–11

Parenting support for families with children aged 5–11: The NSPCC's *Domestic Abuse Recovering Together* (DART) programme works with mothers and children aged 7–11 affected by DVA. DART aims to support the mother and child relationship by improving communication, enabling them to share feelings about the abuse, and reducing problem behaviour. The programme provides separate group sessions for mothers and children as well as sessions for the mothers and children together, taking part in activities designed to strengthen the relationship. An (internal NSPCC) evaluation assessed the impact on mothers and children using a 'before-and-after' programme design and comparing findings for mothers and children on DART with a (small) group of mothers and children who received play therapy in a refuge. Mothers who completed DART reported greater self-esteem, more confidence in parenting and better control over the child's behaviour. Children who completed DART experienced fewer emotional and behavioural problems compared to the non-DART group. Parents, children and professionals interviewed rated the DART programme highly in interview, and the joint mother and child sessions were helpful for developing cooperation and communication. Unfortunately, data at follow-up was sparse, so it is not known if these benefits were sustained over time. The author of the evaluation notes that barriers to improvement included continued contact between the father and child, and some mothers returning to live with the perpetrator after completing DART (Smith 2016).

Therapeutic support for families with children aged 5–11: Evaluations of therapeutic and recovery-focused interventions, usually delivered by specialist domestic violence or mental health services, have drawn heavily on group work and 'talking therapies', usually involving children aged over four. There are some promising findings for parallel mothers' and children's group programmes for children aged four to six. In the USA Graham-Bermann *et al.* (2015) evaluated the impact of parallel group programmes for mothers and 120 children aged four to six who had been exposed to severe domestic violence in the past two years. Using an RCT design, 58 mothers and children were randomly allocated to the intervention group and 62 to the wait list comparison group. The intervention consisted of the *Preschool Kids Club* (PKC) programme, a group programme for young children delivered over five weeks that aims to improve their safety planning, managing feelings and attitudes about domestic violence, with the *Moms' Empowerment Programme* (MEP), which aims to address the social and emotional adjustment of mothers, reducing the possible development of mental health difficulties. Standardized measures of child behaviour and emotional wellbeing were used to assess change from baseline (T1 58 dyads in intervention, 62 in comparison) to post-treatment (T2 50 dyads in intervention, 49 in comparison) and eight months later (T3 36 dyads in intervention, 35 in comparison). Significant improvements were found in the behaviour and emotional wellbeing of children in the intervention group at time three (T3) compared with children in the comparison group. Twenty-three per cent of the children in the intervention group were no longer scoring in the clinical range compared with 8 per cent in the comparison group. Twenty-two per cent were in the normal range in the intervention group compared with 5 per cent in the comparison group.

A systematic review of research by Howarth *et al.* (2016) found psychoeducational group-based interventions delivered to the child were more effective for improving mental health outcomes than other types of intervention. Interventions delivered to (non-abusive) parents and to children were most likely to be effective for improving children's behavioural outcomes. Group-based psychoeducational interventions delivered to children and non-abusive parents in parallel were largely acceptable to all stakeholders. There is limited evidence for the acceptability of other types of intervention.

Supporting children and young people aged 12–17

School and college-based intimate partner violence prevention: Evaluations of school-based DVA prevention programmes that target older children and teenagers focus mostly on partner abuse in young people's own relationships. Most of the evaluation evidence has come from the 'dating violence' prevention programmes in the USA that aim to address gender norms and equality early in life, before gender stereotypes that support abuse become deeply ingrained in children and youth. There are fewer UK-based evaluations, one example being the study of *Relationships without Fear* that found promising changes in attitudes related to DVA (Fox *et al.* 2014). Many of these programmes show changes in attitudes but little evidence of impact on behaviour (Fellmeth *et al.* 2013). Dating violence prevention programmes have been found to be more effective if they are skills-based, interactive, are delivered over multiple sessions rather than in a single session, deliver positive messages to boys, use local data on DVA and culturally specific and relevant information in the curriculum, aim to change attitudes and behaviour rather than just provide information to young people and take a 'whole-school approach' (Stanley *et al.* 2015). An evaluation of prevention programmes developed over the last 25 years found gaps in programmes that target some of the most vulnerable groups of young people such as young people with disabilities, from minority ethnic groups and young people who identify as LGBTQI (lesbian, gay, bisexual, transgender, queer (or questioning) and intersex) (Crooks *et al.* 2019).

The *Safe Dates* programme and more recently the *Dating Matters* programme, both multi-component programmes from the USA targeting children, parents, teachers and school staff, have been rigorously evaluated through experimental design studies (Foshee *et al.* 1998, 2000, 2004; Niolon *et al.* 2019). A four-year evaluation study found risks of perpetration and victimization were significantly lower in the groups exposed to *Dating Matters* compared with those exposed only to *Safe Dates* (Niolon *et al.* 2019).

Support for young people aged 12–17: The systematic review of effective programmes to support children living with DVA by Howarth *et al.* (2016) found no studies that targeted older adolescents between the ages of 15 to 18.

Promoting children's agency and resilience in response to domestic violence and abuse: Messages for practice

In this final section we draw together some of the messages from the above research on DVA experiences for children and young people, resilience and effective responses to look at practice implications when working with children. Listening carefully to what a child or young person says is likely to be far more effective than assuming that all children living with DVA will have the same experiences and needs (Aria *et al.* 2019). Children and young people may also be confused and have mixed feelings about the DVA, lack the words to express their feelings, and need time to process what they have witnessed at home.

Building trust and safety when talking to children[8]

Children and young people may, for a variety of reasons, be unable to talk about the abuse:

> I can't talk to you because if I do my dad will hurt my mum again. (Child, aged 8)

When children present, they often do not have the language to describe their experiences. They all behave and respond differently depending on a number of external and internal factors and influences. The initial assessment by a specialist children's worker is essential to start the unravelling process. Children will more than likely have kept their experiences a secret for a long time, they will have developed coping strategies and, in some cases, will have been threatened not to tell. Often, we are met with a child who is scared, reluctant to talk and who may have normalized the experience in order to protect family members. Trust has to be earned. A child who has experienced abuse has learned that the world is a bad place and that adults can and do behave in ways that hurt and love interchangeably. The practitioner has to prove herself trustworthy and maintain this level of trust throughout the entirety of the relationship.

First, it is essential to establish an environment where the child feels in control and empowered. This means having a private and safe space in which to talk, giving the child time

---

8   This section was written by Amanda Elwen.

and listening without judgement: 'You can talk about anything you want to in here. Even the things you find really hard to talk about.' Telling a child, 'You are not alone. I have worked with 1000s of children who are going through what you are going through and there is nothing you can tell me that I haven't heard before' knocks down the barriers straight away.

Always believe a child from the outset – take what they say as truth; even when your adult brain moves into critical thinking and you know the child is fabricating, understand that they may be fabricating for a million reasons. Never question what they are saying; give them the space to tell their story, their experiences. They have more than likely made sense of it all in their own heads, and you are more than likely the first person they have told; they may have even started to rationalize their experiences. If we, as practitioners, start to question children, we start to close them down, we start to doubt them, and ultimately this leads to them starting to distrust you and the world around them. At the stage of initial assessment your job is simply to encourage the child to share and open up.

Be on their side. Children and young people also want to know that you are going to safeguard and protect them the best way you can, that you are on their side. I can't stress how important this is and how quickly they will figure you out if you are lying. This means empowering a child in the safeguarding process – advocating at multi-agency meetings, asserting their consenting needs to the parents and encouraging them to make informed decisions in respect to the chaos that often surrounds them. It has many positive outcomes, the main one being establishing for the child or young person a sense of control and choice.

Say 'it's not your fault'. Some children will absorb the responsibility; they may feel guilty about their behaviours or they may have been blamed for the violence. If a child is feeling responsible, we must always strive to find ways to let them know that it isn't their fault. Self-blame is something we can help children overcome; if we don't, it can serve as an obstacle to their recovery.

Anti-discriminatory practice. Anyone from a minority or marginalized group knows exactly when someone is behaving oppressively. Children are just as perceptive to this as adults.

If practitioners hold an attitude or belief about, or even lack understanding about a child's identity or lived experience, they have to ask themselves if they are fit to work with this child. If it is at all possible, ask a child who they would prefer their worker to be. For example, a child from South Asian descent may feel better speaking to a worker from a similar ethnic group, or they may think that this might be unsafe. Give the child choices and never make assumptions.

Clarity about roles and responsibilities. It is essential that boundaries are established from the outset; this means being clear about your role and your responsibilities as a practitioner. I really struggle with this as I feel it can sometimes create a barrier from the start. The traditional line goes something like this, 'If I think that you are in immediate danger or you are at risk of harm, I have to refer to children's social care and/or the police.' Sometimes children have been told very clearly not to talk to anyone about the abuse, and certainly not a social worker or the police. In cases like this, the specialist charities are so important because the child does not see workers from these charities as a threat. A child who has been told never to talk and/or has a threat attached to it will test the worker's boundaries endlessly, and more than often will give snippets of information to test what the worker will do with it. I refer to this as a jigsaw piece – every time you see a child, they give you a piece of the jigsaw to look after; essentially they are testing what you will do with that piece of information every time they see you. Over time the child adds to the picture and sometimes as a practitioner you know what pieces are coming next because you can see the picture forming. I can't tell you the number of times myself and my colleagues knew a sexual abuse disclosure was coming, and how frustrating it was, how sensitive we had to be – it is important to take everything at the pace of the child and to resist what you, as an adult and practitioner, want to achieve, which is ultimately a disclosure and the evidence to go with it. The child trusts you to hold the jigsaw piece for as long as is required.

A disclosure then enables the practitioner to respond to the risk and to the impact of any trauma, and the evidence enables the establishment of the facts that can be referred to the statutory services. It is then the role of social workers and the police to investigate cases and make a judgement on whether there should be a statutory intervention and/or a criminal investigation. It is essential that any disclosure discussions are recorded, in writing, and that all concerns and discussions about the child's welfare and decisions made and the reasons for those decisions documented.

Over the years I have implemented age-appropriate creative ways to ensure that children are clear about what I have to do with the information they are sharing. I often start with re-establishing my position as their advocate, saying that everything I do will have their best interests at heart, and that all the way through I will keep them informed, updated and where possible include them in the safeguarding process, if this is their preference. Although practitioners can feel like this creates a barrier, it is important that the child knows that you have rules that you have to follow.

You can adapt the sentence to fit the ability of the child. For example, a ten-year-old will usually understand the following:

> Everything you say to me is confidential; however, if you tell me something that means there is risk to you or a risk to someone else, I will have to tell someone who can help. Your safety and welfare is my main priority, and wherever possible and if you agree, we will do it together.

A five-year-old will understand:

> You can tell me about what is happening at home and I will not tell anyone else unless you want me to. If you tell me something that is really hurting you or hurting someone else, then I will have to tell someone who can help you more.

Safety planning

At first contact, a child's safety is paramount, and a robust risk assessment is always carried out. This gives practitioners a sense of the level of risk to the child and enables us to build a plan of safety around the child, developing a robust safety plan in partnership with them.

An example of a typical safety plan would look at the following:

My safe place inside the house is: . . . .

I need to think about: . . . . (what is the best way to stay safe)

The person I can ring is: . . . .
Their number is: . . . .

If I need to go outside the house, my safe place will be:
. . . .

I will phone the police if I am afraid or I might get hurt. Their number is: . . . .

I will talk to someone I trust about what is happening to me, so that I have a friend I can turn to. This person is: . . . .
Their number is: . . . .

If they are not available, I can also contact: . . . .

I know I can always contact (agency) and speak to my worker, no matter what the problem.

My worker is called: . . . .
Their number is: . . . .

Dates of our next meetings are: . . . .

And the address I need to come to is: . . . .

Children are resilient; they think and more than often have it all figured out before you. Do not be afraid to ask them what they can do to stay safe, and do not be afraid to let them lead. Children and young people may often take an active role in protecting siblings and finding help to end the violence.

> When he got angry with mom... I locked myself into the bathroom and brought mom's phone with me, and then I called my uncle and asked him to come and sort things out, 'cause I was really scared. ('Aranya', in Överlien 2016, p.685)

These children are living daily with abuse, and they have already developed a huge number of coping mechanisms, some healthy and some not so healthy. The impact of DVA and how children cope may not be straightforward. Turning on music loudly to block out the noise, climbing out of the window to find a safe place or turning to friends in gangs to spend time outside the house are some of the things young people may do (Aria *et al.* 2019; Radford *et al.* 2011b). Draw from the research on resilience and protective factors reviewed in this chapter and support young people in developing the healthy ones.

Enabling the child and mother to understand their feelings about the DVA and strengthening support between the mother and child or child, young person and supportive peers is another area in which many practitioners have opportunities to help build resilience. Talking to peers, however, may not be safe for every child. A study of children's experiences of DVA in London found mixed views about whether it was a good idea to talk to friends at school. Talking at school could make things worse:

> …'cause if, I think if you tell them they'll, like even get, it will go even more worser, make more problems too. If you keep it to yourself you feel like you won't have like any problems in your head and like you don't, like you be, you keep quiet. ('Farai', quoted in Radford *et al.* 2011b)

Some children said that 'the mum' could get into trouble if the child talked about the domestic violence at school, or that if the child told other children, 'he' might get bullied (Radford *et al.* 2011b). It is important to listen to what the child says about talking to peers, to their mother or to other members of the family, as this may not be appropriate for all situations.

Peer support[9]

While many practitioners will challenge the use of peer groups in situations where abuse has taken place, we have found that if managed appropriately, the positive outcomes far outweigh the preventable and manageable risks. Peer support and peer education has to be managed carefully, and every child moving from one-to-one sessions to group sessions is assessed for readiness; they also have to sign a behaviour contract.

The role of the practitioner is always to ensure that the group is structured, planned and has clear learning outcomes for every session; children and young people should always gain

---

9   This section was written by Amanda Elwen.

and develop because of their participation, and any developments and outcomes should be documented within individual case notes.

The HARV peer support and education programme supports and provides young people with training and resources that focus on understanding and recovering from the impact of domestic abuse. Our group work aims to enable children and young people to repair and rebuild relational skills. Our peer group would meet three to four times a week; they would have food, watch TV and catch up with each other, often sharing experiences and giving advice on how to manage complex situations. They would go on weekly activities together like bowling or going to the cinema, and every six months we would take 12 young people on a holiday where they could participate in new activities. Our services reflected what the children and young people needed – a safe family environment where they had the opportunity to thrive. As well as social activities we would implement recovery programmes, and every week we would discuss the following themes related to the experience of domestic abuse. Sessions would include:

- How abuse affects our thinking and behaviour.
- Self-esteem – what is it?
- Who's my family?
- Staying safe.
- Protective factors, strengthening resilience.
- Talking positive.
- Ways to handle difficult feelings.
- Healthy relationships and trust.
- Equality.
- Assertiveness vs aggression.
- How do I communicate with others?

The practitioner's role is to make the abusive behaviours conscious and to support the child to change into more positive behaviours, moving from abusive forms of communication to communication that is healthy, such as equality, compromise, respect, listening, etc.

Young people who have accessed our peer support programme are still in contact with each other and continue to support each other as and when needed. The first group of young people are now in their mid-twenties, and out of the initial group of 11 boys, only two have gone on to perpetrate violence.

Building individual resources for children

Schools can play an important role in preventing DVA and in providing help and support to children and young people. Considerable efforts have been made to strengthen the relationship between schools and other agencies such as the police and children's social care through initiatives such as *Operation Encompass*, which enables the police to liaise with schools when children are involved in DVA incidents. Safety plans could take into account children's views of safety in and on leaving school, particularly if they fear post-separation abuse or harassment from a parent. Breakfast clubs and homework clubs can also play an important part in supporting children's education and wellbeing (Lloyd 2018).

Conclusion

Understanding and knowledge about DVA and its impact on children and young people have grown considerably in the past 30 years. While there are still gaps in the research on effective responses to address, particularly in dealing with diversity issues, there are promising indications of the value of taking a lifecourse perspective to consider the impact of living with DVA for children and young people at different ages, how children cope, and how best to support them.

References

Alaggia, R. and Donohue, M. (2017) 'Take these broken wings and learn to fly: Applying resilience concepts to practice with children and youth exposed to intimate partner violence.' *Smith College Studies in Social Work 88*, 1, 20–38. Available at: https://psycnet.apa.org/record/2018-03828-003

Aria, L., Hewood, A., Feder, G., Howarth, E., *et al.* (2019) 'Hope, agency, and the lived experience of violence: A qualitative systematic review of children's perspectives on domestic violence and abuse.' *Trauma, Violence & Abuse*, 1–12. doi:10.1177/1524838019849582.

Austin, A., Shanahan, M., Barrios, Y. and Macy, R. (2019) 'A systematic review of interventions for women parenting in the context of intimate partner violence.' *Trauma, Violence & Abuse 20*, 4, 498–519.

Bair-Merritt, M., Blackstone, M. and Feudtner, C. (2006) 'Physical health outcomes of childhood exposure to intimate partner violence: A systematic review.' *Pediatrics 117*, 2, 278–290.

Bair-Merritt, M., Jennings, J., Chen, R., Burrell, L., *et al.* (2010) 'Reducing maternal intimate partner violence after the birth of a child: A randomized controlled trial of the Hawaii Healthy Start Home Visitation Program.' *Archive of Pediatric Adolescent Medicine 164*, 1, 16–23.

Birchall, J. and Choudhry, S. (2018) *'What About My Right Not To Be Abused?' Domestic Abuse, Human Rights and the Family Courts*. Bristol: Women's Aid. Available at: www.womensaid.org.uk/research-and-publications/domestic-abuse-human-rights-and-the-family-courts

Bowstead, J. (2017) 'Segmented journeys, fragmented lives: Women's forced migration to escape domestic violence.' *Journal of Gender-Based Violence 1*, 1, 43–58.

Boy, A. and Salihu, H. (2004) 'Intimate partner violence and birth outcomes: A systematic review.' *International Journal of Fertility and Women's Medicine 49*, 4, 159–164.

Bradbury-Jones, C. and Isham, L. (2020) 'Editorial: The pandemic paradox: The consequences of COVID-19 on domestic violence.' *Journal of Clinical Nursing 29*, 2047–2049.

Chan, K., Chen, Q. and Chen, M. (2019) 'Prevalence and correlates of the co-occurrence of family violence: A meta-analysis on family polyvictimization.' *Trauma, Violence & Abuse*, 1–17. doi:10.1177/1524838019841601.

Coker, A., Sanderson, M. and Dong, B. (2004) 'Partner violence during pregnancy and risk of adverse pregnancy outcomes.' *Pediatric and Perinatal Epidemiology 18*, 4, 260–269.

Crooks, C., Jaff, P., Dunlop, C., Kerry, A. and Exner-Cortens, D. (2019) 'Preventing gender-based violence among adolescents and young adults: Lessons from 25 years of program development and evaluation.' *Violence Against Women 25*, 1, 29–55.

DfE (Department for Education) (2017) *Statutory Framework for the Early Years Foundation Stage: Setting the Standards for Learning, Development and Care for Children from Birth to Five.* 3 March. Available at: https://assets.publishing.service.gov.uk/government/uploads/system/uploads/attachment_data/file/596629/EYFS_STATUTORY_FRAMEWORK_2017.pdf

DfE (2020) *Keeping Children Safe in Education: Statutory Guidance for Schools and Colleges.* September. Available at: https://assets.publishing.service.gov.uk/government/uploads/system/uploads/attachment_data/file/835733/Keeping_children_safe_in_education_2019.pdf

Domoney, J., Fulton, E., Stanley, N., McIntyre, A., *et al.* (2019) *'For Baby's Sake*: Intervention development and evaluation design of a whole-family perinatal intervention to break the cycle of domestic abuse.' *Journal of Family Violence 34*, 539–551. Available at: https://doi.org/10.1007/s10896-019-00037-3

Eckenrode, J., Campa, M., Morris, P., Henderson Jr, C.R., *et al.* (2017) 'The prevention of child maltreatment through the Nurse Family Partnership program: Mediating effects in a long-term follow-up study.' *Child Maltreatment 22*, 2, 92–99.

Fellmeth, G., Heffernan, C., Nurse, J., Habibula, S. and Sethi, D. (2013) *Educational and Skills-Based Interventions for Preventing Relationship and Dating Violence in Adolescents and Young Adults (Review)*. The Cochrane Library, no. 6.

Finkelhor, D. and Turner, H. (2015) *A National Profile of Children Exposed to Family Violence: Police Response, Family Response, and Individual Impact*. NIJ 2010-IJ-CX-0021. Final Report. Washington, DC: US Department of Justice. Available at: www.ncjrs.gov/pdffiles1/nij/grants/248577.pdf

Foshee, V., Bauman, K., Arriaga, X., Helms, R., Koch, G.G. and Linder, G.F. (1998) 'An evaluation of Safe Dates, an adolescent dating violence prevention program.' *American Journal of Public Health 88*, 1, 45–50.

Foshee, V., Bauman, K., Ennett, S., Linder, G.F., Benefield, T. and Suchindran, C. (2004) 'Assessing the long-term effects of the Safe Dates program and a booster in preventing and reducing adolescent dating violence victimization and perpetration.' *American Journal of Public Health 94*, 619–624.

Foshee, V., Bauman, K., Greene, W., Koch, G.G., Linder, G.F. and MacDougall, J.E. (2000) 'The Safe Dates program: 1 year follow up results.' *American Journal of Public Health 90*, 1619–1622.

Fox, C., Carr, M., Gadd, D. and Sim, J. (2014) 'Evaluating the effectiveness of domestic abuse prevention education: Are certain children more or less receptive to the messages conveyed?' *Legal and Criminological Psychology 21*, 1, 212–227.

Graham-Bermann, S. and Edleson, J. (eds) (2001) *Domestic Violence in the Lives of Children: The Future of Research, Intervention and Social Policy*. Washington, DC: American Psychological Association.

Graham-Bermann, S.A., Miller-Graff, L.E., Howell, K.H. and Grogan-Kaylor, A. (2015) 'An efficacy trial of an intervention program for children exposed to intimate partner violence.' *Child Psychiatry & Human Development 46*, 928–939. Available at: https://doi.org/10.1007/s10578-015-0532-4

HM Government (2015) *What to Do If You're Worried a Child Is Being Abused: Advice for Practitioners*. March. Available at: https://assets.publishing.service.gov.uk/government/uploads/system/uploads/attachment_data/file/419604/What_to_do_if_you_re_worried_a_child_is_being_abused.pdf

HM Government (2016) *Ending Violence Against Women and Girls: Strategy 2016–2020*. March. Available at: https://assets.publishing.service.gov.uk/government/uploads/system/uploads/attachment_data/file/522166/VAWG_Strategy_FINAL_PUBLICATION_MASTER_vRB.PDF

HM Government (2018) *Working Together to Safeguard Children: A Guide to Inter-Agency Working to Safeguard and Promote the Welfare of Children*. July. Available at: https://assets.publishing.service.gov.uk/government/uploads/system/uploads/attachment_data/file/779401/Working_Together_to_Safeguard-Children.pdf

Holt, S., Buckley, S. and Whelan, S. (2008) 'The impact of exposure to domestic violence on children and young people: A review of the literature.' *Child Abuse & Neglect 32*, 797–810.

Hooker, L., Samaraweena, N., Agius, P. and Taft, A. (2016) 'Intimate partner violence and the experience of early motherhood: A cross-sectional analysis of factors associated with a poor experience of motherhood.' *Midwifery 34*, 88–94.

House of Commons (2018) *Domestic Abuse: Ninth Report of Session 2017–19*. HC 1015. Home Affairs Committee. London: House of Commons.

House of Commons (2020) *Home Office Preparedness for Covid19 (Corona Virus): Domestic Abuse and Risk of Harm Within the Home: Second Report of Session 2019–21*. HC321. Home Affairs Committee. London: House of Commons.

Howarth, E., Moore, T.H.M., Welton, N., Lewis, N., *et al.* (2016) 'IMPRoving Outcomes for children exposed to domestic ViolencE (IMPROVE): An evidence synthesis.' *Public Health Research 4*, 10. doi:10.3310/phr04100.

Howe, D. (2005) *Child Abuse and Neglect: Attachment, Development and Intervention*. London: Palgrave Macmillan.

Jaffe, P., Wolfe, D. and Campbell, M. (2012) *Growing Up with Domestic Violence*. Cambridge, MA: Hogrefe.

Jaffe, P., Wolfe, D. and Wilson, S. (1990) *Children of Battered Women*. Thousand Oaks, CA: Sage.

Katz, E. (2015a) 'Domestic violence, children's agency and mother–child relationships: Towards a more advanced model.' *Children & Society 29*, 1, 69–79.

Katz, E. (2015b) 'Recovery-promoters: Ways in which children and mothers support one another's recoveries from domestic violence.' *British Journal of Social Work 45*, i153–i169. doi:10.1093/bjsw/bcv091.

Kitzmann, K.M., Gaylord, N.K., Holt, A.R. and Kenny, E.D. (2003) 'Child witnesses to domestic violence: A meta-analytic review.' *Journal of Consulting and Clinical Psychology 71*, 339–352.

Laing, L. and Humphreys, C. (2013) *Social Work and Domestic Violence: Developing Critical and Reflective Practice*. London: Sage.

Letourneau, N., Fedick, C. and Willms, J. (2007) 'Mothering and domestic violence: A longitudinal analysis.' *Journal of Family Violence 22*, 6, 649–659.

Lieberman, A.F., Ippen, C.G. and van Horn, P. (2006) 'Child–parent psychotherapy: 6-month follow-up of a randomized controlled trial.' *Journal of the American Academy of Child & Adolescent Psychiatry 45*, 8, 913–918.

Lieberman, A.F., van Horn, P. and Ippen, C.G. (2005) 'Toward evidence-based treatment: Child–parent psychotherapy with preschoolers exposed to marital violence.' *Journal of the American Academy of Child & Adolescent Psychiatry 44*, 12, 1241–1248.

Lipsky, S., Holt, V., Easterling, T. and Critchlow, C. (2003) 'The impact of police-reported intimate partner violence during pregnancy on birth outcomes.' *Obstetrics and Gynaecology 102*, 3, 557–564.

Lloyd, M. (2018) 'Domestic violence and education: Examining the impact of domestic violence on young children, children, and young people and the potential role of schools.' *Frontiers in Psychology* 9, 2094.

Lundy, M. and Grossman, S. (2005) 'The mental health and service needs of young children exposed to domestic violence: Supportive data.' *Families in Society: The Journal of Contemporary Social Services 86*, 1, 17–29.

McFarlane, J., Symes, L., Binder, B., Maddoux, J. and Paulson, R. (2014) 'Maternal–child dyads of functioning: The intergenerational impact of violence against women on children.' *Maternal and Child Health Journal 18*, 9, 2236–2243.

McGee, C. (2000) *Childhood Experiences of Domestic Violence*. London: Jessica Kingsley Publishers.

Mejdoubi, J., van den Heijkant, S., van Leerdam, F., Heymans, M., Crijnen, A. and Hirasing, R. (2015) 'The effect of VoorZorg, the Dutch nurse–family partnership, on child maltreatment and development: A randomized controlled trial.' *PLOS One 10*, 4, e0120182. doi:10.1371/journal.pone.0120182.

Mullender, A., Hague, G., Imam, U., Kelly, L., Malos, E. and Regan, L. (2002) *Children's Perspectives on Domestic Violence*. London: Sage.

NICE (National Institute for Health and Care Excellence) (2017) *Child Abuse and Neglect*. NICE Guideline 76. 9 October. Available at: www.nice.org.uk/guidance/ng76/resources/child-abuse-and-neglect-pdf-1837637587141

NICE (2019) *Child Abuse and Neglect*. Quality Standards 179. 12 February. Available at: www.nice.org.uk/guidance/qs179/resources/child-abuse-and-neglect-pdf-75545669305285

Niolon, P., Vivolo-Kantor, A., Tracy, A., Latzman, N., *et al.* (2019) 'An RCT of dating matters: Effects on teen dating violence and relationship behaviors.' *American Journal of Preventive Medicine 57*, 1, 13–23.

Nixon, K.L., Tutty, L.M., Radtke, H.L., Ateah, C.A. and Jane Ursel, E. (2017) 'Protective strategies of mothers abused by intimate partners: Rethinking the deficit model.' *Violence Against Women 23*, 11, 1271–1292.

Olds, D.L., Eckenrode, J., Henderson, C.R., Kitzman, H., *et al.* (1997) 'Long-term effects of home visitation on maternal life course and child abuse and neglect.' *Journal of the American Medical Association 278*, 637–643.

Olds, D.L., Henderson, C.R., Chamberlin, R. and Tatelbaum, R. (1986) 'Preventing child-abuse and neglect – A randomized trial of nurse home visitation.' *Pediatrics 78*, 65–78.

ONS (Office for National Statistics) (2019) *Domestic Abuse Victim Characteristics, England and Wales: Year Ending March 2019*. Available at: www.ons.gov.uk/peoplepopulationandcommunity/crimeandjustice/articles/domesticabusevictimcharacteristicsenglandandwales/yearendingmarch2019

ONS (2020a) *Child Abuse Extent and Nature, England and Wales: Year Ending March 2019*. Available at: www.ons.gov.uk/peoplepopulationandcommunity/crimeandjustice/articles/childabuseextentandnatureenglandandwales/yearendingmarch2019

ONS (2020b) *Homicide in England and Wales: Year Ending March 2019*. Available at: www.ons.gov.uk/peoplepopulationandcommunity/crimeandjustice/articles/homicideinenglandandwales/yearendingmarch2019

Överlien, C. (2016) '"Do you want to do some arm wrestling?" Children's strategies when experiencing domestic violence and the meaning of age.' *Child & Family Social Work 22*, 680–688. doi:10.1111/cfs.12283.

Radford, L. and Hester, M. (2006) *Mothering Through Domestic Violence*. London: Jessica Kingsley Publishers.

Radford, L. and Hester, M. (2015) 'More Than a Mirage? Safe Contact for Children and Young People Who Have Been Exposed to Domestic Violence.' In N. Stanley and C. Humphreys (eds) *Domestic Violence and Protecting Children: New Thinking and Approaches* (pp.112–130). London: Jessica Kingsley Publishers.

Radford, L., Aitken, R., Miller, P., Roberts, J., Ellis, J. and Firkic, A. (2011b) *Meeting the Needs of Children Living with Domestic Violence in London*. London: NSPCC/Refuge/City Bridge Trust. Available at: www.nspcc.org.uk/globalassets/documents/research-reports/meeting-needs-children-living-domestic-violence-london-report.pdf

Radford, L., Corral, S., Bradley, C., Fisher, H., *et al.* (2011a) *Child Abuse and Neglect in the UK Today.* London: NSPCC. Available at: https://learning.nspcc.org.uk/media/1042/child-abuse-neglect-uk-today-research-report.pdf

Radford, L., Corral, S., Bradley, C. and Fisher, H. (2013) 'The prevalence and impact of child maltreatment and other types of victimization in the UK: Findings from a population survey of caregivers, children and young people and young adults.' *Child Abuse & Neglect 37*, 10, 801–813. Available at: http://dx.doi.org/10.1016/j.chiabu.2013.02.004

Radford, L., Richardson Foster, H., Hargreaves, P. and Devaney, J. (2019) *Research Review: Early Childhood and the Inter-Generational Cycle of Domestic Violence.* London: NSPCC.

Rizo, C., Macy, R., Ermentrout, D. and Johns, N. (2011) 'A review of family interventions for intimate partner violence with a child focus or child component.' *Aggression and Violent Behavior 16*, 144–166.

Robling, M., Bekkers, M., Bell, K., Butler, C.C., *et al.* (2016) 'Effectiveness of a nurse-led intensive home-visitation programme for first-time teenage mothers (Building Blocks): A pragmatic randomised controlled trial.' *The Lancet 387*, 146–155.

Sacco, M., Caputo, F., Ricci, P., Sicilia, F., *et al.* (2020) 'The impact of the Covid-19 pandemic on domestic violence: The dark side of home isolation during quarantine.' *Medico-Legal Journal 88*, 2, 71–73.

Schechter, D.S., Willheim, E., McCaw, J., Blake Turner, J., Myers, M.M. and Zeanah, C.H. (2011) 'The relationship of violent fathers, posttraumatically stressed mothers and symptomatic children in a preschool-age inner-city pediatrics clinic sample.' *Journal of Interpersonal Violence 26*, 18, 3699–3719.

Secco, L., Letourneau, N. and Collins, E. (2016) '"My eyes were open": Awakened maternal identity and leaving violent relationships for the infant/children.' *Journal of Family Violence 31*, 619–645.

Sharps, P.W., Bullock, L.F., Campbell, J.C., Alhusen, J.L., *et al.* (2016) 'Domestic violence enhanced perinatal home visits: The DOVE randomized clinical trial.' *Journal of Women's Health 25*, 1129–1138.

Smith, E. (2016) *Domestic Abuse Recovery Together (DART): Evaluation Report.* London: NSPCC.

Stanley, N. (2011) *Children Experiencing Domestic Violence: A Research Review.* Research in Practice. Dartington: Dartington Social Research.

Stanley, N. and Humphreys, C. (2017) 'Identifying the key components of a "whole family" intervention for families experiencing domestic violence and abuse.' *Journal of Gender-Based Violence 1*, 1, 99–115.

Stanley, N., Ellis, J., Farrelly, N., Hollinghurst, S. and Downe, S. (2015) 'Preventing domestic abuse for children and young people: A review of school-based interventions.' *Children and Youth Services Review 59*, 120–131.

Stark, E. (2007) *Coercive Control: How Men Entrap Women in Personal Life.* Oxford: Oxford University Press.

Tajima, E., Herenkohl, T., Moyan, C. and Derr, A. (2011) 'Moderating the effects of childhood exposure to intimate partner violence: The roles of parenting characteristics and adolescent peer support.' *Journal of Research into Adolescence 21*, 2, 376–394.

Timmer, S.G., Ware, L.M., Urquiza, A.J. and Zebell, N.M. (2010) 'The effectiveness of parent–child interaction therapy for victims of interparental violence.' *Violence & Victims 25*, 4, 486–503.

Trevillion, K., Domoney, J., Ocloo, J., Heslin, M., *et al.* (2020) *For Baby's Sake: Final Evaluation Report.* London: King's College London and The Stefanou Foundation.

Usher, K., Bhullar, N., Durkin, J., Gyamfi, N. and Jackson, D. (2020) 'Editorial: Family violence and COVID-19: Increased vulnerability and reduced options for support.' *International Journal of Mental Health Nursing 29*, 549–552.

Waldman-Levi, A. and Weintraub, N. (2015) 'Efficacy of a crisis intervention in improving mother–child interaction and children's play functioning.' *American Journal of Occupational Therapy 69*, 1–11.

WHO (World Health Organization) (2016) *INSPIRE: Seven Strategies for Ending Violence Against Children.* Geneva: WHO. Available at: www.who.int/publications/i/item/inspire-seven-strategies-for-ending-violence-against-children

Chapter 3

Violence and Abuse in Young People's Relationships
FROM RESEARCH TO PRACTICE

Christine Barter and Deidre Cartwright

Introduction

This chapter brings together evidence from research and practice to provide an overview of current knowledge on interpersonal violence and abuse (IPVA) in young people's (under the age of 18) relationships, and how best to support young victims/survivors. The first part of the chapter sets out research findings on the prevalence of different forms of IPVA, including through new technologies, and its subjective negative impact on young people and their help-seeking. This evidence demonstrates both the extent and the complexity of the issues to be addressed in practice. The second half of the chapter builds on this research to provide advice to professionals, working in a multi-agency context, on identifying young people experiencing IPVA; providing a safe, empathetic and consistent response; and referring young people to appropriate specialists and safeguarding services within their local area. The practice advice draws mostly from SafeLives' *Spotlight #3: Young People and Domestic Abuse* (SafeLives 2017a), an online resource that brought together learning from 11 front-line practitioners,[1] research experts[2] and most importantly, 11 young survivors and their parents,

---

1   Janice Stevens, Young LGBT Scotland; Anna Clark, Equation; Di Hunter and Nicola McConnell, NSPCC; Pam Verdhara, Claire Amans, Jamilla Hassan and Hollie Pearson, South Tyneside Young Persons' Violence Advisor (YPVA) service; Amna Abdullatif, Women's Aid; Jo Sharpen, Against Violence & Abuse (AVA); and Helen Bonnick, Holes in the Wall.
2   Professor David Gadd, Dr Christine Barter, Dr Kat Ford and Dr Caroline Miles.

who shared their experiences and views through interviews and written accounts.[3] The findings from *Spotlight #3* also informed the *Safe Young Lives: Young People and Domestic Abuse* report (SafeLives 2017b). In addition, this section references many of the resources developed by the SafeLives Young People's Programme, a two-year programme funded by the Department for Education, to develop a safe, effective and research-based approach to supporting young people experiencing domestic abuse.

International research evidence

Although European evidence on IPVA in young people's relationships has emerged in the last decade, much of our understanding is still derived from the more extensive 'dating' violence research undertaken in the USA. While this evidence is informative, we must be cautious in simply transferring understanding from one country setting to another where disparate cultural and social contexts exist (Stanley *et al.* 2015). In addition, as the recommendations presented later in this chapter are based on UK practice, we will primarily concentrate on UK and European findings, although these will be situated within the wider international context.

Global studies have primarily examined three forms of IPVA: physical, sexual and emotional or psychological. Wincentak, Connolly and Card (2017) and Stonard *et al.* (2014) have undertaken data syntheses to determine international IPVA prevalence rates. Wincentak *et al.*'s (2017) meta-analysis addressed physical and sexual forms of violence (a total of 96 and 31 studies respectively), while Stonard *et al.*'s (2014) research synthesis, based on 52 studies with the majority from the USA, also included emotional and online forms of IPVA. Both evidence syntheses identified that approximately 20 per cent of young people, irrespective of gender, experienced physical violence from a partner. Stonard *et al.* (2014) also revealed that around half of all young people, again, irrespective of gender, reported some form of face-to-face emotional victimization. In respect of sexual violence, both studies identified higher levels of victimization for girls compared to boys. Wincentak *et al.* (2017) applied a narrow definition of coerced sexual intercourse to their meta-analysis, and found that 14 per cent of girls

---

3   All names of survivors and family members used in this chapter have been changed.

and 8 per cent of boys reported this form of victimization. Stonard *et al.*'s (2014) study also showed comparable results when a narrow definition was used of between 2 per cent and 19 per cent for females and 6 per cent for males.

Only relatively recently has IPVA through new technologies been included in prevalence studies. Most international research has focused on specific aspects of abuse through technology, most prominently controlling behaviour and surveillance; emotional online abuse; and coerced sexting (Draucker and Martsolf 2010; Marganski and Fauth 2013; Zweig *et al.* 2013). Stonard *et al.* (2014) found that between 50 per cent and 70 per cent of young people reported some form of IPVA through new technologies. However, they stress that as the evidence in this area is still emerging, findings should be viewed with caution.

In conclusion, Stonard *et al.* (2014) state that IPVA in young people's relationships represents a significant problem, with gender only being a factor in relation to sexual victimization. This gendered experience of sexual victimization continues online, where pressured sexting and unwanted sharing of sexual images was mainly reported by girls (see Draucker and Martsolf 2010; Wood *et al.* 2015; Zweig *et al.* 2013). However, studies that have examined the patterning of IPVA within young people's relationships indicate that girls consistently report higher levels of repeated incidents as well as more severe forms of violence than boys (Foshee 1996; Wolitzky-Taylor *et al.* 2008). International studies have shown that, compared to boys, girls report more negative emotional responses, are more likely to be hurt or require medical attention, while boys are more likely to laugh about the violence perpetrated against them (Foshee 1996; Jackson, Cram and Seymour 2000; Molidor, Tolman and Kober 2000). Similarly, Hamby *et al.* (2012) established that more girls than boys reported physical injury and feeling fear.

So far, we have outlined the international evidence on IPVA in young people's relationships. We now turn our attention to look at findings from two European studies undertaken by the first author (Barter *et al.* 2009, 2017), to provide the wider context in which to view the UK practice learning and recommendations contained in the second half of this chapter.

European research studies

Both IPVA studies (Barter *et al.* 2009, 2017) used a mixed-method approach combining quantitative and qualitative methodologies. In this chapter we will primarily focus on the quantitative survey data. The first survey was undertaken in eight schools across England, Scotland and Wales, and involved 1353 young people aged 13–16; of these, 1185 (88 per cent) reported some form of intimate relationship. The second 2015 survey (Barter *et al.* 2017) was completed in 45 schools across five European countries (Bulgaria, Cyprus, England, Italy and Norway); overall 4564 young people aged 14–17 completed the survey and 3272 reported an intimate partner. The IPVA analysis reported below was only undertaken on the subsample of young people who reported some form of intimate relationship. The surveys measured physical, sexual and emotional forms of IPVA and the subjective impact of these experiences. The surveys used the same questions to measure physical and sexual violence. In the 2009 survey young people were also asked about emotional forms of violence. This was expanded in the later study to delineate between face-to-face and online forms of emotional abuse including controlling behaviours and pressured sexting.

As with all research, some limitations were present. It was not possible to achieve a representative sample across all countries, and due to the length of the survey we could not include some questions, for example, on wellbeing. Nevertheless, the sampling framework ensured a balance by gender, schools from rural and urban areas and localities of economic diversity. We established young people's advisory groups to support both studies to ensure their views and understanding were incorporated into the research process: for example, in the 2015 study young people across the five countries co-developed an online resource for other young people. Findings from both studies have been used to inform policy and practice developments nationally and internationally, including the work of SafeLives.

Findings
Physical violence

The 2009 survey found that more girls than boys reported physical violence victimization, 25 per cent (n=150) compared to 18 per cent (n=100), representing a significant gender difference. The later 2015 survey showed that between 9 per cent and 22 per cent of young women and 8 per cent to 15 per cent of young men across the five countries reported some form of physical violence from a partner (see Table 3.1). Young women in England (22 per cent) and Norway (18 per cent) reported the highest levels: almost one in five reported having experienced physical violence compared to one in ten young women in the other countries.[4]

Table 3.1 Gender and IPVA prevalence

Country	Gender	Physical (%)		Sexual (%)		Emotional (%)		Online (%)	
		No	Yes	No	Yes	No	Yes	No	Yes
Bulgaria	Female	89	11	79	21	59	41	53	47
	Male	85	15	75	25	65	35	57	43
Cyprus	Female	90	10	83	17	69	31	55	45
	Male	91	9	81	19	66	34	57	43
England	Female	78	22	59	41	52	48	52	48
	Male	88	12	86	14	73	27	75	25
Italy	Female	91	9	65	35	59	59	60	40
	Male	87	13	61	39	41	41	54	46
Norway	Female	82	18	72	28	68	32	62	38
	Male	92	8	91	9	81	19	80	20

Sexual violence

In the 2009 survey, 35 per cent (n=185) of girls and 16 per cent (n=93) of boys reported some form of sexual violence (pressured and/or physically forced into sexual activity), most commonly pressured sexual contact. The 2015 survey found that 17 per cent to 41 per cent

---

4   *A note on comparative research:* As European research on adult domestic violence (DV) has shown, the willingness of participants to report their experiences is often heavily influenced by how DV is viewed in different countries (EU FRA 2014). Countries with higher gender equality and greater DV awareness also often report the highest levels of DV. This may be because in these countries DV is viewed as a social and political rather than personal and therefore private problem. The Safeguarding Teenage Intimate Relationships (STIR) expert meetings (Barter 2014) and the young people's advisory groups identified that England and Norway had the highest levels of awareness in respect of interpersonal abuse in young people's relationships, reflecting the European Union Agency for Fundamental Rights (EU FRA) findings for adults across these countries. England and Norway also reported the highest levels of physical and sexual violence for young women in the 2015 survey. It may therefore be that female respondents are under-reporting their experiences of physical and sexual violence, the most stigmatized forms of IPVA, in a social context where awareness of the problem is lower.

of girls and 9 per cent to 25 per cent of boys (see Table 3.1) reported sexual victimization, again most prominently involving sexual pressure. Only participants in England and Norway reported significant gender differences: more girls reported sexual violence than boys. Nevertheless, in general a greater proportion of girls reported their partner/s had physically forced them into unwanted sexual activity compared to boys.

Emotional or psychological abuse

The 2009 study found that 75 per cent (n=428) of girls and 50 per cent (n=289) of boys experienced some level of emotional victimization, which represented a significant gender difference. The most commonly reported acts were verbal abuse, controlling behaviour and surveillance. The qualitative findings from the above study also demonstrated how aspects of male control were often normalized by female partners viewing it as an integral, although often unwanted, aspect of an intimate relationship. Some girls justified their partner's controlling behaviour through discourses of love and protection: their partners did not want them to socialize independently as they may be targets of unwanted, and potentially abusive, male attention. Few of the girls interviewed felt able to substantially challenge their partner's controlling behaviour due to possible negative repercussions. This has important implications for practice, as outlined later, in the second part of this chapter. In contrast, none of the boys interviewed felt that their female partner's attempts at controlling their lives were acceptable. Boys generally stated that their partner's action was ineffective as they simply ignored their demands, told them to stop, or finished the relationship if they continued.

Online abuse

In the 2015 survey we explored the use of abuse through new technologies, which we will call 'online abuse' for brevity. We were particularly interested in determining how online forms of abuse, control and surveillance intersected with more traditional face-to-face aspects of IPVA.

As few survey-based studies had examined this aspect of IPVA, we developed a new set of questions based on the above qualitative interview findings, emergent international studies and recommendations from the young people's advisory groups. The measure sought to address three aspects of online IPVA: abuse, controlling behaviour and surveillance, and lastly, isolation. Young people were asked 'Have any of your partners ever done any of these things using a mobile phone, computer or tablet':

- 'Put you down or ever sent you any nasty messages?'

- 'Posted nasty messages about you that others could see?'

- 'Sent you threatening messages online or by mobile phone?'

- 'Tried to control who you can be friends with or where you can go?'

- 'Constantly checked up on what you have been doing or who you have been seeing, for example, by sending you messages or checking your social networking page all the time?'

- 'Used a mobile phone or social networking sites to stop your friends liking you, for example, pretending to be you and sending nasty messages to your friends?'

Between 20 per cent and 48 per cent of participants reported some form of online abuse (see Table 3.1). Male participants in England and Norway reported the lowest levels. Controlling behaviour and surveillance were the most commonly experienced forms of online abuse, irrespective of gender. When we compared young people's experiences of IPVA, we found that the majority of young people who reported abuse stated that they had experienced both online and offline forms (Barter *et al.* 2017).

Interpersonal partner violence and abuse and subjective impact

We asked participants who reported IPVA to also report the subjective impact of these experiences. We recognized that for some young people certain aspects of IPVA may be perceived as having an affirmative impact, such as feeling loved, and that it was important to understand these dynamics, especially for practice responses. Consequently, survey participants were asked to report on both the negative and affirmative subjective impacts of victimization. Negative impacts included feeling upset, scared, embarrassed, shocked, unhappy, humiliated, bad about yourself, angry and annoyed. Affirmative responses included feeling loved, wanted, protected, good about yourself, thought it was funny and no effect.

Results from both surveys showed a significant gender difference: girls were more likely to report a negative impact compared to boys. Girls most commonly reported that their partner's behaviour made them feel scared, humiliated and upset; in contrast, boys who did identify a negative outcome most commonly reported feeling annoyed or angry (Barter 2014; Barter *et al.* 2009). Boys were much more likely than girls to report affirmative impacts, most commonly stating it was funny. However, for all forms of violence, affirmative responses were provided by young people, although to a much lesser degree by girls. This may testify to the normalization of certain unhealthy relationship behaviours or young people's uncertainty about what is acceptable. Boys' insistence that they found their partner's behaviour funny may be a mechanism for the minimization of the impact of female IPVA due to constructs of hegemonic masculinity that seek to restrict male vulnerability. Alternatively, this may show that girls' use of IPVA generally fails to cause significant concern for male partners (see Barter *et al.* 2017). Nevertheless, this should not mitigate the fact that some boys did report a negative impact. In addition, if boys generally viewed IPVA perpetration by females as amusing, this would make help-seeking more difficult for those who found the behaviour distressing.

However, in both surveys, reports of negative consequences did significantly increase when behaviours were reported to occur frequently or if more than a single form of abuse was reported. This supports earlier findings that it is the patterning of IPVA that requires addressing in practice, and not simply an isolated incidence of, for example, physical violence.

Help-seeking

The survey questions also asked about help-seeking. The results showed very similar patterns; most young people did not tell anyone about their experiences, and those who did tell overwhelmingly talked to a friend or peer. Girls were more likely than boys to talk with someone, possibly reflecting the fact that boys did not view their experiences as constituting a major problem or maybe because they did not feel able to seek help due to embarrassment. In the interviews, girls spoke about the barriers they faced in seeking adult support. These included concerns that: adults would not take it seriously; they would be forced to end the relationship; or that it would not be kept confidential and especially that their parents would be informed. Girls who felt at risk of honour-based violence or forced marriage were particularly worried that their parents or wider families may be told about the relationship, which may put them at further risk of violence.

In comparison, boys mainly stressed that they did not see it as a major issue, and if their partner did not stop, they would end the relationship, although many did state that they found it annoying. These patterns were also borne out in the survey findings: most girls stated that the violence or abuse remained at the same level or got worse while boys mostly reported that it stopped. This indicates that some girls are staying, for various reasons, in abusive relationships while boys are more able to stop their partners' behaviour or decide to terminate the relationship.

Having reviewed the national and international findings, we now turn our attention in the second half of this chapter to look at how professionals can effectively identify young people experiencing IPVA, provide an empathetic and caring response to disclosures, and to consistently support them to access vital specialist domestic abuse and safeguarding services within their local area.

From research to practice: Advice for non-specialist professionals

Every professional has a vital role to play in safeguarding children and young people who are at risk of harm, including those who are experiencing IPVA (HM Government 2018). It is evident from the research presented in this chapter that young people's experiences of IPVA can be severe, life-threatening, complex and greatly impact their developmental health, wellbeing and future relationships. It is imperative, therefore, that all professionals involved in young people's lives, whether they are teachers, school nurses, social workers, healthcare practitioners or sport/club leaders, provide a safe, consistent, effective and empathetic response to young people experiencing IPVA.

In order for individual professionals to confidently and effectively identify and respond to young people experiencing IPVA, they need to be supported by their organization to do so. This should include providing professionals with relevant training for supporting young people experiencing IPVA, complemented by safeguarding policies and procedures with a specific focus on IPVA in young people's relationships. Guidance cannot replace robust training, localized policies and procedures, or the advice and support provided by national and local specialist young people's domestic abuse and child safeguarding services. However, it does use the research outlined in this chapter, alongside the advice provided by young survivors, specialist practitioners and academics through the SafeLives *Spotlight #3: Young People and Domestic Abuse* (SafeLives 2017a) and the resources developed from the SafeLives Young People's Programme, to make key recommendations regarding what a safe, consistent and empathetic response from non-specialist professionals should look like, both at an individual and institutional level. This includes how professionals can:

- Identify a young person experiencing IPVA.

- Create an inclusive and supportive space for the young person to talk about their experiences.

- Ask the right questions and provide a safe, non-judgemental and empathetic response.

- Consider the intersectionality of the young person's additional risks and needs.

- Respond to the young person's immediate safety needs and refer to specialist support services and local child safeguarding arrangements.

- Continue to work alongside multi-agency professionals to offer the young person ongoing support.

For any professional reading this chapter, we advise that you consider how you can build these recommendations into your own practice, and also how you can advocate with your organization's safeguarding leads to facilitate training, policies, procedures and relationships with local domestic abuse and specialist young people's services and child safeguarding services.

Identify a young person experiencing IPVA

There are many barriers to identifying violence and abuse. For IPVA, some of the most common barriers to identification include:

- Young people may not recognize that the relationship is unhealthy or abusive.

- They may feel embarrassed that they are experiencing or perpetrating abuse, causing them to minimize, dismiss or ignore it.

- They may feel responsible for the abuse perpetrated against them. They might want to protect the abusive (ex-)partner from any criminal or disciplinary actions taken against them as a result of disclosing the abuse.

- They could be fearful about how adults and professionals will respond, for example, not believing them, 'overreacting' or not allowing them to see their partner.

- They might fear that telling someone about the abuse will make things worse and lead to an escalation of violence (SafeLives 2017a).

Because of the barriers that often prevent a young person from recognizing and disclosing their experiences of abuse, professionals need to be alert to the signs and symptoms. Any young person above the ages of 12 or 13, irrespective of their gender identity, sexuality, socioeconomic, ethnic, cultural or religious background, can experience IPVA, although risks are higher for girls with older male partners (Barter *et al.* 2009).

Some examples of the changes in young people's lives that may demonstrate IPVA include:

- Any behavioural issues within the classroom or home environment, such as truanting, worsening school performance, getting into trouble at school, being frequently away from home, a sudden loss or change in friendships.

- Any changes in physical or mental health and wellbeing: self-harm, suicidal thoughts, anxiety, depression or eating disorders; use of alcohol or other substances; pregnancy or miscarriage; unexplained and/or repeated physical injury; contracting sexually transmitted diseases.

- Concerning behaviour within the intimate relationship: being constantly with the partner within and outside of the school environment; being isolated from friends and family; having to let the partner know where they are, when and with whom; the abusive partner using social media and other forms of technology to monitor the young person's behaviour, interactions and movements.

This is not an exhaustive list of the signs and symptoms of abuse within a young person's relationship, and it will not reflect the impact of IPVA on every young person's life. However, it is used to highlight that when a young person may experience one or a few of these issues, professionals should consider IPVA as a potential cause or contributing factor. If you do have concerns, consider how to safely and effectively discuss this with the young person you are concerned about.

Create a safe space to talk

It is not just an individual responsibility to create safe environments for young people. The overall organizational context, for example, in schools, can support or challenge abuse and discrimination. Creating a safe environment includes having and implementing safeguarding policies, attention to the physical environment, training and supporting staff in their roles and responsibilities and, in education, supporting girls and boys, and providing them with the skills and knowledge to develop equitable, non-abusive relationships and to respond to abuse should it happen.

As defined within the UK government's statutory guidance for Relationships and Sex Education (RSE) (DfE 2019), the school environment provides a vital opportunity to learn about and address IPVA and provide pupils with the opportunity to talk about their experiences or explore their experience of abuse and access support. Specifically, RSE at a secondary level should clearly and sensitively address grooming, sexual exploitation, female genital mutilation (FGM) and domestic abuse, including coercive and controlling behaviour. This includes a clear message to students regarding how they can access support from trusted adults within the school (DfE 2019). Professionals should also ensure that they use inclusive language and examples when discussing IPVA, which consider both hetero and same-sex relationships, male and female victims of abuse, and young people with different gender identities and ethnicities (SafeLives 2017a [Janice Stevenson, LGBTQI Youth Scotland]).

Professionals should also demonstrate to all young people that they are aware of IPVA, that it is not tolerated, and that they will believe and support those experiencing abuse. Such statements and policies should be as prevalent and vocal within a school or any other young person's environment as policies and statements about bullying, racism, sexism, homophobia and transphobia.

Practice tips: Creating a safe space to talk

- If you are concerned that a young person may be experiencing IPVA, it is important to first familiarize yourself with your organization's policies and procedures, so you know how to provide the right response within your professional environment.

- You may be able to speak with an internal Safeguarding Lead or Domestic Abuse Champion about what this looks like within their professional setting.

- Confidentiality and safety are important for survivors of domestic violence and abuse (DVA), and young people prefer to talk with a trusted adult with whom they have built a relationship. You should consider who the young person is most comfortable with and most likely to speak openly to about their experiences.

- Access a safe and private space in which the young person feels comfortable.

- Ensure that you have given adequate time to have these conversations without cutting the young person off, and make sure to give all your attention by minimizing interruptions from any phone or computer.

- Do not assume a young person will immediately share their experiences. This may take some time.

- Build a rapport. This can be done by spending extra time with the young person and doing other activities together, such as getting a coffee or ice cream or playing a board or card game.

- When beginning a dialogue with a young person about their experiences of abuse, it is important to clearly inform them about the confidentiality of the information shared, particularly within a safeguarding context where you may need to share information without their consent.

- Speak with the young person in a way that is accessible. Some example phrasing includes: 'If we talk about things that concern me, I will need to tell other agencies so that we can help keep you safe. How do you feel about that?' (SafeLives 2017a [Jill Prodenchuk]).

- If IPVA is disclosed, be honest and transparent about how the information shared will be used and provided to other professionals and adults in the young person's life, and what will happen as a result of the disclosure.

- Remain honest and transparent about what you can and cannot do to support the young person.

Resources

SafeLives (2014a)[5] provides detailed guidance on the legal grounds for sharing information in light of the General Data Protection Regulations (GDPR) 2018, including when or if professionals should seek consent to share information (SafeLives 2018).[6]

Ask the right questions

Based on the research presented at the beginning of this chapter, we know that young people will not always recognize that their relationship is abusive or unhealthy. Therefore, by simply asking the question 'Are you experiencing domestic abuse?' or 'Is your relationship abusive or unhealthy?', a professional will not provide the young person with the opportunity to reflect on and describe the abuse in their relationship.

Instead, it is important to ask specific questions about the nature of the relationship that will help the young person to reflect if it is abusive. It may help to start with a conversation about why you are concerned

---

5   See https://safelives.org.uk/practice_blog/top-tips-asking-question
6   See https://safelives.org.uk/sites/default/files/resources/Legal%20Grounds%20for%20 Sharing%20Information%20Guidance.pdf

and why you want to speak with them. This may include the concerning behaviour you have seen in the relationship or changes in the young person's own behaviour or wellbeing. Say, for example, 'I wanted to have a chat with you because I've noticed that you've been missing class more often and handing in assignments late. How are things at home and in your relationships?' Professionals can also use online resources and tools to help the young person recognize any abuse in their relationship and discuss it, such as the Teen Power and Control Wheel and Women's Aid Love Respect website (see below).

Resources

The National Center on Domestic and Sexual Violence (n.d.)[7] has developed the Teen Power and Control Wheel based on the Domestic Abuse Intervention Project's Duluth Power and Control Wheel.

Women's Aid has developed the Love Respect website[8] to support young people to understand the difference between healthy and unhealthy relationships. Professionals can signpost young people to the website, or go through it with them in conversation.

When asking questions specifically about the abuse, it is important to think about the different forms of abuse and how this might make the young person feel. Some examples include:

- 'Has your (ex-)partner physically hurt you or threatened to hurt you? For example, have they: hit, punched, slapped or pushed you or used any objects to hurt you?'

- 'Do you feel scared or frightened of your (ex-)partner? For example, are you afraid they may hurt you physically, or get upset or angry with you?'

- 'Do you feel that your (ex-)partner is controlling? For example, do they control where you go, what you do, who you see? Do they monitor your activities via your phone or social media?'

---

7   See www.ncdsv.org/images/teen%20p&c%20wheel%20no%20shading.pdf
8   https://loverespect.co.uk

- 'Do you think your (ex-)partner is jealous? For example, do they worry or accuse you of being interested in other people or cheating on them?'

- 'Does your (ex-)partner put you down or make you feel bad about yourself? For example, do they say negative things about the way you look or the way you act, or how well you do at school?'

- 'Does your (ex-)partner embarrass you in front of friends and family? For example, do they put you down or tell you off in front of other people?'

- 'Does your (ex-)partner make you do anything that you don't want to or that makes you feel uncomfortable? Do you feel you can say, "no" if you don't want to? For example, have sex or do sexual acts that you don't want to, or drink alcohol or use other substances if you don't want to?'

It is important to confidently ask the young person about the relationship so that they do not sense that the professional is uncomfortable or embarrassed and therefore respond with a similar level of discomfort or shame. Use clear language that will not be misunderstood or confused. For example, if you are talking about consent and sex, do not use euphemisms to describe any aspect of sex or the body. Be relaxed and relatable and use language that is accessible to a young person, rather than using an overly clinical, officious or authoritarian manner.

Provide a safe, non-judgemental and empathetic response

A young person may believe that the abuse is deserved and that it is excusable. The responsibility of the adult professional is to reassure them that the (ex-)partner's actions are abusive, that it is not their fault, and that there is no excuse for abuse. What a professional should not do is minimize, disbelieve, judge or attempt to influence the young person's *choice* to remain in the relationship.

It is possible that the young person disclosing abuse may be either a young victim/survivor or a young person causing harm. In some cases, a young person may be both. A young person causing harm within their intimate relationship may be experiencing domestic abuse in the family home, and vice versa, young victims/survivors of IPVA may be displaying abusive behaviour at home where they could have witnessed

IPVA between parents or carers. Professionals should consider that a young person's experience of abuse may be intertwined with childhood experiences of abuse or trauma. It is important to also explore all aspects of the young person's abusive experience so that you can offer the right support for the individual's needs. All of the same considerations should be made for discussing other aspects of abuse in their life: ask questions that explore the nature of the abuse, listen, believe, validate and support. Some example questions include:

- 'How are things for you at home? Do you feel safe there? Do you feel like you can speak to your parents/carers about your relationship?'

- 'Do you feel scared of anyone else in your life? For example, a parent/carer, siblings, friend or other relative?'

- 'Has anyone else in your life harmed/controlled/threatened you or someone in your family?'

Exploring other risks and needs should cover the young person's relationships with parents/carers, and how parents/carers may play a positive or negative role in helping the young person become safe. Due to the overlap that may occur between a young person's experience of IPVA and domestic or child abuse within the home, it is important to ask young people how they feel about their parents/carers and what additional risks they may present to the young person, particularly if information is shared with the parents/carers about their relationship or the abuse. When the young person has not yet 'come out' to their parents as LGBTQI (lesbian, gay, bisexual, transgender, queer (or questioning) and intersex), or if there may be an additional risk of violence and abuse or forced marriage, informing the parents/carers about the young person's intimate relationship may increase the risk of harm to them.

SafeLives (2014b)[9] provides guidance for supporting young people experiencing domestic abuse who may be at risk of forced marriage.

9　See https://safelives.org.uk/sites/default/files/resources/Forced%20marriage%20-%20 practice%20briefing%20FINAL.pdf

It is also possible that through conversation with the young person about abuse in the home, they may find that an adult carer or parent could be at risk of harm from the young person as well. Information about any threat of abuse or neglect by an adult, parent/carer towards the young person or vice versa should be shared with child safeguarding services.

> Helen Bonnick writes a blog called 'Holes in the Wall', a documentation of parent abuse.[10]

When professionals refer to specialist and safeguarding services, they should clearly state whether the parents/carers/families are aware of the young person's relationship, whether the young person wishes to tell their parents/carers, and if they believe doing so would present a risk to the young person. It is important to always be clear and transparent with the young person that you may have to inform the parents/carers about the relationship/abuse and, if doing so presents a safeguarding risk to the young person or their children, the right steps will be taken to protect them from harm.

Consider and explore the intersectionality of other risks and needs

Not every young person's experience of IPVA is the same. Experiences are influenced by the abusive actions of the (ex-)partner and by the intersectionality of other risks and needs such as mental health, disability or substance use, or personal characteristics such as gender identity, ethnicity, culture, religion and sexual orientation. While this chapter does not provide the space to explore each of these intersections, it is important to consider how these risks, needs and characteristics can impact and increase the risk of harm to the young person or any other adult or children, and how their intersectional risks and needs may prevent them from accessing specialist services.

---

10   See https://holesinthewall.co.uk

SafeLives (2015a)[11] provides research and practice briefings on supporting young survivors with mental health needs.

SafeLives (2015b)[12] also provides research and practice briefings for professionals supporting young survivors who have substance misuse/abuse issues.

For example, a young person's experience of IPVA is a form of trauma, and for many, this is not their first experience of personal trauma or abuse. The developmental impact of experiencing trauma as a child and young person has a devastating toll on their emotional, mental and physical wellbeing and ability to form both short- and longer-term healthy and trusting relationships. Young people who have not yet developed healthy coping mechanisms to respond to the impact of trauma are at a much higher risk of risk-taking behaviour, including problematic substance use and self-harm. As a young person begins to develop unhealthy coping mechanisms, unhealthy relationships and lowered feelings of value and self-worth, they can also be at an increased risk of other forms of violence and abuse, particularly sexual abuse from multiple and adult partners, child sexual exploitation and gang violence.

When speaking to a young person about their experience of IPVA, it is important to explore the impact of abuse and the coping mechanisms and other potential harmful behaviour they have developed. Some example questions include:

- 'It sounds like you've been dealing with a lot; can you tell me about how this has made you feel?'

- 'Have you been feeling sad or low? Have you been worrying more than usual?'

- 'Do you use drugs or alcohol to cope with your feelings?'

- 'Is there anyone else who has hurt you or who you feel afraid of?'

- 'Has anyone else made you do something that makes you feel uncomfortable or that you don't like?'

---

11 See https://safelives.org.uk/sites/default/files/resources/SafeLives%20research%20 briefing%20-%20young%20people%20with%20mental%20health%20issues_0.pdf
12 See https://safelives.org.uk/sites/default/files/resources/Practice%20briefing%20for%20 young%20people%20-%20substance%20misuse%20FINAL.pdf

When a young person shares with you information about other risks and needs that are potentially linked to their experiences of trauma, it is important to offer them support through appropriate specialist services, such as Child and Adolescent Mental Health Services (CAMHS), Young People's Substance Misuse Services or Child Safeguarding Service/Early Help. As Jo Sharpen, a specialist in childhood experiences of abuse and trauma at Against Violence & Abuse (AVA) explains within the SafeLives *Spotlight #3*, it is also important to consider how you can develop a trauma-informed approach with the young person, so that you can ensure that your interactions with them do not cause re-traumatization, but instead, engage and support the young person in a way that is responsive to their needs (SafeLives 2017a [Jo Sharpen, AVA]).

Jo Sharpen's guidance (2017)[13] has been provided as a blog for SafeLives.

Being aware that young people may be experiencing trauma could help professionals to find new and creative ways to engage with them. Examples based on Jo Sharpen's advice include:

- It may take several attempts to meet up with or contact the young person – don't give up and decide they just don't want help. Keep trying to engage and let them know you're always available and your 'door' is always open. Don't show anger, frustration or disappointment when they don't engage, so that they still feel comfortable to approach you when they are ready.

- They may have difficulty keeping schedules of appointments and calls. Think about what you can do to remind and support them to organize their diary. Again, be patient and supportive rather than angry or upset if they miss appointments or cancel.

- Consider their other behaviours from a trauma-informed perspective: is their truanting, lateness or emotional reactions or actions related to their experiences of trauma? How can you help and support them rather than punish or admonish them?

---

13 See https://safelives.org.uk/practice_blog/trauma-informed-response-working-young-people-affected-domestic-abuse

Experiences of and responses to IPVA may also be impacted by the intersection of sexual orientation, gender identity, ethnicity and culture, all of which need to be explored to provide a safe and effective response. For example, an LGBTQI young person's experience of IPVA may greatly influence their experience of abuse and their access to support services. An LGBTQI young survivor may not have 'come out' to their family and friends. This could be used as an abusive tool by the abusive (ex-)partner, as 'coming out' may present additional risks to the young person, including isolation, judgement and shame, as well as 'honour-based' violence and forced marriage. The young person may find it even more difficult to access the support of professionals and specialist services, who they may fear will be prejudiced against them or assume they are not experiencing abuse as they don't fit the heteronormative view of relationships or IPVA. In order to support young LGBTQI survivors, Janice Stevenson from LGBT Youth Scotland makes some key recommendations for professionals, including ensuring that professionals demonstrate that they are inclusive of LGBTQI individuals when talking about IPVA by using clear examples of LGBTQI individuals (SafeLives 2017a).

LGBT Youth Scotland provides detailed guidance on how professionals can support young LGBTQI survivors of domestic violence and other forms of gender-based violence in their Voices Unheard education resource.[14]

SafeLives (2014b)[15] provides guidance for supporting young survivors at risk of forced marriage.

Janice Stevenson (2017)[16] provides guidance on supporting young LGBTQI people experiencing domestic abuse.

The way young men and women experience and respond to abuse may be different, and so their gender should be considered when discussing the abuse. Young men are more likely to minimize and dismiss the abuse.

---

14 www.lgbtyouth.org.uk/media/1473/voices-unheard.pdf
15 See https://safelives.org.uk/sites/default/files/resources/Forced%20marriage%20-%20 practice%20briefing%20FINAL.pdf
16 See https://safelives.org.uk/node/1027

While some young men, particularly in heterosexual relationships, may not feel at a risk of harm or not feel emotionally impacted by the abuse from a female partner, it is still a possibility that they have not been told that what has happened to them is not okay or normal, and that being frightened and emotionally impacted by the abuse is a normal reaction. Young male survivors may minimize or dismiss the abuse, but this does not mean it has not been harmful and had no impact. Professionals should be just as rigorous in their attempts to support and safeguard young men and make them aware that abuse is not okay, it is not excusable and it will not be tolerated.

Respond to immediate safety needs

When a professional becomes aware of a young person's experience of IPVA, they should always prioritize responding to the risk of harm or homicide to the young person(s) and any dependent children. Non-specialist professionals should not attempt to 'take matters into their own hands' by approaching the abusive (ex-)partner or encouraging the young survivor to leave the relationship, as this may increase the risk of harm and homicide. Instead, non-specialist professionals should believe, validate and support the young person, and immediately link them into specialist support and safeguarding services, which can ensure the right safety measures are put into place to support the young person and reduce the risk of harm.

If there is an imminent risk of harm or homicide, the professional should encourage the young person to contact the police, and if they are not able to, the professional should do this for them.

Within the UK, any individual who is concerned about the wellbeing and safety of a young person or child should make an immediate child safeguarding referral. This does not require the consent of the young person, child or parents/carers. Safeguarding concerns are not limited to adult-to-child abuse, and when abuse within a young person's intimate relationship presents a risk of harm to a dependent child or young person, it becomes a matter for child safeguarding (HM Government 2018). Raising safeguarding concerns in cases of IPVA in young people's relationships is particularly important because of the increased risk of severe harm, including homicide, and the associated risks of poorer mental health, problematic substance use, self-harm, child sexual abuse and exploitation, 'honour-based' violence and forced marriage.

High-risk IPVA

Young people aged 16 and over in the UK who are experiencing IPVA are considered to be victims of domestic abuse and can access specialist domestic abuse services and multi-agency safeguarding arrangements. Multi-agency risk assessment conferences (MARACs) have been developed across UK local authorities to bring together multi-agency partners to share information and develop joint safety plans for survivors who have been identified as being at a high risk of severe harm or homicide.

Core MARAC agencies include specialist domestic abuse services, the police, child and adult safeguarding services, housing services, mental health, substance use services, and probation and primary health services. Independent domestic violence advisors (IDVAs) are domestic abuse specialists who play the vital role of advocating for the needs and wishes of the survivor with the multi-agency partners, so that any agreed actions are based on the survivor's needs and risks. Within some local authority areas, young people can access specialist young people's violence advisors (YPVAs) who provide the same role as IDVAs, but are specialists in supporting young people experiencing domestic abuse. Unfortunately, not all local authority areas offer specialist young people's domestic abuse services, and it may be that only adult service provision is offered to the young person.

As child safeguarding services are a core member of the MARAC, this multi-agency arrangement should provide the vital opportunity for child safeguarding to work alongside domestic abuse and other specialist young people's services to support young survivors and their children. However, they do not replace the partnership working that should continue outside of the MARAC process between specialist domestic abuse services and child safeguarding services, and any other professionals involved in the young person's life, such as Early Help Teams, Youth Offending Teams, CAMHS and Young People's Substance Misuse Services.

If a young person is thought to be at a high risk of harm or homicide, a referral should be made to the local MARAC and IDVA services in addition to child safeguarding services. Professionals can refer young survivors (16 and over) to MARAC based on their own professional judgement or by using evidence-based risk assessment tools such as the SafeLives young person's Risk Identification Checklist ('Dash') and the Severity of Abuse grid.[17]

---

17   See https://safelives.org.uk/sites/default/files/resources/Dash%20for%20IDVAs%20FINAL_0.pdf

Resources

SafeLives (n.d., a)[18] provides information for professionals referring to MARAC.

SafeLives (2014c)[19] provides a definition of IDVA work.

SafeLives (2014d)[20] provides a definition of a young person's violence advisor (YPVA).

SafeLives' flowchart on the care/referral pathways for 13- to 18-year-olds (2015c),[21] which includes both MARAC and child safeguarding referral pathways.

SafeLives' guidance notes to accompany the care/referral pathway flowchart (2014e).[22]

SafeLives' detailed guidance regarding the criteria for referring to MARAC based on professionals' judgements.[23]

SafeLives (2018)[24] provides guidance on the GDPR and Data Protection Act 2018.

IPVA risk assessment

The SafeLives young person's Risk Identification Checklist, or 'Dash' (SafeLives 2015d), is an evidence-based tool used by specialist and non-specialist professionals to identify the individual risks of harm to a young person experiencing current domestic abuse either from a family member or from an intimate (ex-)partner. Professionals are advised to complete the 'Dash' questionnaire directly with the young survivor and to complete each of the questions. When a young person has

---

18 See https://safelives.org.uk/practice-support/resources-marac-meetings/resources-people-referring

19 See www.safelives.org.uk/sites/default/files/resources/National%20definition%20of%20IDVA%20work%20FINAL.pdf

20 See https://safelives.org.uk/sites/default/files/resources/Young%20People%27s%20Violence%20Advisor%20suggestions%20on%20role%20-%20case%20management%20FINAL.pdf

21 See https://safelives.org.uk/sites/default/files/resources/YP%20care%20pathway%20FINAL.pdf

22 See https://safelives.org.uk/sites/default/files/resources/Care%20pathway%20guidance%20notes%20FINAL.pdf

23 https://safelives.org.uk/sites/default/files/resources/Marac%20Referral%20Criteria%20-%20Definitions_.doc

24 See https://safelives.org.uk/sites/default/files/resources/Legal%20Grounds%20for%20Sharing%20Information%20Guidance.pdf

'scored' ten or more 'yeses' on the 'Dash', this is considered to indicate that the young person may be at a high risk of harm or homicide, and they should be referred to local YPVA/IDVA services and child safeguarding services. If the score is 14 or more 'yeses', this should additionally trigger a referral to the MARAC. It is important to note that different local authorities have different thresholds for referring to the MARAC that may be higher or lower than 14, and you will need to find out what your local MARAC advises. However, it is also important to note that professionals can refer to the MARAC based on their professional judgement, even if the 'Dash' score is lower than the threshold, but professionals should never use their professional judgement to downgrade a score. The information shared using the 'Dash' is confidential and should not be shared with the abusive (ex)-partner or any other family members/peers. It should only be shared with other professionals for safeguarding purposes, through the MARAC or a child safeguarding referral. SafeLives provides detailed guidance on when and how to complete a 'Dash' with a young person, and what actions to take depending on the outcome.[25]

The SafeLives Severity of Abuse grid (SafeLives n.d, b)[26] should be used alongside the young person's 'Dash' checklist in order to provide a framework for identifying specific features of the abuse *currently suffered* by the client, and to help guide the caseworker and client to address the client's safety in an informed and coherent way.

It is advised that, where possible, professionals who are trained to use the risk assessment tool should complete it with the young person, which could include a Domestic Violence Champion or Safeguarding Lead within the professional's organization. For professionals who are not specialists and who have not been trained to use the form, SafeLives provides detailed guidance for using the risk checklists. Referrals to the MARAC or child safeguarding arrangements can be made without the young survivor's prior consent, but it is advised that

---

25   For the 'Dash' checklist and detailed guidance, see SafeLives (2015d).
26   See www.safelives.org.uk/sites/default/files/resources/Dash%20for%20IDVAs%20FINAL_0.pdf

you do all that you can to support the young person to access support from the YPVA/IDVA, and use the MARAC process to gain further support from multi-agency professionals.

It is important to remember that professionals can only refer survivors of domestic abuse to their local MARAC. For safeguarding purposes, young people causing harm or adult perpetrators should never be informed of the MARAC referral and the young survivor's involvement with specialist services. Sharing this information may place the survivor and any dependent children at an increased risk of harm. MARAC partners should carefully consider how they can offer support to the young person causing harm or adult perpetrator in a way that does not breach the confidentiality of the young survivor and place the young survivor and other children in the family at increased risk. This may be through engaging with the young person causing harm through a professional already involved in the young person's life, who is fully aware of and supported by specialists and safeguarding services to offer support to the young person causing harm.

Young people experiencing IPVA who may not be at a high risk of severe harm or homicide should be referred to child safeguarding services, particularly where there are additional risks and needs. Support can be given by local specialist domestic abuse services and any other specialist services. It is important to find out which specialist services are offered in your area, how to refer to these services, and build relationships with local specialist services for young people. However, young people (who are not at high risk of severe harm or homicide) are not obliged to use specialist services. Professionals should especially consider that where a local area may not provide specialist young people's domestic abuse services, the young person may feel uncomfortable accessing services designed for adult survivors and they should not try to force a young person to use services, particularly if they do not feel they meet their unique needs.

Be part of a multi-agency team around the young person
All professionals have an integral role to play in providing a multi-agency support network around the young person or child who has experienced IPVA. Whether a professional is a school nurse, teacher, sport/club leader or any other adult in that young person's life, they can be a source of ongoing support and safety. Therefore, a professional

should work alongside the young person and specialist domestic abuse and other relevant services to consider what professionals can do within their own environment to make it a place of safety for that individual. For example, for schools this may include changing the student's course schedule so they don't share classes with the abusive partner or see them on campus. This could also mean that schools could 'forgive' the young person's past truanting and give the student added opportunities to perform well, so they can overcome past behaviours linked to their experiences of abuse. Schools could also provide the private space for students to meet with specialist services.

Conclusion

In this chapter we have brought together international and national research findings on the prevalence and impact of IPVA, and outlined key practice messages and recommendations on how best to meet the needs of young survivors. The research evidence, both nationally and internationally, clearly identifies the significance and impact of IPVA in young people's relationships. Within the second half of this chapter we have used the recommendations made by young survivors and expert practitioners to provide guidance for professionals working with young people to safely, effectively and consistently identify the potential signs and symptoms of IPVA and its impact on a young person and build trusting relationships to aid disclosure, provide a safe, effective and empathetic response and refer to specialist and safeguarding services. By believing, validating, supporting and safeguarding young people experiencing IPVA we are much closer to ensuring their wellbeing and safety in childhood as well as providing them with the best opportunities to live a lifetime free of violence and abuse.

References

Barter, C. (2014) 'Researching Young People's Experiences of Intimate Partner Violence: Concepts, Contexts and Consequences.' In N. Aghtaie and G. Gangoli (eds) *Understanding Gender Based Violence: National and International Contexts* (pp.33–49). London: Routledge.

Barter, C., Stanley, N., Wood, M. and Lanau, A., *et al.* (2017) 'Young People's Online and Face-to-face Experiences of Interpersonal Violence and Abuse and their Subjective Impact Across Five European Countries.' *Psychology of Violence 7*, 3, 375–384.

Barter, C., McCarry, M., Berridge, D. and Evans, K. (2009) *Partner Exploitation and Violence in Teenage Intimate Relationships*. London: NSPCC.

Barter, C., Stanley, N., Wood, M., Lanau, A., *et al.* (2017) 'Young people's online and face-to-face experiences of interpersonal violence and abuse and their subjective impact across five European countries.' *Psychology of Violence 7*, 3, 375–384.

DfE (Department for Education) (2019) *Relationships Education, Relationships and Sex Education (RSE) and Health Education: Statutory Guidance for Governing Bodies, Proprietors, Head Teachers, Principals, Senior Leadership Teams, Teachers.* Available at: https://assets.publishing. service.gov.uk/government/uploads/system/uploads/attachment_data/file/805781/ Relationships_Education__Relationships_and_Sex_Education__RSE__and_Health_ Education.pdf

Draucker, C.B. and Martsolf, D.S. (2010) 'The role of electronic communication technology in adolescent dating violence.' *Journal of Child and Adolescent Psychiatric Nursing 23*, 133–142.

EU FRA (European Union Agency for Fundamental Rights) (2014) *Violence Against Women: An EU-Wide Survey: Main Results.* Available at: https://fra.europa.eu/sites/default/files/fra_ uploads/fra-2014-vaw-survey-main-results-apr14_en.pdf

Foshee, V.A. (1996) 'Gender differences in adolescent dating abuse prevalence, types, and injuries.' *Health Education Research 11*, 3, 275–286.

Hamby, S., Nix, K., De Puy, J. and Monnier, S. (2012) 'Adapting dating violence prevention to Francophone Switzerland: A story of intra-western cultural differences.' *Violence & Victims 27*, 1, 33–42.

HM Government (2018) *Working Together to Safeguard Children: A Guide to Inter-Agency Working to Safeguard and Promote the Welfare of Children.* July. Available at: https://assets.publishing. service.gov.uk/government/uploads/system/uploads/attachment_data/file/779401/Working_ Together_to_Safeguard-Children.pdf

Jackson, S.M., Cram, F. and Seymour, F.W. (2000) 'Violence and sexual coercion in high school students' dating relationships.' *Journal of Family Violence 15*, 1, 23–36.

Marganski, A. and Fauth, K. (2013) 'Socially interactive technology and contemporary dating: A cross-cultural exploration of deviant behaviour among young adults in the modern, evolving technological world.' *International Criminal Justice Review 23*, 4, 357–377.

Molidor, C., Tolman, R.M. and Kober, J. (2000) 'Gender and contextual factors in adolescent dating violence.' *Prevention Research 7*, 1–4.

National Center on Domestic and Sexual Violence (no date) 'Teen Power and Control Wheel.' Available at: www.ncdsv.org/images/teen%20p&c%20wheel%20no%20shading.pdf

SafeLives (no date, a) 'Resources for people referring.' Available at: https://safelives.org.uk/ practice-support/resources-marac-meetings/resources-people-referring

SafeLives (no date, b) *SafeLives Dash Risk Checklist for the Identification of High Risk Cases of Domestic Abuse, Stalking and 'Honour-'based Violence.* Available at: www.safelives.org.uk/ sites/default/files/resources/Dash%20for%20IDVAs%20FINAL_0.pdf

SafeLives (2014a) 'Top tips: Asking the question.' April, May. Available at: https://safelives.org.uk/ practice_blog/top-tips-asking-question

SafeLives (2014b) 'Identifying and engaging with young people at risk of forced marriage.' Practice briefing. Available at: https://safelives.org.uk/sites/default/files/resources/Forced%20 marriage%20-%20practice%20briefing%20FINAL.pdf

SafeLives (2014c) 'National definition of IDVA work.' Available at: www.safelives.org.uk/sites/ default/files/resources/National%20definition%20of%20IDVA%20work%20FINAL.pdf

SafeLives (2014d) 'Suggested role profile for Advisors with case management responsibilities (recommended).' Young People's Violence Advisor. Available at: https://safelives.org.uk/sites/ default/files/resources/Young%20People%27s%20Violence%20Advisor%20suggestions%20 on%20role%20-%20case%20management%20FINAL.pdf

SafeLives (2014e) '13–18 referral/care pathway.' Guidance notes. Available at: https://safelives. org.uk/sites/default/files/resources/Care%20pathway%20guidance%20notes%20FINAL.pdf

SafeLives (2015a) 'Young people with mental health issues.' Research briefing for professionals working with young people. Available at: https://safelives.org.uk/sites/default/files/resources/ SafeLives%20research%20briefing%20-%20young%20people%20with%20mental%20 health%20issues_0.pdf

SafeLives (2015b) 'Working with young people who misuse/abuse alcohol or substances.' Practice briefing for professionals working with young people. Available at: https://safelives.org. uk/sites/default/files/resources/Practice%20briefing%20for%20young%20people%20-%20 substance%20misuse%20FINAL.pdf

SafeLives (2015c) '13–18 care/referral pathway.' Available at: https://safelives.org.uk/sites/default/files/resources/YP%20care%20pathway%20FINAL.pdf

SafeLives (2015d) *SafeLives Risk Identification Checklist for the Identification of High Risk Cases of Domestic Abuse, Stalking and 'Honor'-based Violence: Young People's Version with Practice Guidance.* Available at: www.safelives.org.uk/sites/default/files/resources/YP%20RIC%20guidance%20FINAL%20%281%29.pdf

SafeLives (2017a) *Spotlight #3: Young People and Domestic Abuse.* Available at: www.safelives.org.uk/knowledge-hub/spotlights/spotlight-3-young-people-and-domestic-abuse

SafeLives (2017b) *Safe Young Lives: Young People and Domestic Abuse.* Available at: https://safelives.org.uk/sites/default/files/resources/Safe%20Young%20Lives%20web.pdf

SafeLives (2018) 'GDPR & Data Protection Act 2018.' Information sharing. Available at: https://safelives.org.uk/sites/default/files/resources/Legal%20Grounds%20for%20Sharing%20Information%20Guidance.pdf

Sharpen, J. (2017) 'A trauma informed response for working with young people affected by domestic abuse.' SafeLives Blog, 15 March. Available at: https://safelives.org.uk/practice_blog/trauma-informed-response-working-young-people-affected-domestic-abuse

Stanley, N., Ellis, J., Farrelly, N., Hollinghurst, S. and Downe, S. (2015) 'Preventing domestic abuse for children and young people: A review of school-based interventions.' *Children and Youth Services Review 59*, 120–131.

Stevenson, J. (2017) 'LGBT young people's experiences of domestic abuse.' SafeLives Blog, 28 February. Available at: https://safelives.org.uk/node/1027

Stonard, K., Bowen, E., Lawrence, T. and Price, S.A. (2014) 'The relevance of technology to the nature, prevalence and impact of adolescent dating violence and abuse: A research synthesis.' *Aggression and Violent Behavior 19*, 4, 390–417.

Wincentak, K., Connolly, J. and Card, N. (2017) 'Teen dating violence: A meta-analytic review of prevalence rates.' *Psychology of Violence*, 11 April.

Wolitzky-Taylor, K.B., Ruggiero, K.J., Danielson, C.K., Resnick, H.S., *et al.* (2008) 'Prevalence and correlates of dating violence in a national sample of adolescents.' *Journal of the American Academy of Child & Adolescent Psychiatry 47*, 7, 755–762.

Wood, M., Barter, C., Stanley, N., Aghtaie, N. and Larkins, C. (2015) 'Images across Europe: The sending and receiving of sexual images and associations with intimate partner violence in young people's relationships.' *Children and Youth Services Review 59*, 149–160.

Zweig, J.M., Dank, M., Yahner, J. and Lachman, P. (2013) 'The rate of cyber dating abuse among teens and how it relates to other forms of teen dating violence.' *Journal of Youth and Adolescence 42*, 7, 1063–1077.

Chapter 4

Untangling the Web

UNDERSTANDING DOMESTIC ABUSE, MENTAL ILL
HEALTH AND PROBLEMATIC SUBSTANCE USE

Sarah Fox[1] and Jennifer Holly

Introduction

There is a relationship between domestic abuse, mental ill health and problematic substance use, and this coexistence is ever-present within health and social care practice, both nationally and internationally (Fox 2018; Holly 2017). Within GP practices, antenatal clinics, social work offices, psychiatric facilities, domestic abuse agencies and substance use services, individuals often present with co-occurring domestic abuse victimization, problematic substance use, depression, anxiety and other mental health issues (Fox 2018; Holly 2017; Humphreys, Thiara and Regan 2005; Khalifeh *et al.* 2015; Sharps-Jeff and Kelly 2016). Some individuals experience one or two of these issues and some require support for all three. The combination of the three issues is common, and for practitioners who have a child or adult safeguarding role, working with families affected by two or three of these issues at any one time is routine (DfE 2017; Sidebotham *et al.* 2016).

Yet, despite the frequency with which domestic abuse, mental ill health and problematic substance use occur, these issues are responded to separately at both a national policy and local practice level. For example, domestic abuse services are predominantly funded through national and local homelessness and community safety funding streams, while funding

---

1   Sarah Fox is funded by the Society for the Study of Addiction (SSA). The opinions expressed in this chapter reflect the views of the authors and do not necessarily represent the opinions or official position of the SSA.

for mental ill health is funded by the Department for Health and Social Care and the NHS, whereas support for problematic substance use has largely been funded through public health. National policy documents such as the *2017 Drugs Strategy* (HM Government 2017) or *Ending Violence against Women and Girls* (HM Government 2016) further fail to link the issues of domestic abuse and substance use. The policies that derive from government and the subsequent funding sources continue to isolate each issue. This separation further affects front-line service delivery, as practitioners tend to work in an either/or framework, focusing on problematic substance use, domestic abuse or mental ill health rather than supporting the individual holistically.

While each issue has received individual attention from government, researchers and practitioners in recent decades, a specific focus on the interconnections between domestic abuse, mental ill health and substance use is still in its infancy. As such, this chapter will explore the relationship between domestic abuse, mental ill health and problematic substance use. Specifically, it focuses on women's lived experience of these issues. While we know that men are vulnerable to domestic abuse, mental ill health and problematic substance use, and require specialist support to meet their needs, we are choosing to focus on women because statistically they are more likely to experience domestic abuse (ONS 2018), and to report mental health problems as a result of the abuse (Chandan *et al.* 2019). Furthermore women's use of substances has increased over the last decade (PHE and DH 2017), and those who use substances are more likely to experience stigma and shame, especially women who are mothers (Lee and Boeri 2017), which can deter them from accessing support. They are more likely to be the primary caregiver and as such are more likely to encounter social work services when domestic abuse, mental ill health and/or problematic substance use exist in their lives. Furthermore, women are not a homogenous group; they experience domestic abuse, substance use and mental ill health in various ways, based on their identity. While this chapter will not explore the intersectional aspects of women's lives in detail, it is important to consider the place of race, ethnicity, sexuality and disability when exploring the co-occurrence of domestic abuse, substance use and mental ill health because, as Ettorre explains:

> It is important for the reader to be aware that if one is a lesbian, a woman of colour or a disabled woman, for example, having an alcohol

problem is experienced in a different way both personally and socially than it is by women who are less marginalised. (Ettorre 1997, p.19)

This chapter seeks to present an overview of the relationship between domestic abuse, mental ill health and problematic substance use among women. The first section presents an overview of prevalence within the UK, highlighting the need for more statistics that accurately capture the scale of this coexistence of issues. The second section explores the theoretical associations, highlighting the role of self-medication and coerciveness by a perpetrator in women's use of substances. To demonstrate the lived experience of domestic abuse, mental ill health and problematic substance use among women, this section also includes a case study and poses reflective questions. The third section provides an overview of policy throughout the UK, highlighting the gaps in policy and the lack of integration of issues. Following this, the fourth section offers an overview of service provision in the UK, demonstrating the need for more joined-up, integrated, trauma-informed and gender-responsive care. It concludes with a case study demonstrating the impact of siloed service provision on women's lived experiences. Finally, the last section sets out our recommendations for front-line practitioners, commissioners and policy-makers. It is our hope that this chapter will support greater understanding of these interconnected issues and challenge organizations, commissioners and policy-makers responsible for support provision for women.

A note on terminology
Domestic abuse
We advocate for the term 'domestic abuse' because it encompasses the perpetration of both physical and non-physical harms, including:

- Coercive control (a pattern of intimidation, degradation, isolation and control with the use or threat of physical or sexual violence (CPS 2017).

- Psychological and/or emotional abuse.

- Physical or sexual abuse.

- Financial or economic abuse.

- Harassment and stalking.

- Online or digital abuse.

Victim

Throughout this chapter, we use the term 'victim' to denote an individual who has had abuse committed against them by a perpetrator. In practice and research, the terms 'victim' and 'survivor' are used interchangeably. Quite often, an individual may consider themselves as accessing support as a victim and leaving as a survivor; however, others may always identify as a 'victim'.

Problematic substance use

We use the term 'problematic substance use' here to denote 'problems associated with alcohol and other drug use rather than low levels or occasional use which does not lead to social or health-related problems' (Galvani 2015, p.4). We advocate for this terminology in research, policy and practice because terms such as 'addict' or 'drug user' often stigmatize the person who uses substances.

Mental ill health

We refer to 'mental ill health' as a spectrum ranging from mild to severe experiences of emotional distress and psychological impairment including conditions such as anxiety, depression, bipolar disorder and schizophrenia.

Women's multiple disadvantage

The term 'multiple disadvantage' refers to those people who face multiple and intersecting inequalities including gender-based violence and abuse, substance use, mental ill health, homelessness, being involved in the criminal justice system and the removal of children (AVA 2018).

While we chose to use this language, we believe it is important that researchers and practitioners respect the language used by their research participants and those accessing support. For many individuals, the language they use stems from their identity. While we may not use the term 'addict' or 'alcoholic', for example, those within 12-step programmes use this terminology as an expression of their identity. It is therefore vital that we use the language of our clients and be willing to adapt.

Domestic abuse, mental ill health and co-occurring substance use: How common is it?

The co-occurrence of domestic abuse, mental ill health and problematic substance use has received increasing attention in recent years, particularly in the context of safeguarding children and young people. A review of serious case reviews (Brandon *et al.* 2012) was pivotal in bringing these co-occurring issues to the fore. The report highlighted the interrelationship between domestic abuse, mental ill health and substance use among families and found:

> At least one of these characteristics [domestic abuse, mental ill health and/or substance misuse] was evident in the lives of the families at the centre of serious case reviews in 86% of the cases. Almost two thirds of the cases featured domestic abuse, and parental mental ill-health was identified in 60% of cases. Parental substance misuse was evident in 42% of cases. All three factors were present in just over a fifth of the cases and, as in our previous biennial reviews, we argue that it is the combination of these factors which is particularly 'toxic'. (Brandon *et al.* 2012, p.30)

This review was important in illuminating the co-occurrence of domestic abuse, mental ill health and substance use in serious case reviews; critically, however, there are concerns about the use of the term 'toxic trio'. Such terminology is often used to suggest that the victim (usually the mother) is toxic or the main source of risk and can obscure the perpetrator's risk to the safety and wellbeing of the victim and any children in the household (AVA 2013).

More recently, data from the Department for Education (2017) demonstrated how the three issues continue to be a common feature in the lives of children assessed to be 'in need'.[2] For example, of the children assessed to be in need on 31 March 2017, 49.9 per cent were

---

2   Under Section 17 of the Children's Act 1989, a child will be considered to be 'in need' if they are unlikely to achieve or maintain a reasonable standard of health or development, or their health or development is likely to be significantly impaired, without provision of services from the local authority.

living in a household where domestic abuse (directed at the child or another member of the household) occurred. Mental health concerns (the child and/or an adult's) was the second most common factor (39.7 per cent). Similar rates of the child's or an adult's drug or alcohol use were also identified – 19.7 per cent and 18 per cent of cases involved substance use respectively.

In many cases, there is evidence that more than one issue affects families (see Figure 4.1).

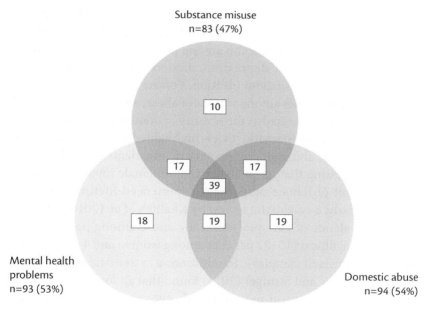

Figure 4.1 Number of families experiencing multiple problems (Sidebotham et al. 2016, p.76).

In a review by Sidebotham *et al.* (2016), 139 serious case reviews (out of 175) involved domestic abuse, problematic substance use by the parents, and/or parental mental ill health at least as a single issue. In 73 cases (42 per cent), two of the aforementioned issues were identified, and in 39 (22 per cent) of the cases, all three issues were present (see Figure 4.1). Encouragingly, this more recent review did not use the stigmatizing terminology of 'toxic trio'. The lack of such a term demonstrates the gradual shift in language within the health and social care sector. However, the term does continue to be used in policy and practice, and it is important that this is challenged.

Although serious case reviews are a valuable source of data in understanding both the relationship between domestic abuse, mental ill health and/or problematic substance use and the impact these issues have on families that come to the attention of the social care system, they are also the most extreme cases.

The broader literature on these co-occurring issues, however, is limited and often focuses *either* on domestic abuse *or* mental ill health *or* problematic substance use, rather than on all three. International studies have demonstrated that victims of domestic abuse are at increased risk of suicidal ideation and attempting to take their own life (Ellsberg *et al.* 2008; Rees *et al.* 2011). Research by Chandan *et al.* (2019) has shown the increased risk of mental ill health among domestic abuse populations, particularly in terms of depression, anxiety, post-traumatic stress disorder (PTSD) and suicidal ideation. Ferrari *et al.* (2016) explored mental health outcomes among victims of abuse, and found that mental health symptoms increased as the severity of domestic abuse increased. Oram *et al.'s* (2013) systematic review highlighted a high prevalence of lifetime domestic abuse among psychiatric inpatients in the UK, with findings suggesting that up to 30 per cent of female inpatients and up to 33 per cent of female outpatients experienced lifetime domestic abuse. Similarly, a systematic review by Khalifeh *et al.* (2016) reported a high prevalence of past year domestic abuse among patients with severe mental illness (15–22 per cent among women and 4–10 per cent among men/mixed samples). In addition, a systematic review from Lagdon, Armour and Stringer (2014) found that all forms of domestic abuse had an impact on mental health outcomes. Specifically this study found a significant association between experiences of domestic abuse and depression, PTSD and anxiety. A further study by Khalifeh *et al.* (2015) compared rates of domestic abuse among 303 individuals accessing NHS community mental health services to those reported by the general population in the British Crime Survey (n=22,606). The study found that 27 per cent of the females accessing mental health support (n=133) had past year experiences of domestic abuse, which was three times more than women in the general population (8.8 per cent). Similarly, 69 per cent of the women using mental health services reported experiencing some form of domestic abuse since the age of 16 – more than two times greater than women in the general population (32.6 per cent). While this study shows that women who experience domestic abuse victimization can be found in mental health facilities, the results should be interpreted with caution. The British Crime Survey, which was used as the comparison group for this study, is limited in its reach when it comes to counting the number of women who have experienced domestic abuse. This is because the survey only includes people aged 16–59. Furthermore, population studies, such as the British Crime Survey, may not elicit honest answers, as participants may not be comfortable disclosing their experiences of abuse in a survey. However, this study does show a relationship between domestic abuse victimization and experiences of mental ill health.

In contrast, much of the research in the UK relating to substance use and domestic abuse is relatively small scale and was conducted some years ago. As such, international findings are often used to denote the scale of the co-occurrence (Cafferky *et al.* 2018; Devries *et al.* 2013; Rees *et al.* 2011). Within the UK, examples of larger, newer studies that shed light on the extent of substance use among survivors of domestic abuse include the Adult Psychiatric Morbidity Survey (APMS) for England and Wales and the DORIS study (Drug Outcome Research In Scotland). Using data from the APMS, Agenda (Scott and McManus 2016) conducted secondary analysis of this national representative study and found that 31 per cent of women who have experienced extensive physical and sexual violence used alcohol problematically, 45 per cent have used drugs, with 8 per cent displaying signs of problematic drug use or dependency. Likewise, nearly a third of women (n=113) in the DORIS study reported experiencing sexual abuse in their lifetime, and two-thirds (n=197) reported past experiences of physical abuse (McKeganey, Neale and Robertson 2005).

Despite the associations found by these studies, within a practice setting, problematic substance use is not frequently disclosed to domestic abuse services. Only 4 per cent of women calling the National Domestic Abuse Helpline in 2016 stated they had a drug or alcohol support need (Women's Aid 2017). Similarly, an analysis of IDVA[3] services found that 5–12 per cent of women accessing support from an IDVA reported using drugs and or/alcohol problematically (Howarth and Robinson 2015). The under-reporting of substance use to domestic abuse agencies is multifaceted. Many women do not reveal their substance use because they may not recognize their use is problematic;

---

3   An IDVA is an independent domestic violence advisor who works specifically with high-risk victims of domestic violence.

they may be wary of social work involvement for fear of having their children removed from their care; and they may be afraid there will be police involvement, especially if they are using illegal substances (Fox 2018).

Systemic factors also have an impact on women's ability to access appropriate support. Across the UK, the majority of domestic abuse refuges do not support women with problematic substance use. Mapping the Maze,[4] a project that included mapping services for women experiencing multiple disadvantage (see below), identified only three refuges across England and Wales that explicitly supported substance-using women (Holly 2017), and reports from Women's Aid (2016, 2017, 2018) have consistently shown that women are being turned away from a refuge if they have problematic substance use. Because of this siloed support, some women do not disclose their problematic substance use in the hope of gaining safety at a refuge, which in effect requires them to prioritize one need over another (Fox 2018).

Understanding the links

Although there is a strong association between domestic abuse, mental ill health and problematic substance use, the direction and nature of the relationships is not as clear.

As research evidence shows, there is a direct relationship between being a victim of domestic abuse and mental distress, with depression, anxiety and PTSD being most commonly identified (Howard, Trevillion and Agnew-Davies 2010a; Humphreys and Thiara 2003; Khalifeh *et al.* 2015; Oram *et al.* 2013; Rees *et al.* 2011; Scott and McManus 2016). For children and young people living with and witnessing domestic abuse, the documented emotional and psychological effects range from irritability and clinginess in infants, to withdrawal, depression, anxiety, eating and sleep disturbances, obsessive behaviour and self-harm in school-age children (Callaghan *et al.* 2015; DH 2009; RCPSYCH 2017).

In the literature, substance use is predominantly viewed as being used by victims as a means to cope with the trauma that they are experiencing (Humphreys *et al.* 2005). This follows the idea of

---

4   Mapping the Maze was a collaboration between two women's organizations in the UK to map provision for women affected by multiple disadvantage and to develop a model of good practice for working with this group of women. Full details of the project and the resulting resources can be accessed at: www.mappingthemaze.org.uk

self-medication (Khantzian 1997), which stipulates that individuals use substances to cope with the feelings associated with traumatic experiences. Khantzian (1997) posits that individuals discover how a substance can relieve painful feelings and self-regulate vulnerabilities. Among women who experience domestic abuse, substances are often used as a coping mechanism to deal with their traumatic experiences and the psychological consequences. For example, research has found that victims may use alcohol to detach from painful experiences when their ability to spontaneously dissociate has been eroded (Herman 2015) or to moderate symptoms of PTSD (Hien, Cohen and Campbell 2005). Many women also refer to substance use as a physical anaesthetic (Fox 2018; Humphreys *et al.* 2005). The theory of self-medication is popularly used to denote the relationship between substance use and coping (Khantzian 1997; Smith 2019).

Importantly, however, women may experience mental ill health and substance use problems prior to domestic abuse victimization. Mental health difficulties may be impacted by other life experiences, such as child abuse, bereavement, breakdown of non-abusive relationships, unemployment, chronic physical health problems and homelessness, as well as being affected by environmental and individual factors. Equally, women's routes into substance use vary: some women start using alcohol or drugs recreationally before developing a psychological or physical dependency; others may begin to drink or use problematically in response to the same types of stressful or traumatic life events that can cause mental health problems. Experiences of mental ill health and problematic substance use may also render a woman at greater risk of then being abused. For example, substance use and mental ill health both increase the likelihood of someone being in an unsafe environment and vulnerable to victimization (Howard *et al.* 2010b). This is especially true of victims who become homeless because of domestic abuse, mental ill health and/or substance use.

Perpetrators have also been documented as using a victim's mental ill health or substance use as a means of abusing them. Research has shown that perpetrators use substances to coerce and control victims (Fox 2018; O'Brien *et al.* 2016; Wright *et al.* 2007). Practice-based evidence suggests that perpetrators may excuse their own abusive behaviour on the basis of the victim's mental health or substance use problems. For example, perpetrators may use a victim's mental ill health as an excuse to isolate the victim – saying she is unable to cope going out by herself, or discouraging her from participating in social activities such as seeing friends or family because she's 'mad' or an 'embarrassment'. Abusers may also use verbal insults relating to mental health or substance use such as 'junkie' or 'nutter' to damage a victim's self-esteem and accuse the victim of causing the abuse by their own erratic behaviour. Perpetrators may insist on controlling the finances, claiming the victim is mentally incompetent or suggesting they will spend it all on drugs or alcohol. Abusive tactics that are more specific to situations where the victim has mental health or substance use problems include:

- Controlling access to substances: alcohol, drugs or prescribed medication.

- Being sexually violent when the victim is intoxicated or lacks capacity to consent.

- Preventing access to substance use or mental health services.

- Using their rights as the named carer or nearest relative for someone with mental health problems to influence the treatment that person receives, including potentially influencing if someone is detained under the Mental Health Act 1983.[5]

The relationship between domestic abuse, mental ill health and problematic substance use is not linear. Domestic abuse can occur before, during or after mental ill health or substance use, and mental ill health and/or substance use can occur in conjunction with, before or after domestic abuse experiences. The three issues are interconnected in various ways, as Figure 4.2 demonstrates. AVA (Against Violence & Abuse, a national charity that conducts research with women who have experiences of domestic abuse, mental ill health and substance use) has developed a working model of association,[6] which may be helpful for practitioners looking to increase their understanding of why these issues so frequently coexist.

---

5   For more information about the rights of mental health carers, please visit: www.mind.org.uk/information-support/legal-rights/health-and-social-care-rights/carers-social-care-rights

6   For more information about AVA's model of association, please visit: www.elearning.avaproject.org.uk and register for the public *Complicated Matters* elearning programme.

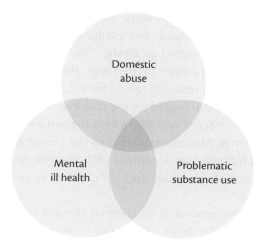

Figure 4.2 The interconnectedness of domestic abuse,
mental ill health and problematic substance use.

To further understand the relationship between domestic abuse, mental ill health and problematic substance use, and that this association is impacted by numerous factors, we have included Michelle's (not her real name) story. Michelle was interviewed as part of a research study exploring support for women with co-occurring domestic abuse and problematic substance use (Fox 2018). While reading Michelle's story, consider the various factors that may have contributed to her continuous use of alcohol and her experiences of domestic abuse.

CASE STUDY 1: MICHELLE

As a child, Michelle experienced abuse and neglect from her parents, who used alcohol heavily. She began drinking at a young age, often taking alcohol from her mum and bringing it into school in the hope that her mum would not be as drunk when she returned. At 13, Michelle experienced sexual abuse at the hands of her mum's partner. She was put into foster care when her mother refused to believe Michelle. From this point, she began drinking heavily and getting into trouble with the police. At the age of 17, while homeless, she met a man whom she said she depended on.

Michelle's partner was physically abusive, controlling and coercive. Throughout their relationship, Michelle drank heavily and experienced continuous domestic abuse. She said she often drank before he came home from work because she knew he would hit her, so the alcohol helped. She explained that after an abusive episode her partner would go to the shop and buy her alcohol as an apology. She had three children with this partner, and one day she reached out to a women's refuge for support. While living in the refuge, however, she arranged for the children to see their dad; social services were contacted, and Michelle was given a warning. Two days before Christmas, Michelle returned to the refuge after consuming alcohol and following an argument with another woman, Michelle was kicked out of the refuge and her children were removed from her care.

Following the removal of her children, she was 'strongly advised' to complete a seven-day detox. On the day of her release from detox she went to court to gain custody of her children, but was denied access. From court, she went to the pub and says her life 'ended up going worse'. She later had two children with a new partner, having been given a second chance by social services. However, her new partner became abusive and Michelle began drinking again. She lost custody of her fourth and fifth child. For a number of years she continued to drink heavily, self-harm and tried to take her own life. She was admitted to a psychiatric hospital where she was detoxed. She was sober for 33 days, but began drinking again. Michelle's drinking soon began to affect her physical health and she described herself as 'a mess'. She wanted to see her children again, and knew she had to stop drinking or risk dying eventually. Following support from her friends, she moved into supported accommodation and began recovery.

Reflective questions for practitioners

1. Think about the various theories discussed so far in this chapter. How do they fit into Michelle's narrative?

2. Is there an underlying cause for her domestic abuse, mental ill health or substance use?

3. As a practitioner, what support would you offer Michelle as she enters supported accommodation?

Policy support for addressing domestic abuse, mental ill health and substance use

A strong central government policy steer is needed to improve responses to women's experiences of mental ill health and problematic substance use. Despite the links between the three issues outlined throughout this chapter, historically, policy-making for each has evolved entirely independently of the others. Unsurprisingly this has resulted in a siloed approach that reflects limited understanding of how issues such as abuse, mental ill health and problematic substance use are interconnected.

Across the UK, national-level policy and strategy responses to co-occurring domestic abuse, mental ill health and problematic substance use remain disjointed, despite the issues spanning the same policy arenas – including health, public health, criminal justice, social care, housing and homelessness. The UK *2017 Drugs Strategy* (HM Government 2017) (which, in terms of policy directives, only covers England), for example, refers to the relationship between substance use and mental ill health and between substance use and domestic abuse, yet both are limited. In relation to domestic abuse, a small section on intimate partner abuse notes that 'women with experience of extensive physical and sexual violence are more likely to have an alcohol problem or be dependent on drugs' and that 'some people accessing substance use services may perpetrate abuse' (HM Government 2017, p.12). Beyond this, there is a loosely worded commitment to 'support[ing] innovative approaches to working with victims and perpetrators, and achiev[ing] sustainable reductions in repeat offending and misuse' (HM Government 2017, p.12).

In Scotland, the most recent drugs strategy, *Equally Safe: Scotland's Strategy for Preventing and Eradicating Violence Against Women and Girls* (Scottish Government 2018) is vocal about the need to address co-occurring substance use and mental ill health, recognizing that the latter can impair a person's ability to recover from the use of substances, a major development since the publication of the 2008 drugs strategy. Similarly, the strategy also acknowledges the role of trauma in substance use, highlighting that 'many people attending alcohol and drug services are thought to have a history of trauma' (2018, p.13), and 'many will have used alcohol and drugs as a means of coping with, and managing, these experiences' (2018, p.36). There is, however, no specific mention of domestic abuse as a form of trauma; the only reference to abuse refers to abuse and neglect of children rather than domestic abuse.

Nonetheless, in response to the increased focus on trauma, a specific commitment to '[d]evelop trauma-informed approaches in alcohol and drug treatment and recovery services' (2018, p.25) has been included in the strategy. The Scottish Government's commitment to developing trauma-informed service provision is a very welcome step forward, particularly as its implementation will hopefully be supported through the creation of the National Trauma Training Framework.[7] This work has been advocated by a collective of organizations across the UK (MEAM 2017b).

By comparison, *Working Together to Reduce Harm: The Substance Misuse Strategy for Wales 2008–2018* (Welsh Government 2008) specifically acknowledges the relationship between substance use and domestic abuse. This strategy commits to working with the All Wales Domestic Abuse Working Group to 'take forward, identify and co-ordinate actions which support jointly the delivery of the domestic abuse strategy and tackle substance misuse' (Welsh Government 2008, p.7). The strategy also outlines measures in relation to women, stating that '[a]ll drug and alcohol specialist services should enquire about domestic abuse at assessment and within ongoing treatment' (2008, p.40), and action should be taken to support vulnerable individuals, including 'pregnant women, victims of domestic abuse, those with mental health problems and the homeless' (Welsh Government 2008, p.33). Whether these intentions have been achieved in practice is unclear. However, a recent mapping exercise – part of the broader Mapping the Maze project – did find substance use midwives to be the most common type of gender-specific support for women using drugs and alcohol in Wales (five midwives were found to be available across Blaenau Gwent, Caerphilly, Monmouthshire, Newport and Torfaen) (Holly 2017). The study did not identify other support specifically for substance-using women in Wales. Equally, the Welsh strategy also clearly addresses dual diagnosis, that is, coexisting substance use and mental health problems, recognizing the impact of substance use on mental wellbeing and the need for services to work together to support people affected by both issues.

The current mental health strategies for both Scotland (Scottish Government 2017) and Wales (Welsh Government 2012) reflect the

---

7   For more information, please visit: https://www.nes.scot.nhs.uk/our-work/trauma-national-trauma-training-programme

aforementioned need to deliver integrated services that meet the needs of people affected by co-occurring mental health and substance use problems. In their own way, each strategy also addresses the issue of trauma and abuse. While the Scottish strategy briefly touches on the fact that trauma can be a risk factor for poorer mental health and links it to their evolving work to address Adverse Childhood Experiences (ACEs), the Welsh strategy goes into more detail. For instance, beyond recognizing domestic abuse and violence against women as potential risk factors for mental ill health, the Welsh strategy talks of health inequalities and that those at most risk of developing mental health problems include 'women subject to violence and children experiencing domestic abuse' (Welsh Government 2012, p.23). Interestingly, in the section on co-occurring conditions, victims of rape, sexual abuse and sexual violence are mentioned as a specific group, and there is also reference to the high levels of mental health problems reported by women staying in refuges.

However, the current Welsh strategy to address violence against women (Welsh Government 2016) makes no mention of substance use or mental ill health except in reference to the impact of children living with these issues alongside domestic abuse. Various groups of survivors are identified as having complex or multiple needs, namely older women, migrants and refugees, black and minority ethnic women, and women offenders. Similarly, *Equally Safe: Scotland's Strategy for Preventing and Eradicating Violence against Women and Girls* (Scottish Government 2018) is almost entirely silent on the subjects of substance use and mental health. The overarching UK Government's *Ending Violence against Women and Girls* (HM Government 2016) includes actions (a) for local areas to work in partnership – including with drug, alcohol and mental health services – to address violence against women and girls; (b) to introduce routine enquiry about domestic abuse in mental health services within the next few years; and (c) to provide centralized funding for services that support survivors who have the most complex needs. More recently, the consultation process for the evolving Domestic Abuse Bill highlighted the need for greater focus on addressing substance use and domestic abuse, and elicited a number of commitments from the Home Office to educate themselves more about the issues and make funding available for training to promote partnership working between substance misuse and domestic abuse services (Home Office and Ministry of Justice 2019).

A final area of policy-making and funding that requires consideration is that around multiple disadvantage. As advocated by the MEAM collective,[8] addressing multiple disadvantage requires providing an integrated package of support to people who face a combination of problems including homelessness, substance use, involvement with the criminal justice system and mental ill health. This approach was influenced in part by research by Bramley *et al.* (2015) who found that 'each year, over a quarter of a million people in England have contact with at least two out of three of the homelessness, substance misuse and/or criminal justice systems, and at least 58,000 people have contact with all three' (2015, p.6). The same report highlighted, however, that only 22 per cent of the people identified as experiencing multiple disadvantage were women, and this was most likely due to the types of disadvantage included in the analysis and particularly the exclusion of experiencing violence and abuse. Following this report, campaigners have (somewhat successfully) sought to raise the profile of women experiencing multiple disadvantage and ensure funding streams include women as a specific target group for interventions around multiple disadvantage. This advocacy has had a positive impact on projects that focus on women with the most severe levels of disadvantage, such as those who are involved in prostitution and/or offending (Holly 2017). However, it has done little to improve how mainstream services respond to those victims of domestic abuse who are affected by problematic substance use and/or mental ill health.

Overall, national policy is fragmented when addressing the three issues that so frequently coexist on the ground. It is disappointing that the strategy documents aimed at tackling domestic abuse are almost silent on substance use and mental ill health, given the links have long been acknowledged within the domestic abuse sector itself and the people delivering victim services. The increased inclusion of trauma-informed provision is a very welcome development as it has the potential to improve how a wide range of services address domestic abuse, problematic substance use and mental ill health. As noted above, however, at present more joined-up approaches to addressing the types of multiple disadvantage discussed in this chapter have largely been delivered through specialized initiatives that focus on people

---

8   The MEAM approach was the first widely recognized model to address multiple disadvantage in England (MEAM 2017a, b). Find out more at: http://meam.org.uk

experiencing the greatest levels of disadvantage. Meeting the needs of all victims who are affected by problematic substance use and/or mental ill health – the majority of whom currently fall between the gaps in services – needs a wholesale shift in how services are designed and delivered. A new vision for service provision that can effectively support women affected by multiple disadvantage is set out in the following section.

Service responses to multiple needs

Research exploring service responses to domestic abuse, mental ill health and problematic substance use consistently demonstrate the positive impact both integrated or coordinated approaches have on outcomes for each of the issues (Bennett and O'Brien 2007; Elliott *et al.* 2005; Morrissey *et al.* 2005; Morton, Holman and Middleton 2015; Torchalla *et al.* 2012). Within the UK health and social care setting, NICE (National Institute for Health and Social Care Excellence) guidelines on domestic abuse recommend multi-agency working between substance use, domestic abuse and mental health services (NICE 2014), recognizing the critical importance of services working together. However, recent changes to funding, particularly the reduction in funding for core health and social care services, has resulted in increased siloed working and greater fragmentation of support pathways (AVA and Agenda 2019). There is, therefore, an immediate need to promote partnership working across both formal mechanisms, such as joint key working, and more informal networking opportunities that allow professionals with different specialisms to get to know and learn from one another. Such initiatives have been recommended for many years (Fox 2018; Galvani 2010; Holly 2017), and in times of increasingly limited resources are even more critical.

Research by women's organizations in the UK have further demonstrated the need for support that is also gender-responsive if it is to be effective in engaging with the majority of victims of abuse who are women (Fox 2018; Galvani and Humphreys 2007; Holly 2017; Holly and Scalabrino 2012). 'Gender-responsive' involves much more than providing a gender-specific space where women can safely access support. Covington (2002) talks of gender-responsive services as being achieved by:

Creating an environment through site selection, staff selection, program development, content and material that reflects an understanding of the realities of women's lives and is responsive to the issues of the clients. (pp.52–53)

Inevitably, this means being trauma-informed, that is, understanding the types of trauma that women commonly experience and the multitude of effects the trauma may have on a woman. Services that are trauma-informed have been described as:

Those in which service delivery is influenced by an understanding of the impact of interpersonal violence and victimization on an individual's life and development. (Elliott *et al.* 2005, p.462)

However, even services specifically set up for women are not always willing or able to address the full range of support needs that women who have experienced trauma may present. As highlighted earlier, for example, very few women who use substances access specialist domestic abuse services. This is unsurprising given that many substance-using victims are aware that only a minority of refuges are able to support women experiencing multiple disadvantage, particularly drug and alcohol use (Harvey, Mandair and Holly 2014; Holly 2017). Moreover, as the Mapping the Maze study demonstrated, support for multiple needs remains siloed, as well as operating on a postcode lottery basis. In many cases, the current system can often re-traumatize women by sending them from service to service, requiring them to retell their story, and failing to identify and prioritize their needs (Sweeney *et al.* 2016). This was the case in Kat's (not her real name) story, outlined in the following case study. As part of the same research as Michelle, Kat also had experiences of domestic abuse victimization, mental ill health and problematic substance use. Kat sought support early on but was met with many barriers and did not receive the support she needed when she wanted it. Read Kat's story below and consider the various barriers she faced when trying to access support.

CASE STUDY 2: KAT

Following a relationship breakdown, Kat was diagnosed with depression and soon began drinking alcohol heavily. She was diagnosed with PTSD due to extensive childhood trauma. She continued to drink, tried to take her own life, and was voluntarily admitted to psychiatric hospital where she stayed for four months. While in hospital, she was referred to a counsellor. Although the counselling sessions helped her deal with her childhood trauma, she explains that she became alcohol dependent, often leaving the counselling session, going home, and drinking to cope with her feelings. Her alcohol use was never discussed in counselling, although she feels her counsellor did know about her drinking. At this time, Kat was also accessing support from a mental health service and a sexual assault charity. Her psychiatrist referred her to an alcohol service; however, they did not support her, telling her there was nothing they could do because she was already accessing other support services. None of these services were alcohol specialists. As no intervention was offered, Kat continued to drink for many years.

After ceasing counselling, Kat met her partner. He was also a heavy alcohol drinker. His control and coerciveness slowly emerged and there were often times of light assault. The couple drank daily, and Kat explains that her ex-partner used to prefer Kat drinking because she was easier to control. Following the second incident of serious assault, Kat called the police. A restraining order was put in place. Kat was offered refuge at that point; however, she was told she would have to stop drinking if she accepted a place. She was not offered any support, a referral, or a number to help her with her alcohol use. As such, she moved in with a friend who was also a heavy drinker. She soon contacted her ex-partner and the relationship began again.

At that point, Kat believed her partner would change. When the abuse began again, she lost hope in leaving because she felt she had tried before and failed. However, she did make contact with a domestic abuse service again, but was unable to access refuge accommodation because she was working and could not afford the rent on her salary. She was not prepared to give up her job. After another serious assault from her partner, Kat decided to leave. She accepted a place in a refuge, and although there was an alcohol-free policy, she drank for the first two weeks in secret, quickly reducing her consumption. She was not offered support for her substance use while in the refuge. Kat's friend informed her about a local alcohol service. She engaged with them and was supported in her sobriety. However, she explained that there was no crossover support between the two services.

Reflective questions for practitioners

1. What systemic barriers are in place prohibiting Kat from accessing support?

2. What would you recommend to the practitioners and services Kat has engaged with?

3. Are you aware of any services in your own locality that could have supported Kat?

4. What can you do in your own practice to support women like Kat?

Recommendations for improving support around domestic abuse victimization, mental ill health and problematic substance use

Throughout this chapter, we have sought to explain how domestic abuse, mental ill health and problematic substance use are intertwined experiences that are, sadly, a common feature of many women's lives. Moreover, we have provided an overview of the current policy and practice landscape that has evolved to support women dealing with these issues. It is clear, however, that much still needs to be done to create an effective response. Our recommendations for progressing towards a joined-up, trauma-informed and gender-responsive package of care for women affected by domestic abuse, mental ill health and problematic substance use are set out below. Many of the recommendations echo the findings of the 2018 National Commission on Domestic & Sexual Violence and Multiple Disadvantage.[9]

Joined-up service delivery

The effect of national policy-making – primarily through the impact this has on local commissioning practices – has resulted in highly siloed services, particularly for women experiencing abuse, mental ill health, problematic substance use and associated problems such

9   For more information about the Commission, please visit: https://avaproject.org.uk/ava-services-2/multiple-disadvantage/commission-domestic-sexual-violence-multiple-disadvantage. The final report of the Commission can be accessed at: https://avaproject.org.uk/wp/wp-content/uploads/2019/03/Breaking-down-the-Barriers-full-report-.pdf

as homelessness and involvement in the criminal justice system. The Mapping the Maze exercise, for example, found a distinct lack of provision in any one area for women experiencing multiple forms of disadvantage. Out of 173 local authorities in England and Wales, only 19 (11 per cent) provided services that address a combination of substance use, mental health, homelessness, offending and complex needs (including domestic abuse) to women (Holly 2017).

As highlighted in Kat's case study, and from the evidence throughout this chapter, fragmented service provision that has rigid eligibility criteria can result in women being unable to access support at the point when they are ready. Not only do services and the wider systems they are located within need to be designed to be more accessible to service users with greater complexity of needs, but services also need to work together more closely. Following on from the MEAM approach to supporting people experiencing multiple disadvantage, 'service navigators' have been recommended as a specific form of service provision to reduce the risk of people seeking support for more than one issue falling through the gaps.

Recommendation 1: Nationally, responsibility for driving forward cross-departmental approaches needs to be held by a cabinet-level minister. This should include overseeing the creation of a funding stream for the overlapping issues addressed in this chapter to invest in service redesign and incentivize local commissioning bodies to pool budgets and jointly commission health and social care services.

Recommendation 2: A duty on local bodies to collaborate with and through the local authority should be created, and local authorities should be held responsible for coordinating joined-up approaches.

Recommendation 3: Joined-up service delivery models such as one-stop shops and co-location of professionals should be invested in. Alternatively, 'service navigator' models, where individuals or teams support service users to navigate systems, should be developed to support survivors to access available services.

Recommendation 4: Commissioners should build incentives into contracts to encourage mainstream services to work collaboratively and ensure that specialist expertise is prioritized.

Recommendation 5: Commissioners should ensure that services provide data on who is being turned away to allow data collection on service thresholds and to inform future commissioning.

Becoming trauma-informed

It is evident that the need for trauma-informed practice is increasingly acknowledged and understood. As already highlighted, the current drug and alcohol treatment strategy in Scotland includes a specific commitment to developing trauma-informed treatment and recovery services. Equally, the UK clinical guidelines for substance use treatment (Department of Health & Social Care 2017) highlight the importance of trauma-informed practice within substance use services and provide a clear framework of principles for trauma-informed care (2017, p.42), as well as including a section on working with victims and perpetrators of domestic abuse in drug and alcohol treatment services. The recent government taskforce on women's mental health has also recommended that service guidelines and specifications used in the commissioning process should promote the adoption of trauma-informed practice in the delivery of mental health services (Department of Health & Social Care and Agenda 2018). But what does it mean to be trauma-informed? Various guidelines and checklists now exist based on the principles of Elliott and colleagues (2005, pp.465–469):

Ten principles of an effective trauma-informed service

1. Trauma-informed services recognize the impact of violence and victimization on development and coping strategies.

2. Trauma-informed services identify recovery from trauma as a primary goal.

3. Trauma-informed services employ an empowerment model.

4. Trauma-informed services strive to maximize a woman's choice and control over her recovery.

5. Trauma-informed services are based on relational collaboration.

6. Trauma-informed services create an atmosphere that is respectful of survivor's need for safety, respect and acceptance.

7. Trauma-informed services emphasize women's strengths, highlighting adaptations over symptoms and resilience over pathology.

8. The goal of trauma-informed services is to minimize the possibilities of traumatization.

9. Trauma-informed services strive to be culturally competent and to understand each woman in the context of her life experiences and cultural background.

10. Trauma-informed agencies solicit consumer input and involve consumers in designing and evaluating services.

Importantly, the key to becoming trauma-informed is recognition that implementation does not rest solely with front-line practitioners. A trauma-informed service is one that is delivered by a provider that is trauma-informed, in an environment and within a culture that is trauma-informed. This may require a strategic programme of organizational change to achieve (see AVA and Solace Women's Aid 2017).

Recommendations for service providers to become trauma-informed are widespread and involve many aspects of running an organization and delivering services. Galvani's (2004) approach to supporting individuals and services recommend:

- Displaying posters and information about domestic abuse, substance use and mental health in the common areas that clients may use.

- Employing a resource box of information on domestic abuse, substance use and mental health, including relevant contacts for local services.

- Ensuring all staff receive basic training on domestic abuse, substance use and mental health.

- Reviewing agency policies to incorporate domestic abuse, substance use and mental health.

- Ensuring questions on domestic abuse, substance use and mental health are incorporated into all forms of assessment.

Broader recommendations to enable implementation of trauma-informed practice as standard across all providers of health and social care services are listed below.

Recommendation 6: National trauma guidelines should be created with funding made available for service providers to become trauma-informed through training and other support. The guidelines should be based on an evidence review of the value and impact of trauma-informed practice in public service settings. They must acknowledge that becoming trauma-informed is not solely about training front-line practitioners about trauma-informed practice, but also requires organization-wide adoption of a trauma-informed culture.

Recommendation 7: Monitoring trauma-informed practice should form part of inspection regimes such as those conducted by the CQC (Care Quality Commission).

Recommendation 8: Care and treatment pathways should be designed to enable a stepped model of care that supports people at crisis point through to support to recover from the long-term effects of trauma. This should include ongoing, low-level, unstructured support that people can engage in as and when they need, such as drop-in centres and sessions.

Recommendation 9: Enquiry about trauma should become standard in all health and social care settings alongside questions about how trauma might have affected an individual and how they have coped with the trauma in the short and long term.

Being gender-responsive

While being gender-responsive does not mean only women-specific, there is a distinct lack of support specifically for women across England and Wales. Exploring service provision for women experiencing multiple disadvantage in 173 local authorities within England and Wales, the 2017 Mapping the Maze survey found that:

- Less than half (49 per cent) of all local authorities in England and five unitary authorities in Wales (22.7 per cent) provided substance use support specifically for women.

- The most popular type of women-specific substance use support was a specialist substance use midwife or a weekly women's group within a generic service.

- 104 local authorities in England and five unitary authorities in Wales provided women-specific mental health support, the majority of which (55 per cent) was aimed at pregnant women or women who had recently given birth.

- Refuge provision was the most commonly cited women-specific homeless support across both countries; however, the majority were unable to support women affected by multiple disadvantage.

It is therefore vital that commissioners and funders support the provision of women-specific services, as treatments that address the specific needs of women have been shown to be more effective (Greenfield *et al.* 2007; Holly and Scalabrino 2012).

Beyond this, however, all services need to be more gender-responsive. The second part of the Mapping the Maze project sought to develop a model of good practice in supporting women affected by multiple disadvantage, as no specific model for the UK existed at the time. Following a consultation with women experiencing multiple disadvantage and a review of the literature from both the UK and abroad, the Mapping the Maze model was devised. Drawing heavily from the voices of domestic abuse victims who are also affected by substance use and mental ill health (see, for example, AVA 2013; Holly and Scalabrino 2012) as well as the work of Covington (2002) and Elliott *et al.* (2005), the Mapping the Maze model (see Table 4.1) aims to provide a framework for services to be both trauma-informed and gender-responsive.

Table 4.1 Mapping the Maze model

1. **Organizational ethos:** *Commitment to delivering trauma-informed and gender-responsive services and interventions.* This means:
- Having specialist knowledge of women's lives and experiences.
- Understanding interrelated needs requiring individual holistic care.
- Recognizing the impact of trauma, particularly in terms of violence and victimization.
- Acknowledging the impact of trauma on a diverse population.
- Accepting survivors – viewing behaviour as adaptation and resilience rather than symptoms and pathology.

2. **Safe and enabling environment:** *Provision of support in places where survivors feel safe and welcome.* This means:
- For women, women-only spaces.
- Feeling physically safe, particularly when survivors may be affected by violence and abuse.
- Prioritizing emotional safety that minimizes the risk of re-traumatization.
- An environment that promotes dignity, self-respect and wellbeing.

3. **Approach to working:** *How interventions are delivered is as critical as what support is facilitated.* This means:
- Safety, respect and acceptance are paramount.
- Trust is a key priority, built through consistent relationships.
- Working with the individual, including being culturally competent.
- Building on strengths and ways of coping.
- Enabling choice and control, which in turn builds self-efficacy.
- Building a plan *with* a service user and *not for* a service user, and working with other agencies.
- Offering time and flexibility.

4. **Organizational practice:** *Structures are in place to enable trauma-informed interventions.* This means:
- Recognizing the challenges of working in a trauma-informed way.
- Providing sufficient staff support – informal and line management/clinical supervision.
- Continued staff development.
- Engaging with partners to develop integrated multi-agency responses.
- Challenging and working to eliminate causes of trauma.
- Being aware of the need to develop cultural competence and address issues relating to equality and diversity.

Source: Holly (2017)

As this model aligns with many of the principles of trauma-informed practice, again, it cannot be implemented by front-line practitioners alone but requires a whole organizational approach that is promoted by local commissioning and national policy.

Recommendation 10: Women-specific services should be made universally available, including domestic abuse and substance use services.

Recommendation 11: Where women-only support is not commissioned, service providers should still seek to deliver this, which may involve some creative thinking to carve out a genuinely women-only space in a mixed-gender service. Alternatively, it might mean employing gender-specific workers who have additional expertise in supporting women affected by abuse, problematic substance use and mental ill health.

Recommendation 12: Large service providers, including health trusts, national charities and for-profit companies, should be required to have a women's strategy that informs their service delivery.

Recommendation 13: Involve women in the design and delivery of services. This includes providing an opportunity to hear the voices of women who are often excluded, such as BAMER women (Black, Asian, minority ethnic and refugee), disabled women and LGBTQI (lesbian, gay, bisexual, transgender, queer (or questioning) and intersex) women.

Conclusion

Women who experience domestic abuse, problematic substance use and/or mental ill heath are not a new population in health and social care. They exist in 'domestic violence survivor agencies, perpetrator programmes and substance use programmes' (Humphreys *et al.* 2005, p.16) as well as GP surgeries, midwifery services, psychiatric hospitals and community outreach programmes. Yet, as this chapter has shown, within the UK, there is a gap in both research and practice regarding the co-occurrence of the three issues. While research shows a definite prevalence of domestic abuse, mental ill heath and problematic substance use, the results from the UK are dated, potentially under-representing the scale of the issue. This is particularly true of women whose experiences are impacted by race, ethnicity, disability and sexuality. It is therefore vital that researchers are innovative in capturing prevalence rates, and include women outside of treatment populations.

The second section presented an overview of the various ways that the three issues can manifest in women's lives. That the relationship between domestic abuse, mental ill health and problematic substance use is not linear was highlighted. Mental ill health and substance use can exist before domestic abuse and can be influenced by domestic abuse. Substance use may be intertwined with domestic abuse, particularly if a perpetrator has been coercive or controlling with drugs or alcohol. To demonstrate the interplay between the three issues, a case study was presented. Michelle's story demonstrated how childhood adversity can have an impact on the normalization of abuse and the desire to be loved. Her substance use was influenced by her domestic abuse experiences as she used alcohol to cope, while also being presented with alcohol by her partner after a violent episode. Michelle's story encapsulates the complex interconnection between domestic abuse, mental ill health and problematic substance use.

Following an overview of prevalence and relationships, the third section highlighted some of the key policy documents from the UK that focus on domestic abuse, mental ill health and problematic substance use. There was a notable difference between English, Welsh and Scottish approaches to multiple disadvantage. This difference highlights the need for a national strategy that responds to the multiple needs of those affected by domestic abuse, particularly women. Implementing a strong policy that responds to the various needs of women affected by domestic abuse is necessary to guide practice because, as Kat's story illustrated, there were multiple gaps in support, despite her readiness and need to engage.

The lack of services that respond to the varied and multiple needs of women affected by domestic abuse was also found by AVA's Mapping the Maze study. Kat's real-life experience showed the impact this gap in support has, as she went from service to service retelling her story. To ensure Kat's experiences are not repeated, a gender-responsive, trauma-informed response is recommended. AVA's Mapping the Maze model (Holly 2017), influenced by Covington (2002) and Elliott *et al.* (2005), highlights four overarching principals that are believed to be necessary when responding to multiple disadvantage. To respond to women who have experience of domestic abuse, problematic substance use and mental ill health, it is vital that services understand how the three issues manifest and interact. To do this, Covington's definition of 'gender-responsiveness' is also advocated because it not only focuses on women-only spaces, but also on the gendered nature of the environment overall. To respond to the specific and multiple needs of women affected by domestic abuse, substance use and/or mental ill health requires a shift in both research and practice from a siloed way of doing to a more holistic approach.

References

AVA (Against Violence & Abuse) (2013) *Complicated Matters: A Toolkit Addressing Domestic and Sexual Abuse, Substance Use and Mental Ill-Health.* London: AVA.

AVA (2018) *Multiple Disadvantage.* Available at: https://avaproject.org.uk/ava-services-2/multiple-disadvantage

AVA and Agenda (2019) *Breaking Down the Barriers: Findings of the National Commission on Domestic and Sexual Violence and Multiple Disadvantage.* Available at: https://weareagenda.org/wp-content/uploads/2019/02/Executive-summary-Breaking-down-the-barriers-web-version-FINAL.pdf

AVA and Solace Women's Aid (2017) *An Evaluation of the Refuge Access for All Project: Creating a Psychologically Informed Environment in Solace Women's Aid Services Across Five London Boroughs.* London: AVA. Available at: https://avaproject.org.uk/wp/wp-content/uploads/2017/09/Peace-of-Mind-Summary-Report.pdf

Bennett, L. and O'Brien, P. (2007) 'Effects of coordinated services for drug-abusing women who are victims of intimate partner violence.' *Violence Against Women 13*, 4, 395–411.

Bramley, G. and Fitzpatrick, S. with Edwards, J., Ford, D., Johnsen, S., Sosenko, F. and Watkins, D. (2015) *Hard Edges: Mapping Severe and Multiple Disadvantage.* London: Lankelly Chase. Available at: https://lankellychase.org.uk/wp-content/uploads/2015/07/Hard-Edges-Mapping-SMD-2015.pdf

Brandon, M., Sidebotham, P., Bailey, S., Belderson, P., *et al.* (2012) *New Learning from Serious Case Reviews: A Two Year Report for 2009–2011.* Research Report for the Department for Education. Available at: https://assets.publishing.service.gov.uk/government/uploads/system/uploads/attachment_data/file/184053/DFE-RR226_Report.pdf

Cafferky, B., Mendez, M., Anderson, J. and Stith, S. (2018) 'Substance use and intimate partner violence: A meta-analytic review.' *Psychology of Violence 8*, 1, 110–131.

Callaghan, J., Alexander, J., Sixsmith, J. and Chiara Fellin, L. (2015) 'Beyond "witnessing": Children's experiences of coercive control in domestic violence and abuse.' *Journal of Interpersonal Violence 3*, 10, 1551–1581.

Chandan, J., Thomas, T., Bradbury-Jones, C., Russell, R., *et al.* (2019) 'Female survivors of intimate partner violence and risk of depression, anxiety and serious mental illness.' *The British Journal of Psychiatry.* doi:10.1192/bjp.2019.124.

Covington, S. (2002) 'Helping Women Recover: Creating Gender-responsive Treatment.' In L.A. Straussner and S. Brown (eds) *The Handbook of Addiction Treatment for Women: Theory and Practice* (pp.52–72). Available at: www.stephaniecovington.com/assets/files/5.pdf

CPS (Crown Prosecution Service) (2017) *Controlling or Coercive Behaviour in an Intimate or Family Relationship.* Available at: www.cps.gov.uk/legal-guidance/controlling-or-coercive-behaviour-intimate-or-family-relationship

DfE (Department for Education) (2017) *Characteristics of Children in Need: 2016 to 2017 England.* London: DfE.

DH (Department of Health) (2009) *Improving Safety, Reducing Harm: Children, Young People and Domestic Violence. A Practical Toolkit for Front-line Practitioners.* London: DH.

Department of Health & Social Care (2017) *Drug Misuse and Dependence: UK Guidelines on Clinical Management.* London: Available at: www.gov.uk/government/publications/drug-misuse-and-dependence-uk-guidelines-on-clinical-management

Department of Health & Social Care and Agenda (2018) *The Women's Mental Health Taskforce: Final Report*. Available at: https://weareagenda.org/wp-content/uploads/2018/12/The_ Womens_Mental_Health_Taskforce_-_final_report1.pdf

Devries, K.M., Child, J.C., Bacchus, L.J., Mak, J., Falder, G. and Graham, K. (2013) 'Intimate partner violence victimization and alcohol consumption in women: A systematic review and meta-analysis.' *Addiction 109*, 3, 379–391.

Elliott, D., Bjelajac, P., Fallor, R., Markoff, L. and Reed, B. (2005) 'Trauma-informed or trauma-denied: Principles and implementation of trauma-informed services for women.' *Journal of Community Psychology 33*, 4, 461–477.

Ellsberg, M., Jansen, H.A.F.M., Heise, L., Watts, C.H. and Garcia-Moreno, C. (2008) 'Intimate partner violence and women's physical and mental health in the WHO multi-country study on women's health and domestic violence: An observational study.' *The Lancet 371*, 1165–1172.

Ettorre, E. (1997) *Women and Alcohol: A Private Pleasure or a Public Problem?* London: Women's Press.

Ferrari, G., Agnew-Davies, R., Bailey, J., Howard, L., *et al.* (2016) 'Domestic violence and mental health: A cross-sectional survey of women seeking help from domestic violence support services.' *Global Health Action 7*.

Fox, S. (2018) 'It's sort of a chicken and egg scenario: Women's experiences of substance use, domestic abuse and support.' Unpublished thesis, Manchester Metropolitan University.

Galvani, S. (2004) 'Responsible disinhibition: Alcohol, men and violence to women.' *Addiction Research & Theory 12*, 4, 357–371.

Galvani, S. (2010) *Supporting Families Affected by Substance Use and Domestic Violence*. Research Report. Available at: https://adfam.org.uk/files/docs/adfam_dvreport.pdf

Galvani, S. (2015) *Alcohol and Other Drug Use: The Roles and Capabilities of Social Workers*. London: Public Health England. Available at: www2.mmu.ac.uk/media/mmuacuk/content/ documents/hpsc/research/Alcohol-and-other-drug-use-report.pdf

Galvani, S. and Humphreys, C. (2007) *The Impact of Violence and Abuse on Engagement and Retention Rates for Women in Substance Use Treatment*. National Treatment Agency for Substance Misuse. Available at: www.ccrm.org.uk/images/ docs/7.3aimpactofviolenceonengagementandretentionrates.pdf

Greenfield, S., Brooks, A., Gordon, S. and Green, C.K., *et al.* (2007) 'Substance abuse treatment entry, retention, and outcome in women: A review of the literature.' *Drug and Alcohol Dependence 86*, 1–21.

Harvey, S., Mandair, S. and Holly, J. (2014) *Case by Case: Refuge Provision in London for Survivors of Domestic Violence Who Use Alcohol and Other Drugs or Have Mental Health Problems*. London: AVA and Solace Women's Aid. Available at: https://avaproject.org.uk/wp-content/uploads/2016/03/Case-by-Case-London-refuge-provision-Full-Report.pdf

Herman, J. (2015) *Trauma and Recovery: The Aftermath of Violence – From Domestic Abuse to Political Terror*. New York: Basic Books.

Hien, D., Cohen, L. and Campbell, A. (2005) 'Is traumatic stress a vulnerability factor for women with substance use disorders?' *Clinical Psychology Review 25*, 6, 813–823.

HM Government (2016) *Ending Violence against Women and Girls: 2016 to 2020*. London: Home Office. Available at https://assets.publishing.service.gov.uk/government/uploads/system/ uploads/attachment_data/file/522166/VAWG_Strategy_FINAL_PUBLICATION_MASTER_ vRB.PDF [updated March 2019].

HM Government (2017) *2017 Drug Strategy*. July. Available at: https://assets.publishing.service.gov. uk/government/uploads/system/uploads/attachment_data/file/628148/Drug_strategy_2017. PDF

Holly, J. (2017) *Mapping the Maze: Services for Women Experiencing Multiple Disadvantage in England and Wales*. London: Agenda and AVA. Available at: www.mappingthemaze.org.uk

Holly, J. and Scalabrino, R. (2012) 'Treat Me Like a Human Being, Like Someone Who Matters': *Findings of the Stella Project Mental Health Initiative Survivor Consultation*. London: AVA. Available at: https://avaproject.org.uk/wp-content/uploads/2016/03/Treat-me-like-a-human-being-SPMHI-survivor-consultation-report-June-2012.pdf

Home Office and Ministry of Justice (2019) *Transforming the Response to Domestic Abuse. Consultation Response and Draft Bill.* London: Home Office. Available at: https://assets.publishing.service.gov.uk/government/uploads/system/uploads/attachment_data/file/772202/CCS1218158068-Web_Accessible.pdf

Howard, L.M., Trevillion, K. and Agnew-Davies, R. (2010a) 'Domestic violence and mental health.' *International Review of Psychiatry 22*, 5, 525–534.

Howard, L.M., Trevillion, K., Khalifeh, H., Woodall, A., Agnew-Davies, R. and Feder, G. (2010b) 'Domestic violence and severe psychiatric disorders: Prevalence and interventions.' *Psychological Medicine 40*, 6, 881–893.

Howarth, E. and Robinson, A. (2015) 'Responding effectively to women experiencing severe abuse: Identifying key components of a British advocacy intervention.' *Violence Against Women 22*, 1, 41–63.

Humphreys, C. and Thiara, R. (2003) 'Mental health and domestic violence: "I call it symptoms of abuse".' *The British Journal of Social Work 33*, 2, 209–226.

Humphreys, C., Thiara, R.K. and Regan, L. (2005) *Domestic Violence and Substance Use: Overlapping Issues in Separate Services?* Warwick: University of Warwick and London Metropolitan University.

Khalifeh, H., Moran, P., Borschmann, R., Dean, K., Hart, C. and Hogg, J. (2015) 'Domestic and sexual violence against patients with severe mental illness.' *Psychological Medicine 45*, 4, 875–886.

Khalifeh, H., Oram, S., Osborn, D., Howard, L.M. and Johnson, S. (2016) 'Recent physical and sexual violence against adults with severe mental illness: A systematic review and meta-analysis.' *International Review of Psychiatry 28*, 5, 433–451.

Khantzian, E. (1997) 'The self-medication hypothesis of substance use disorders: A reconsideration and recent applications.' *Harvard Review of Psychiatry 4*, 231–244.

Lagdon, S., Armour, C. and Stringer, M. (2014) 'Adult experience of mental health outcomes as a result of intimate partner violence victimisation: A systematic review.' *European Journal of Psychotraumatology 5*.

Lee, N. and Boeri, M. (2017) 'Managing stigma: Women drug users and recovery services.' *Fusio 1*, 2, 65–94.

McKeganey, N., Neale, J. and Robertson, M. (2005) 'Physical and sexual abuse among drug users contacting drug treatment services in Scotland.' *Drugs: Education, Prevention and Policy 12*, 3, 223–232.

MEAM (2017a) 'MEAM, Agenda, AVA and Revolving Doors Agency respond to new government Drug Strategy.' Available at: http://meam.org.uk/policy/meam-agenda-and-ava-respond-to-new-government-drug-strategy

MEAM (2017b) *Multiple Needs: Time for Political Leadership.* Available at: www.meam.org.uk/wp-content/uploads/2018/09/Multiple-needs-time-for-political-leadership.pdf

Morrissey, J., Jackson, E., Ellis, A., Amaro, H., Brown, V. and Najavits, L. (2005) 'Twelve-month outcomes of trauma-informed interventions for women with co-occurring disorders.' *Psychiatric Services 56*, 10, 1213–1222.

Morton, S., Holman, M. and Middleton, A. (2015) 'Implementing a harm reduction approach to substance use in an intimate partner violence agency: Practice issues in an Irish setting.' *Partner Abuse 6*, 3, 337–350.

NICE (National Institute for Health and Care Excellence) (2014) *Domestic Violence and Abuse: Multi-agency Working.* Public Health Guidance 50. London: NICE.

O'Brien, J.E., Ermentrout, D., Rizo, C.F., Li, W., Macy, R.J. and Dababnah, S. (2016) '"I never knew which way he would swing": Exploring the roles of substances in the lives of system-involved intimate partner violence survivors.' *Journal of Family Violence 31*, 1, 61–73.

ONS (2018) *Domestic Abuse in England and Wales: Year Ending March 2018.* Available at: www.ons.gov.uk/peoplepopulationandcommunity/crimeandjustice/bulletins/domesticabuseinenglandandwales/yearendingmarch2018

Oram, S., Trevillion, K., Feder, G. and Howard, L.M. (2013) 'Prevalence of experiences of domestic violence among psychiatric patients: Systematic review.' *British Journal of Psychiatry 202*, 2, 94–99.

PHE (Public Health England) and DH (Department of Health) (2017) *Adult Substance Misuse Statistics from the National Drug Treatment Monitoring System (NDTMS)*. Available at: https://assets.publishing.service.gov.uk/government/uploads/system/uploads/attachment_data/file/658056/Adult-statistics-from-the-national-drug-treatment-monitoring-system-2016-2017.pdf

RCPSYCH (Royal College of Psychiatrists) (2017) *Domestic Violence and Abuse – The Impact on Children and Adolescents*. Accessed at: www.rcpsych.ac.uk/mental-health/parents-and-young-people/information-for-parents-and-carers/domestic-violence-and-abuse-effects-on-children

Rees, S., Silove, D., Chey, T., Ivancic, L., *et al.* (2011) 'Lifetime prevalence of gender-based violence in women and the relationship with mental disorders and psychosocial function.' *Journal of American Medical Association 306*, 5, 513–521.

Scott, S. and McManus, S. (2016) *Hidden Hurt: Violence, Abuse and Disadvantage in the Lives of Women*. London: Agenda. Available at: https://weareagenda.org/wp-content/uploads/2015/11/Hidden-Hurt-executive-summary1.pdf

Scottish Government (2017) *Mental Health Strategy 2017–2027*. Available at: www.gov.scot/Publications/2017/03/1750

Scottish Government (2018) *Equally Safe: Scotland's Strategy to Eradicate Violence against Women*. Available at: www.gov.scot/publications/equally-safe-scotlands-strategy-prevent-eradicate-violence-against-women-girls

Sharps-Jeff, N. and Kelly, L. (2016) *Domestic Homicide Review (DHR) Case Analysis*. London: Standing Together and London Metropolitan University.

Sidebotham, P., Brandon, M., Bailey, S., Belderson, P., *et al.* (2016) *Pathways to Harm, Pathways to Protection: A Triennial Analysis of Serious Case Reviews 2011 to 2014 – Final Report*. London: Department for Education. Available at: https://assets.publishing.service.gov.uk/government/uploads/system/uploads/attachment_data/file/533826/Triennial_Analysis_of_SCRs_2011-2014_-__Pathways_to_harm_and_protection.pdf

Smith, P. (2019) 'A qualitative examination of the self-medicating hypothesis among female juvenile offenders.' *Women & Criminal Justice 29*, 1, 14–31.

Sweeney, A., Clement, C., Filson, B. and Kennedy, A. (2016) 'Trauma-informed mental healthcare in the UK: What is it and how can we further its development?' *Mental Health Review Journal 21*, 3, 174–192.

Torchalla, I., Nosen, L., Rostam, H. and Allen, P. (2012) 'Integrated treatment programs for individuals with concurrent substance use disorders and trauma experiences: A systematic review and meta-analysis.' *Journal of Substance Abuse Treatment 42*, 1, 65–77.

Welsh Government (2008) *Working Together to Reduce Harm: The Substance Misuse Strategy for Wales 2008–2018*. Available at: www2.nphs.wales.nhs.uk:8080/SubstanceMisuseDocs.nsf/($All)/6361D5806F16EEDD80257C5B005AC8AF/$File/Working%20Together%20to%20Reduce%20Harm%20-%20SM%20Strategy%202008-2018.pdf?OpenElement

Welsh Government (2012) *Together for Mental Health: A Strategy for Mental Health and Wellbeing in Wales*. Available at: https://gov.wales/sites/default/files/publications/2019-04/together-for-mental-health-summary.pdf

Welsh Government (2016) *National Strategy on Violence Against Women, Domestic Abuse and Sexual Violence – 2016–2021*. Available at: https://gov.wales/sites/default/files/publications/2019-06/national-strategy-2016-to-2021.pdf

Women's Aid (2016) *The Women's Aid Annual Survey 2015*. Available at: www.womensaid.org.uk/research-and-publications/annual-survey-2015/ www.womensaid.org.uk/research-and-publications/annual-survey-2016

Women's Aid (2017) *No Woman Turned Away*. Available at: www.womensaid.org.uk/no-woman-turned-away

Women's Aid (2018) *Survival and Beyond: The Domestic Abuse Report 2017*. Available at: www.womensaid.org.uk/survival-beyond-report

Wright, N.M.J., Tompkins, C.N.E. and Sheard, L. (2007) 'Is peer injecting a form of intimate partner abuse? A qualitative study of the experiences of women drug users.' *Health & Social Care in the Community 15*, 5, 417–425.

Chapter 5

Providing a Better Service for Older Women Experiencing Domestic Abuse

John Devaney and Elizabeth Martin

Introduction

Internationally, it is generally accepted that domestic abuse is a serious issue, and that anyone, regardless of age, gender, education or social class, can be a victim. Despite this, however, most research into domestic abuse continues to focus on younger women, and typically those with young children (Phillips 2000; Straka and Montminy 2006; Walsh *et al.* 2007). This has left gaps in our knowledge and understanding of the experiences of many of those who fall outside this age range. However, there is a nascent and growing body of literature surrounding older women who have been abused (Martin, Devaney and Carney 2018; McGarry, Ali and Hinchliff 2017). This body of work on domestic abuse and older women has the potential to support the development and delivery of policy and services. This chapter will explore our growing knowledge, such as how service providers can better meet the needs of older victims and survivors, establish the full scale and dimensions of the issue, and the challenges service providers face in recognizing when domestic abuse is taking place. We draw on the findings of two studies in Northern Ireland into older women's experiences of domestic abuse, and the experience of developing and managing a service designed specifically for older women.

Scale of the issue

A major contribution to the knowledge base on older people and domestic abuse has been the prevalence study of violence and abuse against older women in Europe, conducted between 2009 and 2011. The study involved 2880 women aged between 60 and 97, of whom over 28 per cent who lived in a private household reported some kind of violence (Louma *et al.* 2011). Emotional abuse followed by financial abuse were found to be the most common forms of violence used against these women, with their partners or spouses being most likely to be the perpetrators. A weakness of the study is that it did not appear to ask participants about whether they were in a same-sex, rather than different-sex, relationship, therefore missing an important opportunity to explore the particular experiences and needs of an important subset of women.

Statistics appear to suggest that as women grow older there is an apparent lowering of risk of being a victim of domestic abuse (ONS 2017a), although Bows' (2018) work on intimate partner homicide involving older victims shows that the risk of physical violence does not disappear altogether. There is a growing realization that domestic abuse does not just 'end' when a woman ages, but rather, violence against women over 50 tends to change in nature, and can be framed as elder abuse by some service providers (Brandl and Cook-Daniels 2011; Penhale 2003). Reflecting on the intersection of domestic abuse and elder abuse, Wydall and colleagues (2018) state that in policy and practice, they are often seen as distinct entities, when in reality the distinctions appear 'ambiguous and blurred'. As Kilbane and Spira (2010) note, the system and service response is differentiated by (a) the definitions and model on which services are based; (b) the type of services offered to the victim and how safety and protection are determined; (c) the specific training of workers; and (d) how incidents of abuse are reported. Yet, they are often dealing with issues relating to the misuse of power and control, between adults within close personal relationships, and whenever issues of poor health and one individual being cared by the other obfuscates clear lines of victim and perpetrator. This is most obviously the case when we include coercive control in our definition of abuse (Stark 2009; Walby and Towers 2018) – seeing beyond physical violence, particularly in situations whereby one individual in a relationship may be perceived to be fulfilling a useful role such as a carer or advocate.

As a consequence, some professionals have been accused of failing to acknowledge the fact that domestic abuse occurs in relationships between older people (McGarry and Simpson 2011). One reason for this could be that that while domestic abuse is already understood to be an under-reported crime, older women are more reluctant to report such incidents compared to younger women. This is due to social and cultural factors, such as shame, and a fear that they will not be believed, or that they have somehow perpetuated the abuse by not speaking up sooner (Blood 2004; Penhale and Porritt 2010; Scott 2008; UN 2013). It can also be the case that the older person themselves does not recognize the behaviour towards them as abuse (Martin 2018; Penhale and Iborra 2014).

Defining being 'older'

In undertaking research in this area, one of the often-repeated questions relates to the age at which a woman becomes 'older'. At one level this may appear straightforward, if seeking to use some universal marker. However, as society has changed, so have our conceptualizations of the ageing process. Children now remain in education and living at home with parents for much longer than 50 years ago; the typical age for women having their first child has similarly increased; and the abolition of a mandatory retirement age in many countries makes our ideas of ageing, and the stages of life, more fluid and shifting. As noted in the introduction to this chapter, most of the existing research about the victimization of women by their current or former intimate partner has focused on younger women, and typically those with young children. As such, most of the research on older women who have experienced domestic abuse has often taken the second half of life as an area of study (Lazenbatt and Devaney 2014), with various studies beginning at the age of 50 or older.

As discussed elsewhere (Martin *et al.* 2018), the experience of ageing is impacted by a number of factors at both a structural and individual level. It has been argued that the degenerative discourse on ageing is especially harmful to women, leading to 'stereotypes of elderly women [which] are particularly negative and demeaning' (Arber and Ginn 1991, p.1). Cruikshank (2013) argues that throughout their lives, women continue to face numerous social and structural constraints in relation to ageing. While the process of ageing has been constructed as problematic for both men and women, becoming old is more problematic for women than it is for men, with many women rendered 'invisible' within society as a result (Bell 2012). Recent work suggests that gender is an important aspect in ageing, with women outnumbering men in older age groups across all European Union (EU) member states (Eurostat 2014; Harper 2014). Gender is a significant indicator of elder abuse in older age groups, with most research suggesting women are more at risk of being victims of this than men (De Donder *et al.* 2016). Women under 65 describe more recurring and serious abuse (Ansara and Hindin 2010; Jonson and Akerstrom 2004), and women over 65 are at greater risk of being victims of domestic abuse than men (Freel and Robinson 2004, 2005; O'Keeffe *et al.* 2007). However, as we discuss later in this chapter, there is a need to differentiate between what is defined as elder abuse and domestic abuse in order to make better-informed interventions that are ultimately more protective and supportive of victims.

Ageing as a gender issue

Blood (2003) helpfully provides a reminder that gender differences and the inequalities that arise from them span the lifecourse. Older women are often 'patronised, marginalised and made to be invisible' (2003, p.40), and this blending of ageism and sexism can magnify and intensify the experience of being a victim of domestic violence due to age and gender. Twenty-three per cent of the total global burden of disease is attributable to disorders in people aged 60 and older (Prince *et al.* 2015), although older women are much more likely to have high support needs compared to men, and for these to exist for longer. As noted by Louma *et al.* (2011), poor physical and mental health increase the likelihood of being victimized. In some European countries nearly 50 per cent of women aged over 65 are now living by themselves, many with poor and enduring health conditions (Beard and Bloom 2015). Women's occupational pensions are, on average, nearly 40 per cent lower than men's, with many disadvantaged by years of paying the 'married women's stamp', and many finding that their pensions end or are significantly reduced on the death of their husband (Betti *et al.* 2015). These structural inequalities, due to gender, which are then compounded by age, limit the range of options for women who have or who are experiencing domestic violence.

The impact of abuse on older women

There is now a robust evidence base relating to the negative impact on women of experiencing domestic abuse, particularly those who are younger. While we do need to disentangle the impact of health as a risk factor for being victimized from the impact on health of being a victim, there is a good evidence base to draw on. For example, Dockerty, Varney and Jay-Webster (2015) report that disabled people are at much greater risk of being victims of domestic violence, and that they experience domestic violence for longer periods of time, and more severe and frequent abuse than non-disabled people (see also Chapter 7 by Ravi K. Thiara and Ruth Bashall). This is important given the higher incidence of poor health and disability among older women.

We also know that women who have been abused by their partners are three times more likely to report depression and to be diagnosed with a mental illness (Calvete, Estıvez and Corral 2007); five times more likely to engage in suicidal behaviour (Pico-Alfonso *et al.* 2005); nine times more likely to misuse drugs; and 15 times more likely to experience problematic use of alcohol (Dutton, Green and Kaltman 2006; see also Chapter 4 by Sarah Fox and Jennifer Holly). Post-traumatic stress disorder (PTSD) and depression, which have substantial co-morbidity with domestic abuse, are the most prevalent mental health sequelae (Sormanti and Shibusawa 2008), with the risk of re-victimization being increased by the higher rates among women of low self-esteem and feelings of inferiority (Simmons and Baxter 2010). Long-term effects for older women who may have experienced trauma over a number of decades include: permanent physical disability, self-harm, self-neglect, loss of confidence, mental health problems, reliance on substances and a significant link to suicide risk and risk of homicide (Lazenbatt and Devaney 2014; McGarry, Simpson and Smith 2011; Zink *et al.* 2006).

A review of the research on the impact of domestic abuse on health by Knight and Hester (2016) concluded that the physical health of older victims may be more severely affected than the health of younger victims. In contrast, there is evidence that older victims may experience less psychological distress in response to domestic abuse than younger victims (Knight and Hester 2016). Evidence suggests that psychological violence, such as name-calling, belittling and threats to harm pets or damage property, is the most common form of abuse for older women (Bows 2015; Sormanti and Shibusawa 2008).

In addition to the direct psychological effects, the abuse may also negatively affect the factors that in other instances could improve mental health and wellbeing, such as contact with family and friends, and being in a supportive and caring relationship (Calvete *et al.* 2007). In relation to the ageing process, older victims of domestic abuse report the increasing isolation over time that they face. This takes a number of forms, including children growing up and moving out of the family home, retirement from work outside the family home, and the death of close family members and friends who may have offered emotional and practical support in relation to the abuse and violence experienced.

There is a small literature in relation to the prevalence and experience of domestic violence within same-sex relationships, with Messinger (2011) arguing that respondents to the US National Violence Against Women (NAVW) Survey with a history of same-sex relationships are more likely to experience verbal, controlling, physical and sexual violence from their intimate partners compared to those in different-sex relationships. However, behaviourally 'bisexual' respondents appear to experience the highest rates of intimate partner violence, and are most likely to be victimized by an opposite-sex partner. Unfortunately, this data is not disaggregated by age, and there is an absence of robust studies exploring the prevalence and experiences of domestic violence among older women who are gay.

Barriers to accessing help

While there are many aspects of abuse that affect all women, it should be recognized that older women can experience different issues and barriers to accessing help than younger women (Band-Winterstein, Eisikovits and Koren 2011; Lazenbatt *et al.* 2010; McGarry *et al.* 2017; Roberto, McPherson and Brossoie 2014). As mentioned, one such barrier is that violence against older women is often framed not as domestic abuse, but as elder abuse (Brandl and Cook-Daniels 2011; Phillips 2000; Wilke and Vinton 2005), with some, such as Wydall and colleagues (2018), arguing that domestic abuse is a subset of elder abuse. The framing of an issue is important in thinking about how we respond. As Wydall *et al.* (2018) highlight, historically elder abuse has been premised on the idea of physical frailty, the lack of capacity and increased dependency. We would argue that this results in a system response that is paternalistic, seeking to step in to protect the vulnerable, which is at odds with the orientation of support services for victims of domestic abuse that seek to empower victims to make decisions and to choose options that they believe will work for them, even if professionals believe otherwise. In this way, domestic abuse should not be seen as either a subset or as an extension of elder abuse, but very clearly as part of the continuum of domestic abuse across the lifecourse.

Additionally, the approach taken by those tackling elder abuse is typically gender-neutral and has been critiqued by some as homogenizing older people (Hightower 2002). It is important to note that as with domestic abuse, women are more likely to be a victim of elder abuse than men. Between 2015 and 2016, for instance, about 60 per cent of referrals to adult safeguarding in England were for women, with only 40 per cent for men (Safeguarding Adults 2016, p.6), which cannot be wholly attributed to women's greater life expectancy. Older women are also more likely than older men to suffer from chronic illnesses, to have a disability (WHO n.d.) and to experience poverty (Estes 2005). In her work on homicide in later life in the UK, Bows (2018) highlights that 77 per cent of intimate partner homicides involving victims aged 60 and above between 2010 and 2015 were women killed by their male partner. As a consequence, they are potentially and actually more vulnerable than men to experiencing abuse and lethal harm.

Although definitions of elder abuse and domestic abuse are broadly similar (see the box on 'Defining domestic and elder abuse' below), there are differences between the two. Elder abuse is an issue that affects older adults, while domestic abuse may have existed in a relationship for many decades. If domestic abuse is suspected, it is important that service providers address the effects of power and domination within these abusive relationships. It is believed by some, such as Wolf (2003) and Teresi *et al.* (2016), that the approach to tackling elder abuse could mirror child protection strategies. Others, however, such as Brandl and Horan (2008), argue that whereas the child protection response does need to take a paternalistic approach to children due to their age, level of development and the subsequent impact of their ability to enact their agency in such a situation, this should not be the case with adults.

Defining domestic and elder abuse

In the UK 'domestic abuse' is defined slightly differently in the four countries, but the essence is similar. The key elements are: 'Threatening, controlling, coercive behaviour, violence or abuse (psychological, virtual, physical, verbal, sexual, financial or emotional) inflicted on anyone (irrespective of age, ethnicity, religion, gender, gender identity, sexual orientation or any form of disability) by a current or former intimate partner or family member' (Department of Health, Social Services and Public Safety and Department of Justice, 2016).

The World Health Organization (WHO) defines 'elder abuse' as 'a single, or repeated act, or lack of appropriate action, occurring within any relationship where there is an expectation of trust which causes harm or distress to an older person' (WHO n.d.). Elder abuse can take various forms such as financial, physical, psychological and sexual. It can also be the result of intentional or unintentional neglect.

As such, there has been a debate about whether elder abuse is a subsection of domestic abuse, or whether it also needs to be seen separately as it goes beyond intimate and family relationships, to include those who care for an older person in either a paid or voluntary capacity.

In a study involving 142 institutions in six European countries, Halicka *et al.* (2018) highlight that the practitioners in their research often stressed that older female victims of domestic abuse required more attention and greater levels of support than younger victims. In general, it was reported that working with older women took longer and required more patience and understanding in working at the woman's pace. In part, this is due to changes associated with ageing, which result in biological, psychological and social challenges. On the other hand, the upbringing, socialization patterns, norms and values of older generations increase the likelihood that older women will feel shame about their situation, remain in abusive relationships for the sake of their family, and seek to avoid the stigma of disclosing their problems to strangers, as these are deeply private matters.

Therefore, in seeking to understand the barriers faced by women in either seeking or accepting help, one must engage with Penhale's (1999) conceptualization of the 'triple jeopardy' of being old, female and abused as leading to increased social exclusion and oppression by society, let alone a current or former intimate partner.

Identifying and responding

The first stage in help-giving is the recognition and response by others. Given that older women report higher levels of psychological rather than physical abuse (Lazenbatt *et al.* 2010), Carthy and Taylor (2018) highlight the challenge for both victims and professionals in identifying such abuse. As a result, signs of domestic abuse may instead be misinterpreted as a result of ageing, or health issues connected to old age. Yechezkel and Ayalon (2013) conducted a study whereby a vignette was used to manipulate the age of the victim. They found that when the abuse was psychological, and the victim was an older woman, social workers were less likely to identify that abuse was taking place. Carthy and Taylor (2018) propose that professionals need training not only about domestic abuse, but also how to identify its various forms, such as coercive control and financial abuse, and its different presentations. The danger is that the needs of some victims may go unrecognized without such training, and that even if a victim is identified, the particularities of the response may not be tailored to their specific needs, especially if the gendered dimension of domestic abuse is not recognized, potentially making the situation worse.

In their research, Lazenbatt *et al.* (2010) held a focus group with service providers about the identification of domestic abuse and response to the needs of older women in the context of domestic abuse. The group consisted of representatives of nine organizations working with older people and survivors of domestic abuse, including the police and social care, and third sector organizations in the domestic abuse and ageing sectors. The participants were recruited via one of the inter-agency Domestic Violence Partnerships in Northern Ireland, multi-agency fora seeking to promote closer inter-agency collaboration at a local level under the direction of the government strategy for domestic violence (Department of Health, Social Services and Public Safety and Department of Justice 2016). The focus group lasted for 90 minutes, and the discussion was audio-taped with the permission of the participants, and the data subjected to content analysis. The areas for discussion were guided by a review of the literature on older women's experiences of domestic abuse, and the themes arising from interviews with 18 women aged 53–70 (mean=61 years) who had, or still were, victims of domestic abuse at the time of the study.

Complexity

The group participants felt that domestic abuse in the second half of life (Leisey *et al.* 2009) is often a more complex issue than that which is dealt with by service organizations working with younger women. The participants stated that older women should not be considered a homogenous group, as some of the women will be living with violence grown old (abuse that began earlier in life and has continued into later life), while for others the abuse may be later in onset, such as a new experience within a pre-existing or new relationship. This is supported by research within the UK that has highlighted the 'silver splicers' and 'silver separators' who start and end relationships in later life. The number of individuals aged 65 and over who married went up by 46 per cent in a decade, from 7468 in 2004 to 10,937 in 2014 (ONS 2017b). Similarly, women in the second half of life may experience the abuse differently and have different needs as their physical and mental health becomes more frail, and as they become in need of greater personal care, or in other cases, assume greater responsibility for the care of the person who perpetrated the abuse on them.

While the physical and emotional consequences of being a victim of domestic abuse are similar for all women, there was recognition that the effects on older women were compounded by increasing age. In later life, the assaults on older women could cause more significant injury. In terms of safety, with advancing age women are more likely to experience increasing isolation as children move away from the family home, retirement from work occurs, and friends and other relatives die. Service providers acknowledged that alongside societal ageist attitudes and erroneous assumptions about older people, there was a significant challenge in shaping the views of professionals about the existence of domestic abuse in later life and the types of service response required. As one senior manager from a local authority social care department noted, she was surprised by how casually some colleagues discussed instances of older women living with domestic abuse, but who did not feel the need to do anything about this unless the woman herself declared the violence and asked specifically for assistance. This reinforces the importance of specialist training in recognizing and responding to domestic abuse among professionals working with older people, and the potential value of routine enquiry, an approach that has been seen to be beneficial for younger women (Lazenbatt *et al.* 2008) and those in contact with mental health services (Howard 2017).

Coming to professional attention

As an initial first step, providers of services acknowledged that domestic abuse could come to their attention through either disclosure by the individual or discovery by other people. The experience to date was that older women were less likely to disclose the abuse they were suffering. For example, while some success has been achieved with younger women in acknowledging that domestic abuse was not necessarily an inevitable part of a relationship, there was still an attitude with older women that marriages were sacrosanct, summed up by the adage 'you've made your bed, now you have to lie in it'. This was compounded by the stigma that some older women felt about disclosing domestic abuse after decades of trying to conceal it, a regular feature of calls by older women to the Northern Ireland Domestic and Sexual Violence Helpline. Some participants questioned whether some older women living with violence grown old even recognized that what they were experiencing was domestic abuse.

There was a view that as women became older, physical violence became less frequent, but that psychological abuse became more entrenched and normative. Women had developed mechanisms for coping with their experiences, even if some of these were detrimental to health, such as reliance on prescription medication, smoking or alcohol consumption (Lazenbatt *et al.* 2010). Contact with health professionals because of poor physical or mental health tended to focus on the symptoms of these behaviours, without enquiring about deeper-seated causal factors through asking questions about domestic abuse or the quality of relationships with partners. The experience of police officers and social care staff was that often the abuse may only come to professional attention as a result of another apparently unrelated crisis. Examples were provided of older women starting to disclose whenever their own health deteriorated (and they became more concerned about their ability to protect themselves), the health of the perpetrator of the abuse deteriorated and women felt less controlled, or women moved into a caring role and the power dynamic shifted.

Complicating factors

Focus group participants discussed the complex interplay of family relationships that influenced if and how adult children dealt with the abuse of their mother, highlighting how, even when family members lived apart, domestic abuse remained a family issue. In some instances adult children appeared to continue to have unresolved emotional issues from growing up with violence within the family. Some children appeared to blame their mother for failing to protect them, and as such had less understanding and tolerance for their mother's situation. In other situations, one sibling may have been more inclined to seek support for their mother, but this created tensions with their other siblings who worried about the potential implications for themselves in terms of the care and support their mother, or their father, might then need. In an example shared with the group, the sons of one woman had tried to encourage their mother to leave a violent relationship with little success. When the woman was subsequently admitted to hospital, she had disclosed the abuse to healthcare staff. Her sons were initially angry as they felt that their earlier offers of 'saving' their mother had been rebuffed in favour of help from strangers. The sons appeared to struggle to appreciate their mother's difficulty in accepting their help as going against societal norms about who is meant to look out for whom in parent–child relationships.

A further complicating factor that is unique to Northern Ireland is the impact of 'The Troubles', the political and community conflict that was at its worse between 1968 and 2000. Some participants stated that in particular areas women may have been unable to summon assistance or to draw attention to their situation as it would necessitate unwanted attention within families and the local community where there was a paramilitary connection.

Responsiveness of services

The responsiveness of services to the issue of older women who are the victims of domestic abuse was discussed. Two key issues for older women related to the significance of the family home, and the availability of resources in order to maintain the standard of living the woman had grown accustomed to. Service providers cited examples of where older women had been extremely reluctant to give up the family home that they had invested so much time in, and which held positive memories alongside less positive ones. This was complicated by the paucity of suitable temporary and permanent housing alternatives for women who did choose to leave, and an underlying fear that the end result would be admission to a residential care home. As noted by some service providers, refuges and hostels for the homeless were often not best suited physically or socially to the needs of older women with physical impairments or the need for less disruption. In the Northern Ireland context there was also a recognition that older women in more rural areas may find it difficult to leave the family home due to the lack of suitable local alternatives and their dependence on their partner for transport, as they either did not drive themselves or local public transport services were limited. In many instances women were anxious that the lease or deeds for the property were only in the male partner's name, a vestige of more patriarchal times. Similarly, many older women were in part financially dependent on their partner, and may have had limited experience of managing financial matters. This could prove problematic whenever an older woman needed to navigate the social security and banking systems. For example, in opening a bank account an individual is required to show proof of identity in the form of utility bills. Many older women reported difficulties in meeting this requirement, as traditionally men had been the ones to sign for these services rather than women.

Examples were provided of how some public services were becoming more responsive to the needs of older women. For example, Women's Aid groups had started to provide smaller self-contained residential units for older women, and the Social Security Agency was mindful of facilitating appropriate parties to liaise on behalf of an older person. Representatives from the community sector had sought to provide services that signposted older women to the most appropriate organizations and professionals to meet their needs. Overall, however, there was a recognition that services for older women living with domestic abuse needed to have a higher profile in both public and professional consciousness, and that services needed to be differentiated based on the specific needs and circumstances of particular groups of domestic abuse victims, rather than a 'one size fits all' approach. These issues would require the forging of new alliances between sectors that have traditionally operated in parallel rather than in tandem. While this is beginning to happen alongside the roll-out of adult safeguarding policies, there is still a need to consider the different dynamics and presentations inherent in domestic abuse.

Domestic or elder abuse?

The final issue discussed by the focus group related to whether the labelling of violence and abuse within intimate relationships as either domestic abuse or elder abuse was likely to shape the service response. Over the past decade there has been a move to develop robust policies and procedures around adult safeguarding. This has been in response to the need to recognize that vulnerability may not be closely related to age, for example, with younger adults vulnerable due to a learning disability, and many older people able to take appropriate measures to safeguard themselves (Penhale 2003). Distinctions between how the abuse of older women should be defined centred on the relationship between the woman and the perpetrator (typically a partner or close relative), and by whether the perpetrator of the abuse lived with the woman or not. One example related to whether the financial abuse of women by their children, both male and female, was domestic abuse or not. This debate was important in starting to unravel some of the theoretical debates about the causes of domestic abuse, and whether the main purpose of service responses should be to protect vulnerable women from abuse and neglect, or to empower oppressed women to make their own informed decisions about their lives. As noted, some older women may choose to remain in an unsatisfactory relationship, and the key issue would appear to be whether this is related to a lack of suitable alternatives or an informed choice about what is ultimately in a woman's best interest.

In conclusion, the focus group both informed the research and also provided a catalyst for one of the organizations, Belfast and Lisburn Women's Aid group, to develop a specific service for older women.

Support for older women

In 2013 Belfast and Lisburn Women's Aid were awarded a grant by the Big Lottery Fund to develop a specialist service in respect of older women who were victims and survivors of domestic abuse. The service comprised two workers engaged specifically to work with older women aged 60 years plus, through both outreach and group work (see 'Case study' below). In addition, the funding allowed for activities to raise awareness among the general population and professionals of the needs of older women and the services available. This included a public awareness campaign, with specifically designed posters and radio slots, and a conference for professionals.

CASE STUDY: ALICE

Alice[1] is 75 years old and has been married for 50+ years. She experienced physical violence, financial control and emotional abuse throughout her marriage. She left her husband on many occasions and even moved out of the country with her children. Her husband always promised to change and begged her to come back – Alice explains that the constant pleading wore her down and she always reunited with her husband eventually.

The physical violence reduced over the years but there was still ongoing name-calling and controlling behaviour. Last year the physical violence started again, but this time Alice felt she couldn't deal with it again and phoned the police. Alice's husband was arrested and Alice went to stay with her sister. The police made a referral to Women's Aid and the outreach worker visited Alice in her sister's home.

Alice contacted a solicitor but decided not to proceed with going to court in case this upset their children – they were angry at their mother for phoning the police. With Women's Aid support, Alice went to the local authority housing department and applied for housing. Within weeks Alice was offered and accepted sheltered accommodation. Alice was very content in her new home, and most of all, she felt safe.

However, within a few weeks her husband was diagnosed with a serious illness requiring regular hospital treatment. He lost a lot of weight and refused to accept any help other than Alice's, saying that he would rather be dead than on his own. Due to this Alice has started to visit her husband again to care for him. Even though he is still verbally abusive and controlling, Alice says she would not be able to live with herself if she abandoned him at this time. At the moment Alice is hoping her husband will recover so that she can reduce her contact with him. Alice still has ongoing support from Women's Aid.

As shown in Figure 5.1, raising awareness of the needs of this group of women, and also having a dedicated service, resulted in two important changes. First, the numbers of older women referred by other agencies and self-referred to Women's Aid increased significantly, from 83 women in the year before the awareness-raising campaign to 95 in the first year of the campaign and 192 in the second year. Importantly, however, due to older women having a service specifically focused on

---

1   Fictional name.

their life stage and particular needs, an increasing proportion of the women accepted help and engaged with the service, up from 64 per cent take-up of services in the year before the service commenced (when older women availed of generic services), to 88 per cent in the second year of the specialist older women's service being operational. In short, more older women are being referred to Women's Aid, and a larger proportion are engaging – resulting in a three-fold increase over two years, from 53 to 170 in the numbers of older women receiving help that is better tailored to their needs.

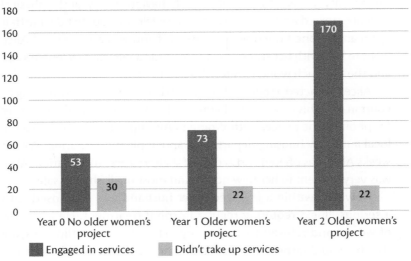

Figure 5.1 Referrals for women over 60 years of age.

Conclusion

Over the past decade there has been an increasing focus on the importance of viewing the experiences and needs of victims of domestic abuse as being heterogeneous. This has been helped by the collection of better data on the epidemiology of domestic abuse, such as the survey on violence against women undertaken by the European Union Agency for Fundamental Rights (EU FRA 2014), to more accurately identify who is affected and in what ways, and how this is similar, and different, for individuals and groups with varying characteristics. In addition, research, such as the study reported here, has been able to focus more closely on the needs of these different groups, to better understand the experiences of individuals, and how their needs might be better met by services that are often keen to help, and open to tailoring their response.

With regard to older women who are victims/survivors of domestic violence, there are some key messages for policy-makers and for those delivering services for this group:

- The need to be clearer about the dynamics and presentation of domestic violence compared to issues that might be more suitably addressed through safeguarding adult processes.

- The importance of providing services that are tailored to the life stage and life experiences of older victims of domestic violence, and the need for services for older people to better recognize the experiences of domestic violence, whether lifelong or recent.

- The value of practitioners in all services asking older people about their experiences of the quality of intimate relationships, both in the past and currently, and being ready to signpost individuals to suitable help.

- The importance of practitioners receiving training that allows them to recognize and engage with women about all forms of domestic violence, and the particular presentations that may appear in later life, such as coercive control within the context of being cared for by a partner.

- Recognition that older people, and those older people with experiences of domestic violence in later life, are seen as a heterogeneous group, and that stereotypical conceptualizations are challenged.

- The value of services working in different sectors, such as victim support organizations and organizations working with older people, to collaborate about their shared goal of improving the quality of life for older people, and promoting their access to suitable services.

Finally, it is positive to see a book such as this that seeks to introduce a lifecourse perspective into the discourse on domestic abuse. It highlights that domestic abuse can affect the life of anyone at any time, but also the need to view how domestic abuse impacts over time and may also change in nature due to the passage of time. This requires a different type of research that moves beyond a point in time, to engage with the temporality of these issues, and the complexity that this brings. However, the most important message is that research can support services, which, in turn, can support individuals and groups who would otherwise be marginalized in the public and professional discourse, and in their ability to access services best suited to their needs. Collaboration between policy-makers, service providers and researchers can both shed a light on a little understood phenomenon and also help inform and shape services that are more attuned to the needs of victims and survivors.

References

Ansara, D.L. and Hindin, M.J. (2010) 'Exploring gender differences in the patterns of intimate partner violence in Canada: A latent class approach.' *Journal of Epidemiology and Community Health 64*, 849–854.

Arber, S. and Ginn, J. (1991) 'The invisibility of age: Gender and class in later life.' *The Sociological Review 39*, 2, 260–291.

Band-Winterstein, T., Eisikovits, Z. and Koren, C. (2011) 'Between remembering and forgetting: The experience of forgiveness among older women.' *Qualitative Social Work 10*, 451–466.

Beard, H.P.J.R. and Bloom, D.E. (2015) 'Towards a comprehensive public health response to population ageing.' *The Lancet 385*, 9968, 658.

Bell, C. (2012) *Visible Women: Tales of Age, Gender and In/visibility*. Newcastle upon Tyne: Cambridge Scholars Publishing.

Betti, G., Bettio, F., Georgiadis, T. and Tinios, P. (2015) *Unequal Ageing in Europe: Women's Independence and Pensions*. Houndmills: Palgrave.

Blood, I. (2003) *A Better Life: Valuing Our Later Years*. York: Joseph Rowntree Foundation.

Blood, I. (2004) *Older Women and Domestic Violence: A Report for Help the Aged/hact*. London: Help the Aged.

Bows, H. (2015) 'Domestic violence "grown old": The unseen victims of prolonged abuse.' *The Conversation*, 15 June. Available at: https://theconversation.com/domestic-violence-grown-old-the-unseen-victims-of-prolonged-abuse-43014

Bows, H. (2018) 'Domestic homicide of older people (2010–15): A comparative analysis of intimate-partner homicide and parricide cases in the UK.' *British Journal of Social Work*, 1–20.

Brandl, B. and Cook-Daniels, L. (2011) *Domestic Abuse in Later Life*. Harrisburg, PA: National Resource Center on Domestic Violence.

Brandl, B. and Horan, D. (2008) 'Domestic violence in later life: An overview for health care providers.' *Women and Health 25*, 41–54.

Calvete, E., Estıvez, A. and Corral, S. (2007) 'Intimate partner violence and depressive symptoms in women: Cognitive schemas as moderators and mediators.' *Behaviour Research and Therapy 45*, 791–804.

Carthy, N.L. and Taylor, R. (2018) 'Practitioner perspectives of domestic abuse and women over 45.' *European Journal of Criminology*, 1477370817749484.

Cruikshank, M. (2013) *Learning to Be Old* (3rd edition). New York: Rowman & Littlefield Publishers.

De Donder, L., Lang, G., Ferreira-Alves, J., Penhale, B., Tamutiene, I. and Luoma, M.-L. (2016) 'Risk factors of severity of abuse against older women in the home setting: A multinational European study.' *Journal of Women and Ageing 28*, 6, 540–554.

Department of Health, Social Services and Public Safety and Department of Justice (2016) *Stopping Domestic and Sexual Violence and Abuse in Northern Ireland Strategy*. Belfast: Department of Health, Social Services and Public Safety.

Dockerty, C., Varney, J. and Jay-Webster, R. (2015) *Disability and Domestic Abuse: Risk, Impacts and Response*. London: Public Health England.

Dutton, M.A., Green, B.L. and Kaltman, S.I. (2006) 'Intimate partner violence, PTSD, and adverse health outcomes.' *Journal of Interpersonal Violence 21*, 955–968.

Estes, C.L. (2005) 'Women, Ageing and Inequality: A Feminist Perspective.' In M.L. Johnson (ed.) *The Cambridge Handbook of Age and Aging* (pp.552–560). Cambridge: Cambridge University Press.

EU FRA (European Union Agency for Fundamental Rights) (2014) *Violence Against Women: An EU-Wide Survey*. Luxembourg: FRA.

Eurostat (2014) *Main Scenario – Population on 1st January by Age and Sex* [proj_13npms]. Available at: https://data.europa.eu/euodp/en/data/dataset/lZgn7QrvVQ23lqxIzMBo9Q

Freel, R. and Robinson, E. (2004) *Experience of Domestic Violence in Northern Ireland: Findings from the 2001 Northern Ireland Crime Survey. Research and Statistical Bulletin 5/2005*. Belfast: Northern Ireland Office, Statistics and Research Branch.

Freel, R. and Robinson, E. (2005) *Experience of Domestic Violence in Northern Ireland: Findings from the 2003/2004 Northern Ireland Crime Survey. Research and Statistical Bulletin 1/2004*. Belfast: Northern Ireland Office, Statistics and Research Branch.

Halicka, M., Halicki, J., Kramkowska, E. and Szafranek, A. (2018) 'Suggestions for prevention measures based on Polish research concerning older victims of domestic violence.' *British Journal of Social Work 48*, 4, 982–999.

Harper, S. (2014) 'Economic and social implications of aging societies.' *Science 346*, 6209, 587–591.

Hightower, J. (2002) *Violence and Abuse in the Lives of Older Women: Is It Elder Abuse or Violence against Women? Does It Make Any Difference?* Background Paper for INSTRAW Electronic Discussion Forum, 'Gender aspects of violence and abuse of older persons, 15–26 April'.

Howard, L.M. (2017) 'Routine enquiry about violence and abuse is needed for all mental health patients.' *The British Journal of Psychiatry 210*, 4, 298–298.

Jonson, H. and Akerstrom, M. (2004) 'Neglect of elderly women in feminist studies of violence, a case of ageism?' *Journal of Elder Abuse and Neglect 16*, 1, 47–63.

Kilbane, T. and Spira, M. (2010) 'Domestic violence or elder abuse? Why it matters for older women.' *Families in Society 91*, 2, 165–170.

Knight, L. and Hester, M. (2016) 'Domestic violence and mental health in older adults.' *International Review of Psychiatry 28*, 5, 464–474.

Lazenbatt, A. and Devaney, J. (2014) 'Older women living with domestic violence: Coping resources and mental health and wellbeing.' *Current Nursing Journal 1*, 1, 10–22.

Lazenbatt, A., Cree, L.F. and Taylor, J. (2008) 'A Healthy Settings Framework: An evaluation and comparison of midwives' responses to addressing domestic violence.' *Midwifery: An International Journal 25*, 622–636.

Lazenbatt, A., Devaney, J. and Gildea, A. (2010) *Older Women's Lifelong Experience of Domestic Violence in Northern Ireland*. Belfast: Changing Ageing Partnership.

Leisey, M., Kupstas, P.K. and Cooper, A. (2009) 'Domestic violence in the second half of life.' *Journal of Elder Abuse & Neglect 21*, 2, 141–155.

Louma, M.-L., Koivusilta, M., Lang, G., Enzenhofer, E., *et al.* (2011) *Prevalence Study of Abuse and Violence against Older Women*. Helsinki, Finland. Helsinki: National Institute for Health and Welfare.

Martin, E. (2018) 'Exploring a Hidden Population at the Intersection of Gender, Ageing, Domestic Violence and Substance Use.' Thesis. Belfast: Queen's University Belfast.

Martin, E., Devaney, J. and Carney, G. (2018) 'Older Women's Experiences of Domestic Violence.' In S. Holt, C. Overlien and J. Devaney (eds) *Responding to Domestic Violence: Emerging Challenges for Policy, Practice and Research in Europe* (pp.309–324). London: Jessica Kingsley Publishers.

McGarry, J. and Simpson, C., (2011) 'Domestic abuse and older women: Exploring the opportunities for service development and care delivery.' *The Journal of Adult Protection 13*, 6, 294–301.

McGarry, J., Ali, P. and Hinchliff, S. (2017) 'Older women, intimate partner violence and mental health: A consideration of the particular issues for health and healthcare practice.' *Journal of Clinical Nursing 26*, 15–16, 2177–2191.

McGarry, J., Simpson, C. and Smith, K. (2011) 'The impact of domestic abuse for older women: A review of the literature.' *Health & Social Care in the Community 19*, 1, 3–14.

Messinger, A.M. (2011) 'Invisible victims: Same-sex IPV in the national violence against women survey.' *Journal of Interpersonal Violence 26*, 11, 2228–2243.

O'Keeffe, M., Hills, A., Doyle, M., McCreadie, C., et al. (2007) *UK Study of Abuse and Neglect of Older People: Prevalence Survey Report*. Prepared for Comic Relief and the Department of Health. Available at: https://natcen.ac.uk/media/308684/p2512-uk-elder-abuse-final-for-circulation.pdf

ONS (Office for National Statistics) (2017a) *Crime in England and Wales: Year Ending March 2016*. Available at: www.ons.gov.uk/releases/crimeinenglandandwalesyearendingmar2016

ONS (2017b) *Marriage and Divorce on the Rise at 65 and Over*. Available at: www.ons.gov.uk/peoplepopulationandcommunity/birthsdeathsandmarriages/marriagecohabitationand civilpartnerships/articles/marriageanddivorceontheriseat65andover/2017-07-18

Penhale, B. (1999) 'Bruises on the soul: Older women, domestic violence, and elder abuse.' *Journal of Elder Abuse & Neglect 11*, 1, 1–22.

Penhale, B. (2003) 'Older women, domestic violence, and elder abuse: A review of commonalities, differences and shared approaches.' *Journal of Elder Abuse and Neglect 15*, 163–183.

Penhale, B. and Iborra, I. (2014) 'The Epidemiology of Elder Abuse'. In P.D. Donnelly and C.L. Ward (eds) *Oxford Textbook of Violence Prevention: Epidemiology, Evidence, and Policy* (Chapter 9). Oxford Medicine Online.

Penhale, B. and Porritt, J. (2010) *Intimate Partner Violence against Older Women*. Sheffield: University of Sheffield.

Phillips, L.R. (2000) 'Domestic violence and ageing women.' *Geriatric Nursing 21*, 4, 88–195.

Pico-Alfonso, M.A., Garcia-Linares, M.I., Celda-Navarro, N., Blasco-Ros, C., Echeburua, E. and Martinez, M. (2005) 'The impact of physical, psychological, and sexual intimate male partner violence on women's mental health: Depressive symptoms, posttraumatic stress disorder, state anxiety, and suicide.' *Journal of Women's Health 15*, 5, 599–611.

Prince, M.J., Wu, F., Guo, Y., Robledo, L.M.G., et al. (2015) 'The burden of disease in older people and implications for health policy and practice.' *The Lancet 385*, 9967, 549–562.

Roberto, K., McPherson, M. and Brossoie, N. (2014) 'Intimate partner violence in late life: A review of the empirical literature.' *Violence Against Women 19*, 2, 1538–1558.

Safeguarding Adults (2016) *Safeguarding Adults 2015 to 2016, Experimental Statistics*. Available at: www.gov.uk/government/statistics/safeguarding-adults-2015-to-2016-experimental-statistics

Scott, M. (2008) *Older Women and Domestic Violence in Scotland, Update*. Edinburgh: Health Scotland.

Simmons, B. and Baxter, J.S. (2010) 'Intimate partner violence in older women: What home healthcare physicians should know.' *Home Healthcare Nurse 28*, 2, 82–89.

Sormanti, M. and Shibusawa, T. (2008) 'Intimate partner violence among midlife and older women: A descriptive analysis of women seeking medical services.' *Health & Social Work 33*, 1, 33–41.

Stark, E. (2009) *Coercive Control: The Entrapment of Women in Personal Life*. Oxford: Oxford University Press.

Straka, S.M. and Montminy, L. (2006) 'Responding to the needs of older women experiencing domestic violence.' *Violence Against Women 12*, 3, 251–267.

Teresi, J.A., Burnes, D., Skowron, E.A., Dutton, M.A., et al. (2016) 'State of the science on prevention of elder abuse and lessons learned from child abuse and domestic violence prevention: Toward a conceptual framework for research.' *Journal of Elder Abuse & Neglect 28*, 4–5, 263–300.

UN (United Nations) (2013) *Neglect, Abuse and Violence Against Older Women*. New York: UN.

Walby, S. and Towers, J. (2018) 'Untangling the concept of coercive control: Theorizing domestic violent crime.' *Criminology & Criminal Justice 18*, 1, 7–28.

Walsh, C., Ploeg, J., Lohfled, L., Horne, J., MacMillan, H. and Lai, D. (2007) 'Violence across the lifespan: Interconnections among forms of abuse as described by marginalized Canadian elders and their care-givers.' *British Journal of Social Work 37*, 491–514.

Older Women Experiencing Domestic Abuse 135

Wilke, D. and Vinton, D. (2005) 'The nature and impact of domestic violence across age cohorts.' *Affilia 20*, 3, 316–328.

Wolf, D.A. (2003) 'Elder Abuse Intervention: Lessons from Child Abuse and Domestic Violence initiatives.' In R.J. Bonnie and R.B. Wallace (eds) *National Research Council, Elder Mistreatment: Abuse, Neglect, and Exploitation in an Aging America* (pp.501–525). Washington, DC: National Academies Press.

WHO (World Health Organization) (no date) *Elder Abuse.* Available at: www.who.int/ageing/projects/elder_abuse/en

Wydall, S., Clarke, A., Williams, J. and Zerk, R. (2018) 'Domestic abuse and elder abuse in Wales: A tale of two initiatives.' *British Journal of Social Work 48*, 4, 962–981.

Yechezkel, R. and Ayalon, L. (2013) 'Social workers' attitudes towards intimate partner abuse in younger vs. older women.' *Journal of Family Violence 28*, 4, 381–391.

Zink, T., Jacobsen, C.J. Jr, Pabst, S., Regan, S. and Fisher, B.S. (2006) 'A lifetime of intimate partner violence: Coping strategies of older women.' *Journal of Interpersonal Violence 21*, 5, 634–651.

Chapter 6

Intersectional Interventions to Prevent Violence against Women in Black and Minority Ethnic Communities

Aisha K. Gill and Gurpreet Virdee[1]

Introduction

This chapter proposes specific interventions to prevent domestic violence and abuse (DVA) and asserts that these interventions must be informed by how and why black and minority ethnic (BME) women are at exceptional risk of DVA and violence against women (VAW) more broadly. It is crucial to note that while VAW manifests in various ways across different class and cultural contexts, victims/survivors' experiences of abuse and victimhood are shaped by their intersectional identities and locations (Crenshaw 1991). Indeed, prior research (Patel 2013; Thiara and Gill 2012) shows that BME women, who are located at the intersection of numerous structural inequalities, face additional issues and pressures that compound their risks of VAW. There are important differences in how VAW is experienced at an individual level, and these influence the responses of both victims/survivors and service providers. For instance, BME women are more likely to suffer abuse not only at the hands of their partners, but also from multiple family members (Gill and Walker 2020). They are also more likely to experience inappropriate professional responses from statutory and voluntary

1   We wish to acknowledge and thank all the staff and clients at the Women and Girls Network (WGN), who generously contributed to the development of this chapter.

agencies. These include lack of coordination, failures in multi-agency cooperation, high levels of stereotyping regarding their identity (for example, some professionals are less likely to consider the fact that BME women may be LGBTQI (lesbian, gay, bisextual, transgender, queer (or questioning) and intersex)) and race. There is also a reluctance to engage with those in BME communities for fear of appearing racist (Izzidien 2008). Misunderstanding or essentializing cultural norms, traditions and values can lead professionals to pathologize BME families, an issue that has been discussed at length in the social care literature (Qureshi, Charsley and Shaw 2012). Professionals widely report that problems in effective service delivery for BME communities in relation to VAW are often the result of inadequate understanding of cultural features (Qureshi *et al.* 2012).

Examining the available literature and analysing the cases of four DVA victims/survivors from BME communities demonstrates how essential it is to centre on key differences in these communities if support mechanisms are to be more accessible, and if preventative activities are to be effective. Critically, support workers must recognize that in BME communities: (a) abuse is often perpetrated by a larger number of family and community members than is typically seen in DVA situations involving victims and perpetrators from other ethnic backgrounds; (b) how communities understand and value differently notions of 'honour'[2] and 'shame' shapes victims/survivors' approaches to reporting and seeking help; and (c) this also impacts the wider community, encouraging a culture of silence on the issue and rendering preventative efforts useless. Therefore, culturally specific work that recognizes these patterns is needed to better support and empower victims/survivors and their communities (Gill and Walker 2020).

One of the most distinctive features of DVA in BME communities is the aforementioned fact that when violence occurs, the abuse is often not – as in many other communities – perpetrated only by the victim's spouse, but also by other family members; it is also more likely that the abuse will be perpetrated by multiple individuals, and this is particularly the case for women of South Asian heritage. In most

---

2   It is important to stress that use of the term 'honour' in relation to 'honour'-based violence and abuse (HBV/A) is not without controversy. Many argue that it is something of a misnomer (Gill 2009; Jiwani and Hoodfar 2012; Meetoo and Mirza 2007; Sen 2005; Vishwanath and Palakonda 2011) and/or a misunderstood term prone to 'exoticization' and 'used as shorthand, to flag a type of violence against women characterized by (claimed) "motivation"' (Welchman and Hossain 2005, p.4).

BME cases of DVA, the violence is primarily aimed at asserting control over a woman's behaviour (Baxi 2014). Patriarchal attitudes reflected in culturally specific norms, such as arranged marriages (Meetoo and Mirza 2007) – where it is not uncommon for the bride to leave her own family and move into her in-laws' home with her husband (Qureshi *et al.* 2012) – make it difficult for victims/survivors to seek external assistance when they are subjected to abuse (Aghtaie 2017). In fact, many victims/survivors fear that seeking help may worsen their situation (Horvath and Brown 2009). In these multi-generational households, all men hold power over women, including male children over their mothers. However, it is also not uncommon for women in positions of authority (usually the mother-in-law, by virtue of her higher status in the familial hierarchy) to exert power over younger women – especially those who have married into the family, given their status as 'outsiders' (Menon 2009). Thus, DVA is both an individual and structural form of violence in BME communities, rooted in deeply embedded structural norms, traditions and values. As a result, DVA in these contexts often goes unreported and unpunished.

Ethnicity, class, gender, sexuality and disability form the basis of systems of power and inequality. These aspects of one's identity thus not only affect individual lives and group interactions, but also the ability of oppressed groups to access power and privilege (Anderson and Hill Collins 2001). Consequently, ignoring intersectionality by emphasizing only one particular identity – such as a person's ethnicity or gender – or by neglecting identities altogether fails to yield a holistic understanding of lived realities. Rather, it assumes that groups of individuals are homogeneous, and adopts a universal approach to understanding multiple discriminations that mistakenly supposes 'sameness or equivalence of the social categories connected to inequalities' (Verloo 2006, p.211). Universalization is problematic because it masks the actual diversity of the individuals and experiences evident in the DVA literature. As Anthias (2013) and Patel (2013) point out, when examining BME women's understandings and experiences of, for example, DVA, specific attention must be given to the intersecting sociocultural forces at play.

The four case studies discussed here – which are drawn from the Women and Girls Network (WGN) case files – demonstrate this by showing how ethnicity, gender and inequality can adversely impact BME women and girls. Each case discussion begins with a brief overview of the woman's situation and then explains the roles played by social services, the police, the courts and the many other organizations and agencies that deal with and support BME women and girls who experience DVA and the ongoing trauma associated with it. The cases highlight some of the major barriers BME women in violent domestic situations face to reporting their abuse, and the challenges they must negotiate to obtaining the various forms of support they need. Finally, the case discussions detail key lessons regarding the most effective safeguarding and prevention strategies that practitioners and statutory authorities can employ to best assist such women.

CASE STUDIES

Milena

Milena is in her mid-twenties. She came to the UK from Macedonia on a spousal visa to join the man she had recently married, who had the right to remain in the UK. Very quickly after Milena arrived in the UK, her husband began forcing her to take drugs, became very controlling, and turned physically and sexually violent. On two separate occasions, Milena was physically assaulted and left unconscious. In the midst of one attack, Milena managed to call the police and escape into the street. Once the police arrived, Milena made a statement about the most recent incident she had suffered and her husband's ongoing abuse. The statement was written with the help of an interpreter, who spoke one of Milena's second languages rather than her mother tongue.

Housing

Milena was unable to access refuge accommodation because of her no recourse to public funds (NRPF) status. As it was unsafe for Milena to return to the home she shared with her abuser, the police found her temporary accommodation for a few days and put her in touch with a specialist Violence Against Women and Girls (VAWG) advice service. This service managed to find Milena a place in a religious hostel for vulnerable and homeless women in London, and referred her to an independent sexual violence advisor (ISVA) for ongoing support. Although seemingly safe, the Christian hostel had a very strict regime: residents were expected to undertake chores, wake up at a certain time each day and attend church. Milena also shared a room with a number of other women. This made the hostel a particularly unsuitable place for someone experiencing ongoing trauma-related symptoms; consequently, Milena felt forced to leave the hostel. Eventually, she was supported by a friend outside London while she made her asylum application. She then moved into a hostel far from London, where she currently resides. Moving to a different city was not her preferred choice, as she has no support system in her new location. Since arriving, she has relied on a local church for ongoing financial support because she is unable to work and receives little in the way of benefits.

Health and specialist services
Milena has experienced ongoing trauma-related symptoms, including flashbacks and anxiety. She has received good medical support from her GP and specialist counselling from a VAW organization in the city where she now lives. She has also maintained contact with an ISVA, who will support her in court in the area where the abuse took place. This support has provided Milena with some reassurance and consistency in the lead-up to the daunting task of giving evidence in court.

Immigration
Milena's asylum application process (which is ongoing) has compounded her traumatic DVA experiences and inhibited her recovery. Her abuser has threatened to kill her and members of her family living back in her home country, and the prospect of returning to this country makes Milena fear for her own and her family's safety. Consequently, in addition to her abuse, relocation and upcoming criminal proceedings, Milena faces the constant threat of deportation and/or destitution if her asylum application fails.

Criminal justice
Milena's abuser was charged with physical and sexual assault; his case was due to reach court 18 months after Milena's initial report. Unfortunately, as she was unable to make her statement in her mother tongue, it was inaccurate, and Milena has recently been informed that it must be rewritten with the aid of a new interpreter before the court hearing. The need to make a new statement has created additional anxiety for Milena about court proceedings and the use of interpreters while giving evidence.

Challenges

Milena's negative experiences have been exacerbated because of the intersecting issues she faces as an asylum-seeking woman. It is important to consider here how responses to 'culturalized' forms of violence (that is, honour-based violence or forced marriage) have been increasingly dealt with via draconian immigration initiatives (Gill and Walker 2020; Patel 2012): for example, the primary purpose rule, the one- and two-year immigration rule, the raising of the minimum age of marital sponsorship from 18 to 21 and the NRPF rule. Irrespective of how these initiatives have been politically framed, they have had a hugely detrimental impact on (im)migrant women suffering violence and abuse (Sharma and Gill 2010) because they have created a 'discursive spill over' between VAW and immigration policy fields (Rolandsen Agustín 2013, p.144).

While years of campaigning on this issue by women's rights groups such as Southall Black Sisters (SBS) have prompted many of these controls to be repealed or amended, the NRPF rule remains one of the most controversial by-products of anti-immigration rhetoric for BME victims/survivors of VAW in the UK. Introduced as part of the Immigration and Asylum Act 1999, the NRPF rule was intended to restrict the amount of public funds available to recently arrived immigrants under the premise that these individuals should be self-sufficient rather than relying on the state benefits to which British citizens are entitled (Home Office n.d.). However, a side effect of this rule is that many women on temporary work permits, student visas or spousal visas who are also being subjected to abuse are unable to claim the public funds necessary to access support such as refuge accommodation (Carline and Easteal 2014). Without these vital funds, victims/survivors must risk either staying with the perpetrators, thus prolonging their abuse, or making themselves homeless (Carline and Easteal 2014).

The Destitution Domestic Violence (DDV) concession has gone some way towards supporting women trapped in this situation. Introduced in April 2012, it allows DVA victims/survivors a temporary variation in their immigration status and access to vital public funds while they apply for indefinite leave to remain (ILR) (Carline and Easteal 2014). Nonetheless, applicants face considerable difficulties meeting the high burden of proof necessary to be granted ILR. Not only is the process of applying for ILR complex (especially for those with limited English language skills), but the level of evidence required to prove that the victim/survivor's relationship has broken down as a *direct* result of abuse can be exceptionally hard to supply (Carline and Easteal 2014). These problems are compounded by the timeframe of applying for the DDV concession. As Hubbard, Payton and Robinson (2013, p.51) explain:

> The timescale of the DDV means that women who have limited or no understanding of English, who are traumatized by abuse, and have not been able to gain support from statutory or voluntary bodies, may struggle to meet the requirements in time [...] [thus delaying their] ability to access protection from violence.

Ultimately, then, even if BME women do find the courage to report their abuse, Milena's case highlights some of the numerous barriers women such as her face to obtaining service provision and justice. The restrictions Milena is up against in terms of receiving benefits or having the right to work mean that she has not been able to access safe, specialist accommodation that is available to other women in the UK; nor has she been able to find a place of physical, emotional or psychological safety. She has also had to move far away from her support systems, and will have to travel a considerable distance to provide evidence in court while living with the ongoing fear of retribution, deportation and destitution.

Key lessons

- The challenges of disclosing abuse, coercive control in relation to marriage arrangements, sexual abuse and domestic violence, and obtaining support are compounded by the asylum process, which can prevent women from achieving physical, emotional or psychological safety.

- Religious institutions are sometimes relied on to give practical support for women with NRPF. Further, some professionals mistakenly assume that women of a certain ethnic background would prefer to stay in a religious hostel. However, support and accommodation from these institutions should be considered carefully, as they may be unsuitable for women who are subject to social stigma or managing the ongoing effects of trauma, or who hold different religious beliefs from those of the institution.

- When making statements for criminal or civil proceedings, women must be able to choose their interpreter based on that individual's gender and competence in the complainant's first language. Women whose first language is not English must be given the chance to review their own initial statements, preferably with a trusted interpreter, at an appropriate time when they are not in crisis. Guidance by Sheffield Council (2016) highlights that in sexual abuse or DVA situations, it would be inappropriate, or would present an additional risk to the victim/survivor, to have a family member interpreting. Because of these risks, those working in specialist BME services and the VAW sector more broadly should make use of interpreters approved by a particular body and by the victim/survivor.

- When women are forced to move to a different location because of their immigration status, services should attempt to find alternative support in the new location, and to ensure that the women are able to re-engage with trusted practitioners in their original location if they are required to return and give evidence in court.

Tanisha

Tanisha is a 15-year-old BME girl from an African Caribbean background. She currently lives with foster carers and attends a local pupil referral unit (PRU). Her father is serving a prison sentence for grievous bodily harm (DVA offence), and her mother has a history of severe depression and anxiety. Tanisha is the youngest of three children; her older brother and sister are gang-involved and the family has a history of domestic violence.

Challenges

Tanisha was referred by the PRU because she was considered 'out of control' following several incidents of violent outbursts, unprovoked attacks directed at her peers and aggression aimed at PRU teaching staff. Tanisha was self-harming on site. She used blades to cut herself, overdosed several times and was found on a few occasions with a ligature that she could have used to hang herself. An essential driver of Tanisha's outbursts was her peers calling her gay – Tanisha identified as gender fluid and, as a very young child, decided daily if she was to be a girl or a boy. However, Tanisha's understanding of her gender was dismissed by a few professionals as ridiculous and attention-seeking, which both undermined Tanisha's identity and reinforced these professionals' stereotypical conceptions of Tanisha based on her ethnicity. While the teaching team stated in their reports that they 'accepted' Tanisha was very bright, they also noted that her increasingly risky behaviour was affecting her peers and teachers; as a result, Tanisha was faced with permanent exclusion from the PRU. The referral information was accompanied by reams of paperwork chronicling a lifetime of Tanisha's involvement with professionals. The chronology reveals the following:

- When she was 4 years old, Tanisha and her siblings were the subject of a child protection plan (CPP) because of domestic violence, and Tanisha's mother was considered unable to protect her children.

- At 6 years old, Tanisha faced repeated suspensions from her school for bad behaviour and her mother was urged to make Tanisha change schools.

- At 7 years old, Tanisha started being placed with a number of temporary foster carers because her mother was no longer able to cope with her.

- At 9 years old, Tanisha was diagnosed with autistic spectrum disorder by her GP.

- At 11 years old, Tanisha was diagnosed with attention deficit hyperactive disorder and prescribed Ritalin. Once again, she was placed in temporary foster care (prior to this placement, she had been sent back to the family home).

- At 13 years old, Tanisha seriously attacked a boy at school, who was hospitalized. Tanisha was arrested and sentenced to one year in a secure children's home.

- At 14 years old, Tanisha had a temporary foster placement referral to Child and Adolescent Mental Health Services (CAMHS) and was diagnosed with conduct disorder and borderline personality disorder.

Therapists' interventions

In this case, it was essential to begin unpacking what had happened to Tanisha instead of what was 'wrong' with her. The critical 'why' question here relates to the numerous opportunities authorities missed to consider the adversity to which Tanisha had been exposed throughout her childhood, and the cumulative effect of this adversity during the critical milestones of her development. The professionals who had contact with Tanisha (especially social care services) lacked curiosity about her specific circumstances and endemic racism in the system – that is, their reactions were perhaps based on their stereotypical ideas of who Tanisha was based on her ethnicity. Consequently, Tanisha was labelled the problem, and her 'badness' was accepted as an explanation rather than her vulnerability and distress being understood and addressed. Here, the senior therapist at the WGN shares her reflections:

> My journey with Tanisha was based on trauma-informed care, so identifying and working with her strengths was an essential part of the process, and involved appreciating her tenacity, courage, confidence, humour, intelligence and vitality. This also meant validating her tools for survival and considering her anger her greatest ally. Embracing her anger as a protective factor, a source of strength and positive energy offered Tanisha a different perspective, a way of exploring the deep, powerful emotions of her pain and sadness and reframing others' interpretation of her defiance and aggression as acts of resistance to oppressive environments – feelings and acts that contributed to her resilience and ability to survive. This work emphasized developing Tanisha's emotional literacy and introducing safe, creative means of expression and problem-solving skills. Giving Tanisha a psychoeducational perspective was essential to contextualizing her responses and adaptations to traumatic events and environments and dismantling her pathologizing disordered diagnoses. Although liberating, this perspective also gave Tanisha responsibilities – if she was not mad or bad, she had to make decisions to control her responses, consider their consequences and become accountable for her actions.
>
> The state machinery failed Tanisha by giving her limited expectations of a positive future and predicting a downward trajectory of

lifelong mental health disability and frequent contact with the criminal justice system. To counter this prognosis, it was vital that the WGN staff explicitly communicated high expectations of Tanisha and emphasized her potential. Slowly, Tanisha internalized this perspective and began talking of her ambitions to be an actor/teacher/social worker/nurse, building her optimism and intention to forge a positive future. This new sense of purpose introduced greater stability into her life and had positive results for her at the PRU and in her foster placement.

Reflecting on and disclosing details of events was not as crucial for Tanisha as understanding her reactions to trauma and asserting control over her responses. For example, WGN provided Tanisha with a vital space in which her gender status was accepted and affirmed. This normalizing of her gender ensured that she was able to explore and feel comfortable with it, which, in turn, led Tanisha to explore her identity as a young BME woman more deeply and connect with the strength, richness and pride of her ancestral heritage rather than the stereotypical sense of oppression associated with her minority status.

The senior therapist at WGN who worked with Tanisha observed that their relationship was not always easy:

> I could not assume and rely on a shared bond because of our mutual cultural identity and had to learn to withstand the therapeutic rollercoaster by holding on tight and remaining seated. Hopefully, our work together has become a template for future patient–therapist healthy relationships, modelling care, compassion, acceptance, genuineness and safety.

This case demonstrates what can be achieved with clients such as Tanisha when an appropriate approach is taken.

Olivia

Olivia arrived in the UK from Iran with her partner on a fiancée visa. After her arrival, her partner became very controlling and financially, emotionally, physically and sexually abusive. After a year of ongoing mistreatment and isolation, and a physically violent incident, Olivia called the police and reported the physical abuse. Her husband was then given bail on the condition that he did not contact Olivia, which gave her the opportunity to end the relationship.

As Olivia felt unable to describe or name her experiences of sexual violence when speaking to the police, they referred her to a specialist domestic violence worker. After talking with this worker and preparing statements with a solicitor to whom the domestic violence agency had referred her, Olivia felt more confident discussing this aspect of her experiences. Her solicitor explained that Olivia's treatment at the hands of her husband amounted to rape, and advised her to report this to the police, which she did. The police then referred Olivia to an ISVA for specialist support.

Health agencies and specialist services

Olivia received a package of support from specialist agencies. This included a domestic violence service, an ISVA at a rape crisis centre, and support and counselling from a specialist BME organization. Olivia's contact with the specialist BME organization was particularly crucial, as it enabled her to receive the support she needed in her first language and with the appropriate cultural sensitivity and understanding. Although prior to reporting Olivia felt unable to discuss her experiences with the GP, she did eventually disclose and found the GP to be supportive and understanding. She received a high standard of care from the hospital for her injuries, including reconstructive surgery and a psychological assessment.

Interpreters

Olivia complained to the police and to her domestic and sexual violence workers after realizing that some of the interpreters were translating her incorrectly. This discovery left Olivia feeling reluctant to engage with the interpreters. Securing accurate interpreting remains a huge source of concern for her in terms of her being able to give evidence in court.

Housing

Olivia is currently unable to access any financial or housing support because of her NRPF status. She has been forced to remain alone in the property she previously shared with her abuser, and relies on specialist services for food bank vouchers and money, as she has no access to income or benefits. Olivia also lives in a constant state of fear that her abusive partner (who still lives in the same city) will return or somehow find a way to make her leave the property, in which case she will become destitute and homeless. Olivia has experienced ongoing flashbacks and nightmares that are exacerbated by being in the environment where the abuse took place. The perpetrator has made indirect threats to Olivia via a neighbour. Olivia also greatly fears returning to her home country because she believes that the perpetrator's family and/or his connections (that is, the police) could hurt her.

Criminal justice

While Olivia found her engagement with specialist services and health agencies positive, she did not have a similar experience with the criminal justice system. Her abuser was initially charged with a relatively low-grade assault, which Olivia knew to be incorrect. She raised this issue with the police and obtained evidence proving the severity of her injuries, but nothing was done – the police informed her that the decision to increase the severity of the charges rested with the Crown Prosecution Service (CPS). On the day Olivia was due to give evidence at the magistrates' court, she presented her case to the barrister (whom she met for the first time that morning), who agreed with her; the case was adjourned and the perpetrator was charged with the higher offence. Because of Olivia's tenacity and self-advocacy, the case will now be heard in the Crown Court.

However, Olivia's rape investigation was pursued separately from the other domestic violence offences. The police discontinued the rape investigation after the perpetrator argued that the encounter was consensual, and the police decided that they did not have enough evidence to prove otherwise to the level required for a jury to convict in a Crown Court (that is, beyond reasonable doubt). This is poor practice, as the CPS recognizes that consent cannot be freely given in certain circumstances – for example, when there are threats of violence or when someone is detained (CPS 2017). If the rape allegations were considered alongside evidence of other forms of domestic violence, this connection could challenge the perpetrator's defence that the sexual abuse was consensual. Olivia and her ISVA raised this issue with the police, and initially Olivia was going to challenge the decision to discontinue the rape investigation through a Victim's Right to Review (VRR) process. However, after the police cancelled several meetings, Olivia decided that the emotional and mental stress of pursuing this course of action was too great.

Key lessons

- Referrals to specialist BME women's services are crucial for ensuring that women's emotional and practical needs are appropriately addressed.

- Sexual violence services should be engaged at the first opportunity to ensure that women can make informed decisions about reporting this form of abuse to the police, and that they receive specialist support to improve their experience of disclosure and support-seeking.

- Interpreters must be used carefully and appropriately, and women should be given the chance to review and comment on their initial statements with a trusted interpreter at a time when they are not in crisis.

- The police and the CPS must address the issue of sexual offences being investigated and prosecuted in isolation from other related domestic abuse offences, as this practice prevents successful prosecution and devalues women's experiences.

Zahra

Zahra is in her mid-thirties. She was raised in the Middle East and came to the UK when she was in her twenties to be with her husband, a UK national. After Zahra arrived in the UK, her husband was physically and sexually violent towards her – his actions included forcing Zahra to drink alcohol, after which he raped her. She left the marriage, despite pressure from her family to stay – divorce was seen as bringing shame to the family and community. By this point, Zahra had two children, aged seven and nine; her ex-husband continues to have contact with them.

Zahra remarried a couple of years after divorcing her abusive husband, but within a year, her new partner became highly controlling and aggressive. This behaviour soon escalated to high levels of violence, including degrading acts of sexual violence and an incident in which Zahra's husband suffocated her and she passed out. Social services became involved with the family after the children's school raised concerns regarding Zahra's older child's behaviour. Zahra's second husband then left the UK and moved back to his home in Europe. He continues to harass and intimidate her.

Counselling

Zahra was initially referred to the NHS for counselling. However, her GP referred her to a different counselling service on the basis that longer-term counselling was considered more suitable because of the nature of the violence she had suffered. At Zahra's assessment, she presented with a number of trauma symptoms. These included, but were not limited to, high levels of anxiety and depression; intense feelings of shame and guilt; coping mechanisms, such as banging her head against the wall; excessive use of alcohol; and intense feelings of fear and hopelessness. She reported two suicide attempts, both of which had occurred during her first marriage. She experienced flashbacks, intrusive and recurring thoughts, and symptoms of dissociation in which she reported not feeling a part of her body. The length and intensity of Zahra's symptoms are consistent with complex post-traumatic stress. At the time of her assessment, Zahra was on a number of medications and had been diagnosed with fibromyalgia; she had also been prescribed anti-depressants at the end of her marriage and had been using them on and off for about two years.

Social care

Social services became involved with the family in the first instance following the concerns raised by the school Zahra's children attended. Zahra's second (current) husband had left the UK, and Zahra was often unsure where he was living, but felt pressured by social services into reporting him to the police – she admitted that she thought this action left her vulnerable to retaliation from his extended family. The social worker raised a number of concerns for Zahra's safety and referred her to a domestic abuse service for safety planning.

Community support

Lack of family support left Zahra and her children further isolated. She felt a deep sense of guilt about her alcohol use, which conflicted with her religious and spiritual beliefs. Living in temporary accommodation, Zahra often felt unsafe in her environment and fearful of being targeted by men in the area. She took a part-time job as a teaching assistant, but felt pressured to leave, as it was thought that her English was not good enough. Zahra felt bullied and harassed at work, but lacked the confidence to challenge her employer.

Safeguarding and risk

The risk to Zahra was both internal and external. Her self-harming behaviour was frightening to her, but helped her cope, and her contact with her ex-husband left her feeling fearful and triggered memories of rape and violence. Zahra was afraid of her children having any contact with her current husband, and admitted feeling conflicted about her relationship with him and feelings towards him. Now, having left one marriage and her culture, Zahra still wants to make her second marriage work and has at times considered resuming the relationship.

Challenges

Zahra's experiences have created a painful internal world that is the result of years of abuse by two perpetrators, neither of whom has been held accountable. However, the statutory services focused on Zahra and her actions rather than on her abusers and their actions. The family was left in poor and unsafe housing situations, and there were few financial resources available to support them or enable them to move forward with their lives. Zahra's experiences of racism and discrimination in the workplace, coupled with being ostracized from religious and social institutions, left her feeling isolated and distressed.

Key lessons

- The effects of violence should be understood in the context of complex and multiple traumas that have long-lasting emotional and psychological consequences – post-traumatic stress disorder, depression and substance misuse are just some of these effects (WHO 2013).

- Social and cultural circumstances are compounded by women's loss of community and family support in the aftermath of abuse, a loss that subsequently makes them vulnerable to further victimization. Emotional and social support, which play a key role in alleviating feelings of horror and aloneness caused by experiences of violence and in enhancing feelings of safety, are integral to victim recovery (Herman 1997).

- Safety planning should be holistic and address both internal and external circumstances. Holistic responses, such as body therapy and group work, should be provided to address the effects of trauma on the body (Ogden, Minton and Pain 2006).

Analysis of the cases
Language barriers and the use of interpreters

Language barriers inevitably create additional obstacles for a non-English speaking BME woman in terms of her ability to access appropriate support. When that support is not available in their first language, BME women often rely on interpreters when dealing with service providers or the police and other statutory bodies. Interpreters thus play a critical role during this part of a woman's journey. However, as is evident from the case studies, women who are allocated interpreters face a number of serious challenges. These include having multiple interpreters, being misinterpreted, having testimonies incorrectly translated and needing statements to be rewritten because of inaccuracy. As a result of these experiences, the women in the case studies reported increased anxiety, stress and concern at how their DVA experiences were being represented.

Interpreters must therefore be selected appropriately, and this selection process must consider not only a woman's first language but, where possible, her specific dialect – the different nuances of dialect can significantly affect how something is understood and interpreted. Ultimately, interpreters must have the appropriate skills and training to ensure impartiality; they also need to possess an awareness of and sensitivity to the issues and power dynamics at play within the survivor-interpreter relationship. Women must feel they can trust the interpreter to present their story honestly and accurately. This means they should be given a choice of interpreter – for example, they should be able to choose either a male or female interpreter. Women must also have every opportunity to review and comment on any statements written and prepared on their behalf with the aid of interpreters in order to ensure that these statements accurately represent what the women have said. This review process should take place when women are not in crisis, and with the support of a trusted interpreter.

Insecure immigration status and NRPF

As the case studies illustrate, the consequences of violence and abuse are further exacerbated by the intersecting issues faced by women seeking asylum, women with NRPF or women with insecure immigration status. The limitations and restrictions placed on these women mean they cannot access the safe, specialist accommodation available to other women in the UK when they experience DVA. This inequality forces many women to remain in violent situations for fear of being deported or left destitute. For example, in Olivia's case, she had to remain in the property she had previously shared with the perpetrator of her abuse, which resulted in a high level of trauma and a constant state of fear that he would return. The other women in the case studies were forced to accept inadequate, temporary and often inappropriate accommodation, such as staying in a B&B for a few nights, staying with a friend or being allocated a place in a non-specialist hostel. Once this initial support ceases, there are few safe and long-term housing options for women with NRPF whose immigration status remains unresolved.

Austerity and cuts to legal aid, welfare benefits, housing and social services have all created additional barriers that continue to adversely affect BME women, who experience intersectional multiple disadvantage and discrimination – in particular, BME-specific domestic abuse services have been disproportionately affected by cuts compared with 'generic' domestic abuse services (Batty 2019). In turn, these women are re-victimized by the state/system, which, in its inadequate treatment of this vulnerable group, continues to enable perpetrators of DVA to keep victims/survivors in a constant state of fear. A more coordinated and collaborative multi-agency response must be undertaken in cases where women are destitute and face multiple barriers. Ensuring this coordinated approach means that the different needs with which each woman presents can be effectively met – for example, women with insecure immigration status (that is, NRPF) require more accessible women-only spaces and immediate referral to a specialist service so they can attain advocacy support at the earliest opportunity.

Exclusions from such safety and support enshrined under the NRPF law do not meet obligations imposed by the Convention on the Elimination of All Forms of Discrimination Against Women (CEDAW), the International Covenant on Civil and Political Rights (ICCPR), the International Covenant on Economic, Social and Cultural Rights

(ICESCR), the United Nations Convention on the Rights of the Child (UNCRC) and the European Convention on Human Rights (ECHR)/ Council of Europe standards – but women's access to this safety and support should depend on their experience of domestic abuse, not their visa status (Threipland 2015). Under current NPRF restrictions, the responsibility for helping women with NPRF cannot rest entirely with charitable organizations that have limited resources – statutory services must be more accountable for vulnerable victims/survivors in order to avoid further compromising these women's safety.

Children and young people

Clear evidence highlights children's reluctance to disclose their experiences of violence; as a result, they lose access to essential support (Office of the Children's Commissioner 2015). Failure to identify children who are victims/survivors of abuse has grave consequences, as exemplified in Tanisha's case study. Unrecognized abuse leads to the emergence of trauma symptoms that become deeply rooted because they go untreated. Typically, child clients are stigmatized early on, with negative labels that characterize their behaviour as disruptive, non-compliant, aggressive or the outcome of a learning challenge. If left without appropriate intervention, early experiences of violence can become a gateway to further vulnerability and polyvictimization; both these risks can extend into adult life and threaten future health and wellbeing. Over the years, such clients are likely to receive numerous diagnoses of conditions such as attention deficit hyperactivity disorder (ADHD), anxiety, major depression, psychosis and bipolar disorder, and be prescribed a variety of medications. They often have heavy involvement with various health and social care services, with few or none of these focusing on the adversity, vulnerability and distress these young people have faced during their critical developmental stages.

At present, support services for young people are skewed more towards boys and young men than girls and young women. Many youth workspaces are often targeted at addressing 'problems' among boys and young men – for example, tackling youth offending or engaging at-risk youth in this gender group. However, organizations such as the WGN have created specialist services for young women: WGN's model for working with young women is intersectional, feminist and gender-responsive, establishing safe and accessible environments for service delivery and emphasizing engagement that is rooted in empowerment, autonomy and collaboration.

These challenges in the youth workspace could be mitigated in a number of ways. These include improved multi-agency partnerships that place young women at the centre of their responses and interventions; increasing public awareness of specialist services through outreach programmes; giving practitioners relevant training and development opportunities; and ensuring a collaborative strategy among the relevant organizations or agencies that enable young women to shape the services on offer, thus ensuring a 'by and for' model. Further, it is essential for the relevant professionals to do this regular review or reflecting on intervention and service outcomes with young women. We must ensure that an intersectional approach is used here to obtain strong and effective responses for all victims/survivors.

Continuum of violence

Women often experience multiple forms of violence and abuse that are complex and interlinked, and the effects of these differ for each woman. There is a continuum of violence, and practitioners must consider all aspects of this continuum when supporting BME women and girls to ensure that all their needs are appropriately met within a holistic framework. Each of the women in our case studies experienced multiple forms of violence and abuse over time; any assessment of needs and risk must thus consider the totality of these experiences. The needs of gendered violence survivors are best met via services that are survivor-centred, gender-specific and trauma-informed, and that give women decision-making autonomy. A trauma-informed perspective means practitioners are alert to the power dynamics of DVA in a particular relationship and context, the impact this has and how a woman may have coped. It is important not to medicalize DVA as not all women will necessarily experience trauma symptoms that need specialist mental health support.

In Olivia's case, the police investigated the sexual violence she suffered separately from the domestic violence committed against her. This is an approach best avoided: the police and the CPS must instead address multiple and complex offences in an interconnected way. If they fail to do so, they risk re-traumatizing women, threatening successful prosecutions and ultimately, minimizing women's experiences of violence.

Further, close correlations exist between different forms of violence and abuse – for example, domestic and sexual violence. In 2015, 2078 out of a total of 15,816 sexual offences reported to the Metropolitan Police Service (MPS) were flagged as domestic violence cases (London Sexual Violence Needs Assessment 2016).

Independent support through qualified independent domestic violence advisors (IDVAs) and ISVAs and specialist case workers is critical to improving survivors' awareness of their rights and options, increasing their confidence in the criminal justice system and criminal justice processes (including the role of statutory agencies), improving their immediate and long-term safety, and ensuring that they are given the means to access all the support they require.

Counselling and therapeutic support

As explained in the case studies, some women were referred to counselling by their GP. Most often, referrals are made to the Improving Access to Psychological Therapies (IAPT) programme. In principle, this programme can be useful for women, as after six to eight weeks of cognitive behavioural therapy (CBT) they may have better control over anxiety symptoms and benefit more from long-term therapy. Ongoing therapeutic interventions are still necessary for most women who access the IAPT programme. However, BME women face an additional disadvantage in that they are often unable to access any form of therapeutic intervention.

It is our experience that women who have experienced chronic violence will present as what we would consider chronically dis-empowered – that is, as a result of their experiences, they have long-standing difficulties that include intense psychological distress, an entrenched sense of despair and severe regression with frequent hospital admissions; they are also highly symptomatic. Such conditions can be resistant to change, which means that short-term interventions such as those offered by the IAPT or mental health services cannot adequately address them. Because these interventions focus on daily functioning or managing clients at crisis point, they are not resourced to deal with clients' underlying experiences. Short-term counselling interventions generally do not work with those who have suffered chronic violence, as these clients often have intense difficulties with managing relationships and may present with hostile projection.

However, there are effective interventions for women experiencing these conditions – WGN's services offer a best practice and more long-term approach to facilitating recovery for victims/survivors.

Women and Girls Network's best practice perspective

WGN aims to make a significant difference to clients' quality of life. It offers empowerment, healing and transformation for women and girls moving on from violence and abuse, thus enabling survivors to become thrivers. WGN's clinical model is gender-responsive, trauma-informed and recovery-oriented; its therapeutic interventions are focused on direct management of trauma sequela, are individually determined, complex, multimodal and holistic, and follow the unique trauma pathway. The independent nature of counselling is paramount for women, a high proportion of whom have had negative experiences with statutory services, including the police, social services, GPs and the education system. Such negative experiences can lead to distrust in these institutions.

WGN's counselling services are for women and girls who have experienced any form of violence, and are delivered via a culturally sensitive framework that offers appropriate therapeutic interventions. Every woman who requests counselling is first assessed to ascertain whether counselling is the right intervention for her at that time, and to identify the best counselling approach. WGN knows that safeguarding is enhanced when practitioners build strong and trusting relationships. This means WGN practitioners are clear about confidentiality, honest about and consistent with the support they offer, and able to ensure that women are given opportunities to meet with a practitioner. WGN approaches women as experts in their own lives, and its practitioners focus on women's agency, strengths and resilience. They remain non-judgemental at all times and help women understand and consider their options so that they can make their own decisions. WGN believes that safeguarding is enhanced when women can control their own decision-making.

Flexibility is essential when supporting women who have experienced domestic and sexual violence, especially when they are homeless or moving to safe accommodation. WGN provides interim support for women if they move within areas or relocate to an entirely new locale, as moving into a safe but unfamiliar place can result in increased isolation and rapid deterioration in emotional wellbeing that places women at further risk. This is particularly the case for LGBTQI women, who may lose the vital support of their local LGBTQI community if they are forced to relocate, and who may also face the additional disadvantage of homophobia, biphobia or transphobia in their new area.

WGN also provides an intensive individualized care package intended to address a number of life areas, to engage interventions to manage trauma responses and to enable recovery for women surviving experiences of gendered violence. This care package offers strengths-based, multimodal, phased interventions that reinforce self-protective attributes aimed at promoting safety and stabilization. WGN's wraparound provision of care incorporates a holistic response directed at facilitating recovery at the mental, emotional, behavioural, interpersonal, spiritual and physical levels. Considered interventions and care models also extend therapeutic goals beyond simply reducing symptoms – rather, they work to restore general wellbeing and quality of life. The wraparound model integrates a comprehensive range of services to facilitate healing, including practical assistance from advice and advocacy services that address legal, health and practical needs; multifocal therapeutic services that use contemporary trauma-focused interventions, such as eye movement desensitization and arts therapy; and therapeutic group work delivered by clinical practitioners and aimed at those affected by gendered violence and related trauma manifestations, including self-harm, suicidal ideation and eating disorders.

Ultimately, the purpose of this chapter is not to deny the importance of culture in the context of gender-based violence in BME communities; on the contrary, we regard culture as necessary to identifying the contextual differences between different women's experiences of violence. But it is essential to recognize that *all* violence is shaped by culture. Nonetheless, while culture is an important element in the perpetration of, for example, 'honour'-based violence, forced marriage and female genital mutilation (FGM), it must not be viewed as the principle or sole causal factor. Rather, culture must be viewed as *one of a number* of intersecting sociocultural forces at play (Gill and Walker 2020). These intersectional identities and locations – not only culture, but also gender, race, class, sexuality, disability, etc. – shape how victims/survivors experience violence and abuse, and

BME women, in particular, face numerous intersecting inequalities that compound their risk of VAW. Intersectionality must, therefore, be the foundation on which effective responses to VAWG are built (Day and Gill 2020). By ignoring intersectionality and instead emphasizing the importance of culture and cultural difference, we fail to achieve a holistic understanding of the lived realities of BME victims/survivors and their intersectional needs. For numerous such victims/survivors, the threat of violence from an intimate partner is one form of oppression among many—racism, homophobia, transphobia, Islamophobia, classism, ableism or oppression based on migration status do not exist in isolation from partner violence, but often intersect and reinforce one other (Day and Gill 2020). By adopting an independent, critical perspective that centres BME survivors' needs, women's organizations have the potential to establish an intersectional approach to safety that offers genuine empowerment to end *all* forms of oppression and violence against *all* survivors.

References

Aghtaie, N. (2017) 'Rape within heterosexual intimate relationships in Iran: Legal frameworks, cultural and structural violence.' *Families, Relationships and Societies* 6, 167–183.

Anderson, M. and Hill Collins, P. (2001) 'Introduction.' In M. Anderson and P.H. Collins (eds) *Race, Class and Gender: An Anthology* (pp.1–9). Belmont, CA: Wadsworth.

Anthias, F. (2013) 'Cultural Difference.' In M. Evans and C.H. Williams (eds) *Gender: Key Concepts* (pp.15–29). Oxford: Routledge.

Batty, D. (2019) 'Marai Larasi: "I'm hurt that this country neglects BME women".' *The Guardian*, 12 February. Available at: www.theguardian.com/society/2019/feb/12/marai-larasi-bme-women-services-domestic-violence

Baxi, P. (2014) *Public Secrets of Law: Rape Trials in India*. New Delhi: Oxford University Press.

Carline, A. and Easteal, P. (2014) *Shades of Grey – Domestic and Sexual Violence Against Women: Law Reform and Society*. Oxford: Routledge.

CPS (Crown Prosecution Service) (2017) *What Is Consent? Guidance for Investigators and Prosecutors*. Available at: www.cps.gov.uk/sites/default/files/documents/publications/what_is_consent_v2.pdf

Crenshaw, K. (1991) 'Mapping the margins: Intersectionality, identity politics, and violence against women of color.' *Stanford Law Review* 43, 6, 1241–1299.

Day, A.S. and Gill, A.K. (2020) 'An intersectional approach to improving domestic violence responses.' *British Journal of Criminology* 60, 4, 830–850.

Gill, A.K. (2009) '"Honour" killings and the quest for justice in black and minority ethnic communities in the United Kingdom.' *Criminal Justice Policy Review* 20, 4, 475–494.

Gill, A.K. and Walker, S. (2020) 'Examining Violence Against Women and Girls through an Intersectional Lens.' In S. Walklate and K. Fitz-Gibbon (eds) *Emerald Handbook of Criminology, Feminism and Social Change* (pp.157–179). Bingley: Emerald Publishing Limited.

Herman, J. (1997) *Trauma and Recovery*. New York: Basic Books.

Home Office (no date) *Victims of Domestic Violence without Indefinite Leave to Remain*. Available at: https://www.gov.uk/government/publications/application-to-settle-in-uk-form-setdv

Horvath, M. and Brown, J. (2009) 'Setting the Scene: Introduction to Understanding Rape.' In M. Horvath and J. Brown (eds) *Rape: Challenging Contemporary Thinking* (Chapter 1). Cullompton: Willan.

Hubbard, A., Payton, J. and Robinson, A. (2013) *Uncharted Territory: Violence Against Migrant, Refugee and Asylum-seeking Women in Wales.* Wales Migration Partnership and Cardiff University. Available at: https://www.cardiff.ac.uk/news/view/research-reveals-uncharted-territory-on-violence-against-women-in-wales-27806

Izzidien, S. (2008) *'I Can't Tell People What Is Happening at Home': Domestic Abuse within South Asian Communities – The Specific Needs of Women, Children and Young People.* London: NSPCC.

Jiwani, Y. and Hoodfar, H. (2012) 'Should we call it "honour killing"? No. It's a false distancing of ourselves from a too-common crime: The murders of females.' *The Montreal Gazette.* Available at: https://www.pressreader.com/canada/montreal-gazette/20120131/281831460623735

London Sexual Violence Needs Assessment (2016) *Sexual Violence LCPF Co-Commissioning Workshop.* Available at: www.london.gov.uk/sites/default/files/mopac_lcpf_co-commissioning_workshop_sv_july_2017.pdf

Meetoo, V. and Mirza, H. (2007) 'There is nothing "honourable" about honour killings: Gender, violence and the limits of multiculturalism.' *Women's Studies International Forum 30*, 3, 187–200.

Menon, N. (2009) 'Sexuality, caste, governmentality: Contests over "gender".' *Feminist Review 91*, 94–112.

Office of the Children's Commissioner (2015) *'If It's Not Better, It's Not the End' – Inquiry into Child Sexual Exploitation in Gangs and Groups: One Year On.* London: Office of the Children's Commissioner.

Ogden, P., Minton, K. and Pain, C. (2006) *Trauma and the Body: A Sensorimotor Approach to Psychotherapy.* New York: W.W. Norton & Company, Inc.

Patel, P. (2012) 'The use and abuse of honour-based violence in the UK.' *Open Democracy.* Available at: www.opendemocracy.net/5050/pragna-patel/use-and-abuse-of-honour-based-violence-in-uk

Patel, P. (2013) 'Multi-Faithism and the Gender Question: Implications of Government Policy on the Struggle for Equality and Rights for Minority Women in the UK.' In Y. Rehman, L. Kelly and H. Siddiqui (eds) *Moving in the Shadows: Violence in the Lives of Minority Women and Children* (pp.41–58). Farnham: Ashgate.

Qureshi, K., Charsley, K. and Shaw, A. (2012) 'Marital instability among British Pakistanis: Transnationality, changing conjugalities and Islam.' *Ethnic and Racial Studies 37*, 2, 261–279.

Rolandsen Agustín, L. (2013) *Gender Equality, Intersectionality, and Diversity in Europe.* New York: Palgrave Macmillan.

Sen, P. (2005) '"Crimes of Honour", Value and Meaning.' In S. Hossain, and L. Welchman (eds) *'Honour': Crimes, Paradigms and Violence Against Women* (Chapter 2). London: Zed Books.

Sharma, K. and Gill, A.K. (2010) 'Protection for All? The Failures of the Domestic Violence Rule for (Im)migrant Women.' In R.K. Thiara and A.K. Gill (eds) *Violence Against South Asian Women: Issues for Policy and Practice* (pp.211–236). London: Jessica Kingsley Publishers.

Sheffield Council (2016) *Guidance for the Use of Interpreters in Situations Involving Domestic Violence and Abuse.* Available at: https://sheffielddact.org.uk/domestic-abuse/wp-content/uploads/sites/3/2016/08/Sheffield-Guidance-for-Use-of-Interpreters-in-situations-of-Domestic-and-Sexual-Abuse-FINAL-May-16.pdf

Thiara, R.K. and Gill, A.K. (2012) *Domestic Violence, Child Contact and Post Separation Violence: Issues for South Asian and African-Caribbean Women and Children: A Report of Findings.* London: NSPCC.

Threipland, C. (2015) *A Place to Call Home. A Report into the Standard of Housing Provided to Children in Need in London.* London: Hackney Community Law Centre and Hackney Migrant Centre.

Verloo, M. (2006) 'Multiple inequalities, intersectionality and the European Union.' *European Journal of Women's Studies 13*, 3, 211–228.

Vishwanath, J. and Palakonda, C. (2011) 'Patriarchal ideology of honour and honour crimes in India.' *International Journal of Criminal Justice Sciences 6*, 1–2, 386–395.

Welchman, L. and Hossain, S. (2005) 'Introduction: "Honour", Rights and Wrongs.' In S. Hossain and L. Welchman (eds) *'Honour': Crimes, Paradigms and Violence against Women* (pp.1–22). London: Zed Books.

WHO (World Health Organization) (2013) *Responding to Intimate Partner Violence and Sexual Violence against Women: WHO Clinical and Policy Guidelines*. Geneva: WHO.

Chapter 7

Addressing Domestic Violence and Abuse against Disabled Women

Ravi K. Thiara and Ruth Bashall

Introduction

It is now widely established that violence against women and girls across the lifecourse is prevalent across the globe irrespective of geography, ethnicity and age (WHO 2013). Despite it being a worldwide problem affecting around one in three women, a differentiated understanding reveals that disabled women are disproportionately affected by structural and interpersonal violence (Shah, Tsitsou and Woodin 2016; Thiara *et al.* 2012; WHO 2013). However, in spite of increased research enabling a more nuanced insight into this issue over the last decade and a half, practice remains under-developed and frequently inadequate. While structural, political and welfare responses to disabled people continue to raise alarm, of concern to this chapter is that disabled women who experience domestic violence and abuse (DVA) also continue to fall between the cracks in current policy and practice. As part of a trajectory of societal responses to disabled people, much of this fails to view them as victims of DVA, serving to further marginalize their experiences. This chapter examines the prevalence of domestic violence against disabled women, their experiences, and the consequences of such abuse.[1] It also focuses on the ways in which services respond, and highlights important issues for practice.

---

1   Several direct quotes from women describing the abuse they were subjected to are used throughout the chapter, and may cause upset.

Impairment or disability – medical and social model

As noted by Mohamed and Shefer (2015, p.2) 'the normal/abnormal binary is profoundly interwoven into existing power and privilege', serving to entrench the marginality of disabled people. Despite decades of activism by disabled activists, dis/ability discourse remains pervasive, reinforcing normative notions of ability–disability – ideal bodies, minds and psyches – and affects us all through marking the conditions for inclusion and exclusion.

What 'disability' signifies has been contested for decades. Mainstream views of disability – as individual impairment – were challenged by disabled activists who shifted emphasis to societal barriers – the social (Oliver 1996). These two ways of defining disability – the medical and social model – are now well known. The former views disability as a medical condition that prevents an individual from living a 'normal' life and something that requires treatment. Such individualizing discourses have been challenged for being essentialist, for reducing agency, for emphasizing vulnerability as a fixed condition and reinforcing power over disabled people. The social model of disability disrupts the focus on the individual and, making a distinction between impairment and disability, locates the 'problem' in the disabling social and material conditions experienced by disabled people to underline the contexts which re/produce marginalization and stigma. That it is the way that society is organized, not the impairment itself, which excludes disabled people from full participation in society is underlined. According to Public Health England (PHE 2015, p.6), which has adopted the definition developed by the disabled people's movement:

> Disabled people are excluded from society by various barriers: social and cultural discrimination; negative attitudes; limited social support; inaccessible transportation, public buildings, information formats, products and built environments; inflexible organizational policies, procedures and practices; lack of services; problems with service delivery; and a lack of involvement.

The social model of disability, despite multiple interpretations and challenges (Shakespeare and Watson 1997), is central to any analysis of the nature and impact of DVA and disabled women (see Corker and Thomas 2002; Swain *et al.* 2004).

Definitions of disability

The *Equality Act* defines disability as:

> ...a physical or mental impairment that has a substantial and long-term adverse effect on a person's ability to do normal daily activities.

The *United Nations* defines disability as:

> ...a long-term physical, mental, intellectual or sensory impairment which in interaction with various barriers may hinder their full and effective participation in society on an equal basis with others.

What is the difference in the two definitions? Which one is a medical model and which a social model?

Understanding disablism and domestic violence and abuse

It is estimated that around 25.7 per cent of the population in England and Wales has a disability or a long-term illness (over one in four) (ONS 2018a) and there are more disabled women (23 per cent) than men (20 per cent) in the UK (Sisters of Frida 2020). A substantially higher number of impairments are acquired throughout the lifecourse rather than congenital, which can shape the impacts of stigma and exclusion. Those who are born disabled find themselves caught up in the system earlier, which means they are more likely to be excluded from having an equal life. Women are adversely impacted by disability due to their social location; for instance, they may be poorer and less well educated than males; gender roles are more pronounced for disabled women; they may be denied opportunities for risk-taking and learning; they are more at risk of forms of violence and abuse such as sexual abuse and DVA; and they are more likely to be de-sexualized (Sait *et al.* 2009). Stigma, marginalization and 'othering' typically form women's 'experiences of being in the world' (Mohamed and Shefer 2015, p.3).

The common assertion that domestic violence affects all women regardless of class, 'race'/ethnicity, age, dis/ability and sexuality has obscured understanding of the differentiated ways that DVA affects different groups of women. An important way to understand the impact of violence against disabled women is to examine the intersection of different forms of oppression and discrimination, such as disablism, racism and sexism/misogyny, ageism and homophobia that interact simultaneously and contribute to structural inequality and systemic injustice. This way of understanding complex experiences is encapsulated by the concept of intersectionality, and is critical to a nuanced understanding and explanation for disabled women's experiences of DVA (see Thiara, Hague and Mullender 2011).

Intersectionality

The term was coined by Crenshaw (1991), a Black feminist in the USA, but was also prevalent in Black feminism in the UK in the 1970s. Viewed through an intersectional lens, gender sexism alone is insufficient to understand a woman's experiences as consideration of 'race'/ethnicity, dis/ability, class and sexuality, and societal attitudes toward each of these, is necessary to fully understand her position within society. Intersectionality suggests that the re/production of power and privilege and of marginality is not a simple linear process but complex and contradictory. It is reflected at the material and discursive levels and thus in policies, procedures and practices. The intersection of multiple systems of power and domination shape individual and collective experiences and struggles.

In seeking to place Black and minoritized women within discourses of disablism and sexism and to explain multiple oppression, Vernon and Swain (2002) have talked about compounded disadvantage, while Chenoweth (1997) speaks of 'simultaneous discrimination'. Drawing on some of this earlier work, Nixon has coined the term 'compound oppressions' (2009) to refer to the intersection of disablism and other forms of oppression. This intersection also leads to a denial of disabled women's identities and experiences; they become 'the disabled', with no gender, faith, culture or sexuality.

Further, the marginalization of disabled women in society has been termed a 'continuum of disempowerment' to take account of the multiple and intersecting levels of exclusion, stigma and disempowerment – institutional abuse, DVA, parental control and societal marginalization – throughout the lifecourse (Bashall and Ellis 2012). The continuum recognizes the 'multiple and continuous violations through the systems, structures and attitudes of society' to which disabled people are subjected as well as the reluctance of professionals concerned to acknowledge the inherent disablism in society (Bashall and Ellis 2012, pp.109–110).

Talking about violence against disabled people

Language can both reflect and influence how we think about an issue. Disability rights activist, Stephen Brookes, recommends that:

We should avoid saying:

'Motiveless crime' – if we mean the motive is not known or is not clear to us.

'There is no evidence' – if we mean there is insufficient evidence.

'Vulnerable victim' – when we mean someone was in a vulnerable situation that was exploited by the offender...

'Bullying' – use of this word understates the seriousness of incidents that often involve intimidation, persecution, terror, fear, harassment i.e. behaviours amounting to criminal offences. Even 'mere' ridicule, mimicking, exclusion can amount to causing serious harassment, alarm or distress, particularly if repeated.

'Has a mental age of' – comparison of an adult person with a child is often considered to be demeaning and unhelpful. Better practice is a reference to the person's level of social functioning and understanding. (Brookes 2010, p.6, cited in Bashall and Ellis 2012, pp.110–111)

Disability and domestic violence and abuse

The connection between disability and DVA is complex such that a disability can be a risk factor for DVA and/or DVA may lead to or worsen an existing impairment (PHE 2015). Literature on disabled women started to emerge in the 1980s and highlighted the ways in which disabled women were infantilized, viewed as helpless victims, and seen as asexual and incapable mothers (Asch and Fine 1988). Research over the last two decades has specifically highlighted the ways in which disabled women experience DVA and found them to be at heightened risk of physical, sexual and emotional abuse (Brownridge 2006; Groce *et al.* 2009; Thiara *et al.* 2012) and to have less social protection from abuse. The earlier focus on women with physical and sensory impairments has been addressed in recent years to also include women with learning or intellectual disabilities (McCarthy, Hunt and Milne-Skillman 2017; McCarthy *et al.* 2019; Pestka and Wendt 2014). Deaf women and those who have sensory, cognitive or communication impairments, serious long-term mental health issues or those who live in institutions are generally missing from existing research (Thiara *et al.* 2012). Little is also known about particular groups of disabled people such as those from Black and minoritized groups and LGBTQI (lesbian, gay, bisexual, transgender, queer (or questioning) and intersex) communities. It is widely accepted that those who are positioned at the intersection of multiple forms of power and discrimination experience greater risk and barriers. Thus, it is important to not homogenize disabled people and recognize the diverse ways in which situational risk is created, reinforced and experienced by different groups and the implications this has for professional responses. Further, it is worth noting that the under-reporting of DVA to key agencies and professionals means that the rates of DVA experienced by disabled people are considerably higher than research suggests (Shah *et al.* 2016). It is possible from existing research to reveal how disabled women experience DVA, their responses to this, the barriers to help-seeking and responses received from support services.

The Crime Survey of England and Wales (CSEW) has repeatedly found that those with a long-term illness or disability were more likely to be victims of all types of DVA compared to non-disabled people. Disabled women were almost three times more likely to experience DVA (16.8 per cent compared to 6.3 per cent) than non-disabled women and disabled men were over two-and-a-half times more likely (9.8 per cent compared to 3.5 per cent) to be victims of DVA than non-disabled men (ONS 2018a). Disabled women were twice as likely to be victims of sexual assault than non-disabled women (5.3 per cent compared with 2.7 per cent in 2016–17), while there was no significant difference among men (1.0 per cent compared with 0.8 per cent) (ONS 2018b). Others elsewhere have also highlighted that disabled women experience greater physical, sexual, emotional and financial abuse than non-disabled women (Barrett 2009; Martin *et al.* 2006). Research on women with learning or intellectual disabilities has noted heightened rates of multiple forms of severe abuse, which includes the use of weapons, by peers, partners, family members and caring staff (Walter-Brice *et al.* 2012; McCarthy *et al.* 2017), much of which continues after the relationship has ended. Martin *et al.*'s (2006) study revealed that women with an intellectual disability were four times more likely to experience sexual abuse or assault compared with the general population, and Frohmader (2002) found that over two-thirds of women under 18 were subjected to sexual abuse. In relation to DVA, this body of research has highlighted 'severe and frequent violence from partners, including brutal physical assaults, sometimes involving weapons and occasionally resulting in life-threatening injuries' (McCarthy *et al.* 2019, p.72). Also reported were high levels of fear including fear of being killed, which continued after the relationship ended (McCarthy *et al.* 2017).

The higher risk of DVA for women with mental illness has been highlighted (Trevillion 2012), with research finding that women in such situations were more likely to experience violence in the past year – more than one in three had experienced DVA and one in twenty had experienced sexual violence. Women with anxiety disorder were over four times more likely and women with a depressive disorder were over two times more likely than women without this to experience DVA (Trevillion *et al.* 2012). Studies also show that disabled children are three times more likely to be sexually abused than non-disabled children, and that disabled girls are significantly more likely to be sexually abused (Kelly, Regan and Burton 1991; Sobsey, Randall and Parrila 1997; Sullivan and Knutson 2000). A recent study has highlighted the high levels of abuse in disabled young people's relationships, but also that they face barriers in getting help, and subsequently remain invisible. Moreover, this research noted the targeting of disabled young people for sexual and criminal exploitation (Goff and Franklin 2019).

Experiences of domestic violence and abuse

CSEW figures on DVA record individual incidents reported to the police and provide no information about patterns and effects of abuse. Context and impact of DVA are increasingly recognized to be significant when considering the effects of DVA, and this suggests that when coercive control is considered, the differences between men and women are more apparent (Myhill and Kelly 2019). While it is accepted that men also experience DVA by female and male intimate partners, it is acknowledged that women in the general population are subjected to greater repeated physical violence, severe overlapping violence and coercive control. They also experience greater fear of their perpetrators and sustain more physical injuries (Hester 2013). Consequently, gender differences also exist within disabled people's experiences of DVA, such that disabled women are significantly more likely to experience DVA than disabled men, as noted earlier (PHE 2015).

Research in Europe, North America and Australia indicates that not only do disabled women experience higher rates of DVA, they also experience more frequent and severe abuse over a prolonged period (see McCarthy *et al.* 2017; SafeLives 2017; Thiara *et al.* 2012). International literature, alongside that in the UK, repeatedly highlights that disabled women are subjected to greater levels of abuse and in additional ways (Hague *et al.* 2008; McCarthy *et al.* 2017; Shah *et al.* 2016). Given that disabled people are significantly more likely to be threatened with violence and to be physically abused, the experience of DVA encompasses wider contexts and is perpetrated by a wider range of people (SafeLives 2017). This can include intimate partners, who may also be their carers (partner-carers), family members, friends, paid and unpaid carers or personal assistants and healthcare professionals. Thus, when disabled women with physical and sensory impairments require greater support with daily living, the likelihood of DVA also increases (Shah *et al.* 2016; Thiara *et al.* 2012). Similarly, for women with learning or intellectual disabilities, rejection in childhood and a search for belonging in adult intimate relationships creates vulnerability to exploitation and abuse (Petska and Wendt 2014). As already noted, disabled women's location at the intersection of multiple forms of marginality also has to be considered, such that barriers and exclusion from education and employment, which result in higher levels of poverty, itself a form of structural violence, all increase the likelihood of them experiencing DVA.

You know the same opportunities are not there for Deaf (or disabled) people. We're forced to become dependent to a certain extent because the facilities aren't there... You don't have the educational opportunities that other people have and training and job opportunities. (Hague *et al.* 2008, p.36)

Being isolated, having reduced support networks, societal devaluing and a lack of awareness about what constitutes an abusive relationship caused by a lack of education about safe relationships (or any relationship at all) all create situational risk and increase the likelihood of DVA for many disabled women. This is also a barrier to help-seeking as women are likely to normalize abuse (internalized devaluation has been widely highlighted), stay with abusive partners because they seek loving relationships or simply have no other options (Eastgate *et al.* 2011; Walter-Brice *et al.* 2012). This is something which perpetrators are often very well aware of; they deliberately target isolated disabled women in the first place and then further isolate them to enhance their power, something that is recognized by some health and social care professionals who come into contact with women (McCarthy *et al.* 2019). This makes the need for professionals to recognize DVA and create avenues for positive support for women all the more vital. Although disabled women are more likely to be subjected to DVA by intimate partners or partner-carers, frequent contact with care providers in institutions exposes many of them to additional forms of DVA from different potential abusers (Shah *et al.* 2016). For some disabled women this can result in abuse that is 'lifelong' (Hague *et al.* 2008).

The strong links between DVA, disability hate crime and targeted abuse against women ('mate crime') with intellectual disabilities has been highlighted by McCarthy (2017), who argues for the need to make connections across all three rather than treating them as discrete forms of violence and abuse in disabled women's lives (Landman 2014).

Mate crime is where people with learning disabilities are befriended by those who are intent on abusing and exploiting them and its dynamics are very similar to the relationships many of the women with learning disabilities in our study found themselves in, that is, meeting someone who appears to like them, who then very quickly inveigles their way into their life and home and starts exerting power and control, through intimidation and violence. (McCarthy *et al.* 2017, p.277)

In such situations, it can be difficult for women with learning or intellectual disabilities to resist the manipulation and pressure, especially if they yearn connection with others and have little confidence to assert their wishes. Clearly, there are lessons for professionals here in recognizing women's compromised ability to make choices in the face of coercive pressure and control:

> Notions of 'choice' can be masked by people's lack of, or poor, experiences. When people live in poverty, in poor housing and in social isolation, as many of those with mild learning disabilities do…it is not surprising that some seek and maintain relationships which are damaging. (McCarthy *et al.* 2017, p.277)

Cuckooing, targeted abuse – domestic violence and abuse versus 'mate crime'

There is a lot of mention of mate crime in the UK, although there is no statutory definition of this. The term commonly refers to the befriending of people perceived to be vulnerable, with the aim of taking advantage, exploiting and/or abusing them for the perpetrator's purposes. People with learning disabilities resist the term 'mate crime' and instead refer to cuckooing, abuse and targeting of disabled people.

'Cuckooing' refers to when a perpetrator takes over the home of a vulnerable person and treats it as his/her own (Gravell 2012). The victims of such crime often do not perceive what is happening to them as abuse, because of their strong desire for friendship and acceptance (McCarthy 2017, p.598).

> Targeting people in vulnerable situations (due to disability status in this instance) is a key feature of hate crime, which often includes high levels of humiliation, cruelty and violence. There is great similarity in the dynamics and forms of abuse perpetrated in contexts of hate and mate crime with those of DVA. (McCarthy 2017, p.598)

Research has also noted the perpetration of abuse by paid carers who have access to disabled women in their homes, and has highlighted the erosion of privacy as well as the contradictions created for those disabled women who rely on carers for their daily care needs, which 'increases the situational vulnerability to other people's controlling behaviour and can exacerbate difficulties in leaving an abusive situation' (PHE 2015, p.13; Thiara *et al.* 2012). Disabled women are frequently reluctant to take any action for fear of being left without care and being institutionalized (Martin *et al.* 2006), or of being subjected to oppressive safeguarding procedures where they may fear they will be blamed.

These range of factors result in experiences of DVA that are different and additional for disabled women (Bashall 2016). Women across much existing research report greater coercion and control, as well as more pervasive and wide-ranging abuse, which is frequently linked to their disability and their situation of marginalization. Research has highlighted the ways in which withholding of medication, control of mobility or communication aids, denial of personal care items, control of finances, destruction of communication aids and deprivation of food are all used as part of the perpetration of DVA by those who are intimate partners, family members or meant to be providing care and support (Thiara *et al.* 2012). Women repeatedly state that being disabled affected the *extent* and *nature* of DVA, and that it was common for abusers to use their impairments as part of the perpetration of abuse (Hague *et al.* 2008; McCarthy *et al.* 2017). Such tactics serve to increase power and control over women and create more and complex barriers to end abuse. In many cases there may be a professional failure to recognize coercive control and threats to harm women.

> There was slapping on the face, chucking me out of the wheelchair. And he grabbed me round the neck. He did slam me into my food a few times.
>
> Because I can't feed myself and often he would go out in the evenings and I wouldn't have eaten anything for a 24-hour period or more. So that wouldn't have happened to anybody that could feed themselves. And it's much easier to hurt me you know. I've got weak bones, I've got weak muscles. (Quoted in Hague *et al.* 2008, p.37)

> He used to take the piss out of me because of my learning disability. He used to show me up in front of his mates if I couldn't work something out. He'd say 'you're useless, you can't do nothing'...
>
> He said not to talk to boys, he told me 'don't wear sexy clothes'. If I

did, he would hit me. He wouldn't let me see my friends. (Quoted in McCarthy *et al.* 2017, p.274)

Research on women with physical and sensory impairments has exposed the neglect and humiliation disabled women are subjected to that is related to specific impairments.

> Oh yes, he would drag me along the floor because I couldn't walk or get away that was how it would start, the way it always went. He'd insult me with all those names, 'you spassy' and so on, who'd want to marry you. And he smashed me against the wall, shouting insults, 'you cripple', all that sort of thing.
>
> Once he threw me on the floor with my dinner and said 'that's where you eat your dinner, that's where you belong'. (Quoted in Hague *et al.* 2008, p.42)

Threats, intimidation and enforced isolation from family, friends and sometimes children are part of an array of tactics used against disabled women to control and enforce subservience. Women's lack of knowledge about support services, reduced support for independent living, inaccessible alternative housing and manipulating a woman's anxiety and beliefs all form part of the tactics used in the perpetration of DVA. While abuse by family members and paid or unpaid carers is rarely recognized, the actions of partner-carers are often couched in such a way that gives emphasis to the 'caring hero', a construct that can hold much sway among family members and professionals, rather than the manipulation of women's impairments, to reinforce their dependence and the perpetrator's control. Recognizing situations where this is occurring and challenging the narratives created by abusive partner-carers and/or family members is the role of professionals who come into contact with disabled women.

> Because they become your carer and they make you believe that you need them because of your disability. And they do everything. 'And I'm making life so much easier for you.' You know and I thought it was wonderful. Nobody had taken care of me in that way. No one. You know, and it was like, god, he'll do the ironing. He'll cook. He'll clean. And bit by bit though he was taking everything. He was buying my clothes. He was telling me who I could see. Where I could go. I mean part of that is about being a woman, but a lot of it was being disabled.

> Non-disabled women don't have that problem. He always made a thing
> about not pushing me out in my wheelchair. He'd carry me out to the
> car. Just to emphasize it more. (Quoted in Hague *et al.* 2008, p.41)

Dominant views of disabled women as asexual, undesirable and dependent, incapable of fulfilling the ideal of womanhood and motherhood, reinforce violence and abuse in their lives, including sexual violence (Begum 1992; Thiara *et al.* 2012). As noted by Shah *et al.* (2016), the objectification of disabled women's bodies across the lifecourse creates opportunities for multiple forms of abuse. Such constructions not only deny them their sexuality but also limit their exposure to learn about such issues, and means they are less likely to understand boundaries, recognize abuse, know their rights as well as how and where to report abuse (Nosek, Howland and Hughes 2001; Shakespeare 2014).

> People pity him because he is taking care of you and so noble. So people
> are reluctant to criticize this saint or to think he could be doing these
> terrible things. And possibly as well as that there's a sort of I think an
> idea...people don't really 'see' disabled women. And people don't easily
> see a disabled woman as a wife, partner, and mother. So I think for
> some people it's hard to think well this might be a woman who's being
> sexually or physically abused by her partner...because disabled women
> don't have sex, do they? (Quoted in Hague *et al.* 2008, p.43)

The normalization of violence against disabled people in various forms has been highlighted by disability activists, who point to the acceptance of 'mercy killings', 'infanticide of disabled newborns, denial of medical care because someone's life is judged to be "not worth living", everyday violence in state institutions, and hiding disabled adults and children in the family home out of fear and shame' (Bashall and Ellis 2012, p.109). Such social, institutional and professional practices have tended to attract limited political concern and are viewed as a normal aspect of their lives by disabled people. That the dynamics and nature of DVA perpetrated against disabled people is characterized by high levels of coercive control by multiple people in diverse contexts disrupts our normative definition of domestic violence, which has been challenged by many disabled people. It has been powerfully argued that existing definitions are inadequate in capturing the structural and interpersonal violence disabled women are subjected to across the lifecourse, in particular violence and abuse by paid or voluntary carers in someone's home or private life and violence that happens in a residential or semi-residential setting but is still 'home' to the victim.

Those relationships are, while in some ways formal, also intimate. So why are they not considered to be domestic violence and dealt with as such? Why is an abusive relationship with a partner, or with a family member who acts as an unpaid carer…considered to be any more intimate than an equally abusive relationship with someone who is a paid worker, or even a volunteer, who has got to know the disabled person? Boundaries in such situations are fluid, and the perpetrator may be closer to and know more about the disabled person than actual family members. (Bashall and Ellis 2012, p.114)

Situational risk serves to entrap disabled women in abusive situations. Women in the UK mentioned the following:

- Not being able to escape because the woman cannot leave the house without assistance or use a refuge because of poor access.

- Not being able to see or hear an attack coming.

- Perpetrators communicating with services on the woman's behalf – for example, a hearing abuser controlling a Deaf woman's contact with Deaf/Sensory services and interpreting for her.

- Denying access to support services, medical and social care (this is common, as in 'we can manage' when in fact it is about control).

- Perpetrators using the impairment to make the abuse worse, for example by depriving the woman of sleep, mismanaging or denying her medication, placing obstacles in her way so she has 'accidental' falls.

- Perpetrators targeting disabled women and in particular, women with learning disabilities, cognitive impairments or high mental health support needs because they know these women will not be believed. This is disability hate crime.

- Humiliation and verbal abuse regarding being disabled, making the experience even worse.

- Lack of training and jobs so they could not be independent in the way they would be if they weren't disabled.

- Making women believe they could not go out at all during the COVID-19 crisis.

Consequences of domestic violence and abuse

Research has extensively highlighted the consequences of DVA for women's physical and psychological wellbeing (Campbell 2002). These effects are likely to be compounded for disabled women since the frequency, severity and length of time in DVA is greater. Experiences of abuse across the lifecourse – bullying at school, child sexual abuse, sexual assault, DVA – are considered to increase disabled women's risk of compromised mental health (Conder, Mirfin-Veitch and Gates 2015, p.577). Erosion of self, low self-esteem and humiliation have been reported across the various research exploring disabled women's experiences of DVA (Hague *et al.* 2008; McCarthy *et al.* 2017). In line with non-disabled women, self-harm and suicidal thoughts have been commonly found (Taggart, McMillan and Lawson 2008, 2009). They are 35 per cent less likely to report positive health than disabled women who have not experienced DVA; they are also more likely to experience anxiety, depression, panic attacks and feelings of worthlessness than those who are non-disabled (Khalifeh *et al.* 2015). DVA can also result in the onset of debilitating secondary conditions (Hassouneh-Phillips and McNeff 2005).

> I lost who I was, my identity really. He left me with some things, and up to this day I can't get them out of my head… I feel not very good about myself in that sense. And I feel that can be just as bad, even worse than being physically abused.
>
> But the verbal abuse was so…difficult, so deeply undermining. I mean I thought at least he's not beating me to pulp but then you just feel worse and worse about yourself. (Quoted in Hague *et al.* 2008, p.46)

The extent, nature and consequences of DVA highlight the need for greater action to prevent and address DVA against disabled women from government, health and social care, domestic violence/violence against women and girls (VAWG) support services and other third sector organizations.

Responses to domestic violence and abuse and help-seeking

But you don't say anything as a disabled woman, I felt so ashamed that this was happening, so I didn't tell anyone, didn't ask anyone for help. I'd just be stranded. Most able-bodied women could get out of the house or drive your own car. If you are disabled you might not be able to, I couldn't.

Quoted in Hague *et al.* (2008, p.43)

Alongside structural inequalities and also being prevented by abusers from doing so, disabled women encounter several obstacles to seeking support. In general, social isolation, limited support networks, a constrained ability to defend themselves against the abuse, to recognize what is happening as DVA, communication difficulties, reduced ability to assess risk, and to also escape their situations have been highlighted (Hague *et al.* 2011; McCarthy *et al.* 2019; Pestka and Wendt 2014). Some with learning or intellectual disabilities may not understand or recognize potential signs of risk and abuse, for instance (Hague *et al.* 2011; McCarthy *et al.* 2017). Several barriers to women reaching out for help and in securing safety and support have been documented.

Barriers to help and safety

- A lack of accessible services.

- Inappropriate skills and attitudes among professionals and services that mirror wider societal attitudes.

- An adult safeguarding system that fails to address the risks from domestic abuse or follow processes to keep the victim/survivor safe.

- Absence of education for disabled children and young people about safe relationships, and of ones that feature their different bodies or ways of being, life experiences and situations.

- Absence of accessible awareness campaigns featuring the different bodies and experiences of disabled women.

- An ensuing lack of knowledge about sources of help and support.

- A lack of accessible refuge spaces and poor national information about access to refuges – not only for women with physical impairments who may need basic facilities such as an accessible bedroom, shower room or cooking facilities, but also for neuro-diverse women who may need adjustable lighting or may find a busy refuge causes them sensory overload. Few refuges have protocols in place if a woman needs a care worker or personal assistant to provide care for her at the refuge.

- An absence of information about specialist DVA services in the places they go to if they can leave the house (Radford, Harne and Trotter 2006; Shah *et al.* 2016; Thiara *et al.* 2012).

Disabled women have been found to be largely unaware of refuges and/ or other forms of help with DVA or to not regard refuges as places that they can be housed in; women with learning or intellectual disabilities especially do not have access to accessible, understandable information, indicating that these gaps need to be addressed if responses to such women are to be strengthened (McCarthy *et al.* 2017). Phoning for help may not be an option for Deaf or disabled women. Moreover, in the absence of alternative accommodation and support options, 'leaving' is often not a viable option for many who have housing that is adapted to their needs. It may not be straightforward to transfer care packages to new areas and across local authorities. Women often worry about their care and health needs, and decide 'better the devil you know'. There are also specific constraints placed on women with insecure immigration status. Indeed, leaving an abusive relationship can come at great cost – not only leaving an adapted home but also their pets, neighbours, supportive family and the community – and may make women think twice. Giving up a home after years of struggle to be appropriately housed and establish independence, in the face of few alternatives, is a huge sacrifice to make for many disabled women. Given such factors, there is a need for professional understanding to be improved about the complexity of 'leaving' an abusive relationship for a disabled woman.

Even when disabled women seek help for DVA, they are frequently left feeling responsible for the abuse (Walter-Brice *et al.* 2012). Being subjected to the punitive actions of children's services that remove their children, professionals colluding with perpetrators, fear of losing their independence and being judged as inadequate mothers are all experiences reported by women in their journeys of help-seeking (McCarthy 2019; Thiara *et al.* 2012). Since disabled women consider accessibility not only in terms of physical access but also a broader sense of attitudes and sensitivity to their needs, any sign that this is absent can lead to a fear of reaching out.

Women may feel ashamed or embarrassed to look for help or they may not want to be defined only as a 'vulnerable victim'. Given societal views of disabled people, reaching out for help can create great anxiety:

> One way it made it worse was like it was hard for me to talk to other people and hard to be understood, and like I would just feel so pathetic, like I was going to be pitied and I was pathetic anyway because of not hearing and speaking like other people. And in getting away – well, I didn't feel I could for a while... (Quoted in Hague *et al.* 2008, p.42)

Fear and/or actual experiences of racism prevent Black and minoritized disabled women from looking for help. In these situations, and especially where they have had negative experiences with statutory services, they believed they could only rely on themselves – 'the only choice I've had is to find my own way really...it's really me helping me out really'.

> When I have opened up about something I haven't been understood. They just didn't know where I was coming from. If anything, I felt like they were being very disrespectful not hearing me... I've had that experience and I don't want that again. The help that I need isn't out there... I'm not afraid to say that anymore. I'm being judged by the colour of my skin before anything. (Quoted in Hague *et al.* 2008, p.53)

Finding an appropriate LGBTQI service that understands their situations as disabled women is a key issue for lesbian, bisexual and trans disabled women.

Key factors in women making the decision to take action to change their abusive situation is being able to access a supportive organization – those accessing services run 'by and for' disabled survivors state the organization 'gets me as a disabled women, as who I am', becoming more confident, an escalation in abuse and wanting to protect their children. However, like non-disabled women, attempts at separation can create greater danger. For those women who are unable to leave their accommodation, the experience of post-separation violence is likely to be graver as they remain easy targets for their abusers.

Barriers to accessing support

Not only do disabled women experience higher rates of DVA, they also experience more barriers to accessing support from the 'system' – domestic violence services, disability organizations and from health and social care agencies (Hague *et al.* 2011). In particular, the separation of domestic violence and safeguarding responses to disabled women experiencing DVA creates a disconnect in responses and reinforces systemic barriers that constrain disabled women's options. While DVA is seen as a crime and processes focus on helping women keep safe and regain their independence while punishing perpetrators, safeguarding adult procedures focus on protection, minimizing harm and social care solutions, including institutional ones, and rarely prioritize women regaining their independence (Thiara *et al.* 2012). Although these procedures have been tightened up and a greater focus placed on the adult with safeguarding needs, knowledge and practice remains uneven and inadequate (LGA and ADASS 2015) alongside an unwillingness to see family carers of disabled people as potential abusers. If a disabled woman is seen as an 'unreliable witness', if they are non-verbal or have learning or intellectual difficulties or mental health issues, any investigation may result in little or no action, giving a clear message to disabled women that violence against them is not taken seriously. The likelihood of disabled women subjected to DVA being channelled through safeguarding processes, where professional voices become prominent at the expense of their own, has been highlighted to point to the discrepancy in the ways in which different groups of victims/ survivors are responded to. Adult services all too often fail to follow basic safety DVA procedures, and invite the victim/survivor and the abuser to the same meeting to 'discuss' the safeguarding. This leaves a disabled woman at heightened risk of further abuse, and means she may not speak out again.

Women's attempts to reach out for help from their informal networks and/or formal services are frequently experienced as negative, although positive responses have been highlighted where agencies and professionals provide the thought and awareness about their situations that women value. Research in the UK and elsewhere highlights how the wider marginalization of disabled women leads to inadequate attention and provision within sectors that would be expected to provide safety, support and protection. Failure on the part of agencies to respond to DVA against disabled women is common (Shah *et al.* 2016; Thiara *et al.* 2012). Gaps persist within health and social care services and within both disability and specialist DVA support services (Chenoweth 1997; Nixon 2009; Thiara *et al.* 2012). In particular, disabling attitudinal barriers among the range of services and professionals result in further trauma for women. Instead of being supported to end DVA, disabled women are left unprotected through minimal police and social services interventions other than the removal of their children, or they are not believed and/or blamed by professionals (McCarthy *et al.* 2017; Walter-Brice *et al.* 2012).

A lack of professional curiosity and a failure to look at presenting issues (often depression) as anything other than those connected to the disability have been found to be common among professionals. In cases of women with learning or intellectual disabilities, it has been shown that even when professionals were indirectly aware of DVA, they failed to act because women did not directly ask for help (McCarthy *et al.* 2017). Although some disabled women identified a single positive response from a professional, in the main their needs are not understood, leaving them feeling unsupported and unheard. This can include the police assuming they cannot make an arrest when the abuser is the partner-carer or when professionals visit women in their homes they only focus on the impairment and the woman's ability to deal with it. Conversely, when professionals were aware of the dynamics of DVA and had taken positive action to support and connect women with appropriate services, this was reported to make a substantial difference to their ability to change their situations.

The importance of a proactive response by professionals has been repeatedly underlined (Hague *et al.* 2011; McCarthy *et al.* 2019). This includes giving information about abusive relationships and indicators of DVA to all disabled women (even if they are not in contact with statutory services), including when they are young

(McCarthy *et al.* 2019), always seeing the woman alone, and asking questions such as 'do you feel safe?' In particular, the role of health and social care professionals and the police is considered to be crucial especially, as highlighted by McCarthy *et al.* (2019), many women with mild learning or intellectual disabilities do not meet the eligibility criteria and fall through the net:

> Vulnerable women relying on support from abusive men to survive, because of a lack of social care provision is a serious issue which needs addressing. Professionals and support staff (and indeed wider society) need to keep a watchful eye and respond proactively if they are concerned that a woman may be at risk from domestic violence. (McCarthy *et al.* 2019, p.79)

Among the services valued by disabled women are advocacy, specialist DVA therapeutic support and empowerment groups based on feminist principles which, through connection with other women, reduce physical and psychological isolation and create friendship networks (Walter-Brice *et al.* 2012).

In order to appropriately assess disabled women experiencing DVA, Stay Safe East (an organization run 'by and for' disabled people) has developed the following risk assessment to be used as an addition to the widely used 'Dash' (2016, 2020a).[2] It is a tool to enable practitioners to identify the specific risks that arise from the power the abuser/s hold over a victim/survivor because she is disabled. Practitioners will also need to be informed about the particular forms of DVA perpetrated against disabled victims/survivors, and of the specific nature of targeted abuse and control, as discussed earlier in the chapter.

---

2   Stay Safe East usually only shares this risk assessment with practitioners who have been trained by the organization. However, in the light of COVID-19 and the very high risks faced by disabled survivors, a decision was made to share this more widely, especially with partner organizations.

Domestic abuse risk assessment
Stay Safe East additional disability-related questions

1. General information
This page is not part of the scoring risk assessment but is used to find out if the victim is a disabled person and has access or support needs which are essential to keeping them safe.

	Yes	No	N/K
Are you a disabled person? If yes, please tick the relevant box(s) ☐ Physical disability ☐ Sensory impairment ☐ Deaf ☐ Learning difficulty ☐ Mental health issuesAutism, Asperger's or other neuro-diverse condition ☐ Other long-term health condition (please state)			
Are any children in the household disabled? If yes, please give details:			
Are any other adults in the household who are affected by domestic violence elderly or disabled people? If yes, please give details:			

Access, support and communication needs
Please use this box to include any information about the victim's needs – *for example, if she/he needs personal care or other daily assistance, transport, information in large print, or a British Sign Language interpreter. This is especially important if the victim has communication needs (e.g. does not use the phone) which impacts on the ability of professionals to contact them.*

If the victim says 'yes' to any of the above questions, please go to the next page and ask the disability risk assessment questions.

2. Disability risk assessment				
Tick the box if the factor is present. Please expand on any 'yes' answers. Please note the examples in brackets are not to be read out, but can be used as prompts.	Yes	No	N/K	Source if not the victim
D1. Do you rely on [perpetrator]…for practical help or for communication? (For example, washing, dressing, help with eating or taking medication, help with getting out of the home or with travelling, managing money, communication of the victim's speech, British Sign Language, etc.) If yes, please give details:				
D2. Do they use this to control you? (For example, refusing you medication or help to eat, doing things deliberately to make your condition worse etc.) If yes, please give details:				
D3. Is…refusing to let you access support relating to your disability needs? (For example, refusing to let carers, personal assistants, GP or social workers into the home, or controlling your access to support services.) If yes, please give details:				
D4. Is…abusive to you/your child directly because of your/your child's disability? (For example, calling you names, mocking your disability, blaming you, etc.) If yes, please give details:				
D5. Are there any concerns around the victim's capacity to make her/his own decisions? Please note: if the victim is deemed not to have full capacity, or if there is any doubt, a referral must be made to Adult Safeguarding.				
D6. Any other factors relating to the victim's disability or their situation which might put them at risk? Please give details:				
Total 'yes' responses out of 6 disability risk assessment questions				
Note: Please do not add this score to the standard SafeLives risk assessment. Please note the score under your reasons for referral to a multi-agency risk assessment conference (MARAC).				

Even while these issues in professional responses endure for disabled women, further challenges and precarity are created during a pandemic, such as COVID-19 (see Sisters of Frida 2020; Stay Safe East 2020b). COVID-19 has amplified existing inequalities faced by disabled women, and it is likely that the increase in DVA has also impacted particularly acutely on disabled women. Structural inequalities, dependence on care providers without routes to help during lockdown periods as well as social isolation clearly create greater risk for disabled people, which also have an intersectional impact. This is further exacerbated by restricted access to advocates, health and medical services, social care and support, essential information, and a lack of support with accessing food. A rise in hate crime, including race hate crime, has also been highlighted (Sisters of Frida 2020; Stay Safe East 2020b).

A great deal of development is required if the double jeopardy for disabled women is to be broken – that they experience greater levels of DVA and thus have a greater need for support but there is far less provision to help them. However, services can address this by closing knowledge and attitudinal gaps, by improving accessibility and identification and by providing more opportunities for disclosure and support. Training and knowledge development among all professionals and services, improving joined-up and integrated working between key services such as the police, adult social care, specialist disability services and DVA services, and direct engagement with disabled women are key to strengthening responses to abused disabled women.

Disabled women have been writing, actively organizing and campaigning on both disability and DVA issues for decades. They have established many 'by and for' organizations over the years, and many continue to provide support services to disabled people and to challenge established stereotypes, poor practice and the gap in national policy and strategy so that disabled women who experience DVA can benefit from the same support and access to justice as other victims/survivors. These organizations include Sisters of Frida,[3] Stay Safe East,[4] Disabled Survivors Speak Out and the SignHealth Domestic Abuse Service.[5]

Research has flagged a number of promising practice issues for professionals who interact with disabled women, which are shown on the following page.

---

3   www.sisofrida.org
4   www.staysafe-east.org.uk
5   https://signhealth.org.uk/with-deaf-people/domestic-abuse/domestic-abuse-service

Women with learning or intellectual disabilities

There is a clear role for healthcare and social care professionals in helping women with learning disabilities who are experiencing DVA.

> There is nothing about having a learning disability which protects women from domestic violence. (McCarthy *et al.* 2017, p.279)

Staff involved with women with learning disabilities have been urged to be aware where women are involved with men who have no learning disabilities, mental health issues, problematic drug/alcohol consumption, as well as those who are unemployed and start to live in with women at an early stage of the relationship.

Professionals are also urged to take note when women in a new relationship:

- Become more isolated from friends, family, professionals and children.

- Have less money than before.

- Show signs of physical injury, likely to indicate multiple forms of abuse.

Additionally, professionals can play a crucial role in:

- Proactively asking women if they need help.

- Giving women information about available specialist support, legal provision and other options and help them to access these.

- Supporting women to develop their social networks and independence.

Good practice

A social model approach seeks to remove barriers for disabled women at all stages through an inclusive approach to accessibility and usability of processes and services from the outset – viewing disabled women as equals and not 'add-ons' to services. The following are key dimensions of removing barriers.

1. Removing barriers
Prevention

- Organizations must reach out to disabled women and girls where they live in ways that are accessible and relevant.

- Have an inclusive approach to independent living that does not leave disabled women dependent on the goodwill of those who would control their lives.

- Challenge assumptions of service providers and wider society about disabled people and women.

- Raise awareness among disabled women about what domestic violence is and where to get help, and reporting all forms of domestic violence, hate crime and abuse.

Information

- Inclusive, accessible and relevant information about domestic violence.

- Information about access to services that are inclusive and reflect them.

Reporting and getting help

- Accessible places for disabled women to report domestic violence and to get help where they can trust they will be listened to.

- Safe and appropriate options for refuge that meet a range of needs.

- Inclusive refuge services – not just in terms of physical access, but types of services available – 24-hour staffing or staff trained to communicate with women with learning disabilities and where bullying towards disabled women in refuges is challenged.

- Additional accessible options to help keep women safe and not to exacerbate issues faced.

- Institutional care is rarely an appropriate option for women fleeing domestic or sexual violence.

Tailored holistic support that is appropriate to needs

- Advocacy and therapeutic support that understands disabled women's needs and the social care system and is linked with organizations. Partnership working between domestic violence and disability advocates is an excellent way to address this.

Justice for disabled women

- Police investigations must treat the woman as a reliable witness, not a 'vulnerable adult', and keep her at the centre of the process. This requires trained police officers who understand disability equality and who have access to services to meet disabled women's needs.

- Ensure support to a disabled woman as a witness through appropriate intermediaries[6] and special measures; this has helped obtain convictions in rape cases involving people with learning difficulties.

Short- and long-term recovery

- Counselling services that are appropriate and accessible to disabled women, social model-based, and where possible, involve peer support.

- The social care system needs to be flexible to provide long-term support while a woman recovers from the violence and learns new independent living skills.

Learning and training

- At a time when resources are limited, sharing of skills between domestic violence organizations and disabled

---

6   Intermediaries are independent professionals, not advocates, and are there to give advice to the police and Crown Prosecution Service (CPS) to help achieve more productive interviews and at court to get best evidence at trial. They can facilitate the communication process in court, advise on how a witness communicates and their levels of understanding, and how it would be best to question them to get best evidence. People with learning disabilities must have a 'responsible adult' in any police proceedings, including where they are a witness or providing a statement.

people's organizations can help improve practice responses.

- Training must address attitudes and assumptions about disabled women.

2. An inclusive approach to all forms of violence against women and a single approach to domestic violence against all women

A single approach does not mean a uniform approach as different women require different forms of support, and responses must be tailored to diverse needs.

A wider definition of domestic violence

- Definitions of domestic violence need to reflect the specific reality of disabled women's lives. A new definition of domestic violence would include:

  - Any form of abuse, physical, psychological, financial, sexual or otherwise that happens in a domestic or intimate setting and is perpetrated by partners, family members, paid or unpaid carers, and others who have close contact with the victim.

Situational risk, not individual vulnerability

- To tackle all forms of violence against disabled women and men, it is essential to move away from the idea that there are groups or individuals who are in themselves vulnerable to an understanding of 'situational vulnerability'.

Revising risk assessment procedures to include disabled women's lives

- Current domestic violence risk frameworks should be used for all violence against disabled people but widened to include the specific and unique risks faced by disabled women, such as:

  - Social isolation and no contact outside their immediate

family and/or paid carers, or if living in residential care, outside their paid 'carers' and other professionals.

- Dependence on relatives or a partner for all or most care or support needs or to go out.

- Dependence on family or partner to speak – interpret or communicate.

- Rarely or never goes out of the home.

- Threat of institutionalization is being used (including of sectioning under the Mental Health Act).

- Abuser control over medication or disability equipment.

• This approach focuses on situational vulnerability rather than vulnerability because of an impairment. Disabled women are not exempt from risk factors such as a perpetrator using their pregnancy as a means of control, 'honour'-based violence or forced marriage.[7]

3. 'Nothing about us without us': partnerships with disabled people's organizations and disabled women at all levels in policy and practice

• At an individual level, whatever the level of impairment, a disabled woman's wishes must be respected; she must be listened to and supported to make her own decisions.

• At a strategic level, disabled women must be involved in formulating policies, strategies and protocols around domestic violence.

• Involvement cannot happen by asking disabled women to attend established forums and working groups, but processes need to be made accessible and relevant. Key areas of involvement are:

---

7   The Home Office (2010) has produced guidance on tackling forced marriage against people with learning difficulties. Research showed that women and men with learning difficulties from South Asian and other communities were at high risk of forced marriage by families, who saw marriage as a means of providing a carer and continuing support, or of facilitating the entry into the UK of the spouse, or even of 'curing' the disabled person.

- Board membership of domestic violence services.

- Local strategic safety partnerships.

- National strategic boards on domestic violence.

- Police and CPS independent advisory groups.

- Serious case reviews or domestic homicide reviews where the victim is a disabled woman.

• Disabled women and disability organizations should be involved as partners in equality impact assessments and audits at a local level to establish what the gaps are in practice and approach.

Adapted from Bashall and Ellis (2012, pp.126–132)

Key tips: Responding to disabled women

✓ Do not accept a situation at face value; show professional curiosity.

✓ Look beyond the impairment and for any signs of DVA – depression may not always be a response to the impairment but the effects of abuse.

✓ Ask women in a safe way about their situation – but you may have to do this a number of times after you have built up trust.

✓ Speak directly to women and not through carers, partner-carers and/or family members.

✓ Help and support women to find accessible and appropriate help from a service that understands issues for abused disabled women.

✓ Ensure women have specialist advocacy from a specialist DVA-VAWG service or a disability organization.

Disabled women urge organizations and professionals to increase their knowledge and understanding to better respond to their situations and needs, as part of giving greater visibility to the issue.

- Be aware of it.

- Don't patronize.

- Don't assume – quite possibly the experience of abuse has been worse (than disclosed), but don't assume.

- Don't define a woman by her disability – take her impairment on board in assessing the situation, but don't define her by it.

- Don't have a 'special' different tone of voice.

Disabled women highlighted the following for good practice:

- Be informed about disabled women's needs.

- Take advice from and consult with disabled women.

- Develop accessible services.

- Provide accessible, well-publicized domestic violence services (including refuge accommodation) that disabled women know about.

- Ensure choices are offered beyond institutionalization if no refuge space is available.

- Develop accessible alternative accommodation, both temporary and permanent, as well as support to use it.

- Develop disability equality schemes and reviews with input from disabled women.

- Take disabled women seriously and do not patronize them.

Conclusion

The complex nature of disabled women's DVA experiences, inadequate professional responses and absence of specialist services suggests that fundamental change is required at multiple levels across different sectors if effective support and protection is to be offered to disabled women. Even provisions that exist for disabled people, such as the safeguarding agenda, need to be more effective in responding appropriately to disabled women who are subjected to DVA. An intersectional analysis provides an important framework for considering and understanding the cross-cutting issues for disabled women affected by DVA, including structural inequalities, social attitudes, marginality within the domestic violence and disability movements, and responses from a raft of statutory service providers. In considering the experiences of disabled women, an emphasis is placed on the importance of redefining what we understand as DVA, the contexts in which it occurs and the perpetration of abuse, as well as the responses to such abuse. In highlighting the barriers and challenges encountered by abused disabled women in seeking help and support, the chapter has also identified areas in which the response of diverse professionals can be strengthened.

References

Asch, A. and Fine, M. (1988) 'Introduction: Beyond Pedestals.' In M. Fine and A. Asch (eds) *Women with Disabilities: Essays in Psychology, Culture and Politics* (pp.1–37). Philadelphia, PA: Temple University Press.

Barrett, K. (2009) 'Intimate partner violence, health status and health care access among women with disabilities.' *Women's Health Issues 19*, 94–100.

Bashall, R. (2016) *Recognising and Supporting Disabled Victims of Domestic Abuse*. London: SafeLives. Available at: https://safelives.org.uk/practice_blog/recognising-and-supporting-disabled-victims-domestic-abuse

Bashall, R. and Ellis, B. (2012) 'Nothing About Us Without Us: Policy and Practice.' In R.K. Thiara, G. Hague, R. Bashall, B. Ellis and A. Mullender (eds) *Disabled Women and Domestic Violence: Responding to the Experiences of Survivors* (pp.106–136). London: Jessica Kingsley Publishers.

Begum, N. (1992) 'Disabled Women and the Feminist Agenda.' In H. Hinds, A. Phoenix and J. Stacey (eds) *Working Out: New Directions for Women's Studies* (pp.61–73). London: Falmer.

Brownridge, D. (2006) 'Partner violence against women with disabilities: Prevalence, risk and explanations.' *Violence Against Women 12*, 9, 805–822.

Campbell, J. (2003) 'Health consequences of intimate partner violence.' *The Lancet 359*, 1331–1336.

Chenoweth, L. (1997) 'Violence and Women with Disabilities: Silence and Paradox.' In S. Cook and J. Bessant (eds) *Women's Encounters with Violence: Australian Experiences* (pp.21–39). Los Angeles, CA: Sage.

Conder, J.A., Mirfin-Veitch, B.F. and Gates, S. (2015) 'Risk and resilience factors in the mental health and well-being of women with intellectual disability.' *Journal of Applied Research in Intellectual Disabilities 28*, 572–583.

Corker, M. and Thomas, C. (2002) 'A Journey around the Social Model.' In M. Corker and T. Shakespeare (eds) *Disability/Postmodernity: Embodying Disability Theory* (pp.18–31). London: Continuum.

Crenshaw, K. (1991) 'Mapping the margins: Intersectionality, identity politics and violence against women of color.' *Stanford Law Review 43*, 6, 1241–1299.

Eastgate, G., van Driel, M.L., Lennox, N. and Scheermeyer, E. (2011) 'Women with intellectual disabilities: A study of sexuality, sexual abuse and protection skills.' *Australian Family Physician 40*, 4, 226–230.

Frohmader, C. (2002) *There Is No Justice, There's Just Us: The Status of Women with Disabilities in Australia*. Canberra: Women with Disabilities Australia.

Goff, S. and Franklin, A. (2019) *We Matter Too: Disabled Young People's Experiences of Services and Responses When They Experience Domestic Abuse*. Nottingham: Ann Craft Trust, University of Nottingham.

Gravell, C. (2012) *Loneliness and Cruelty: People with Intellectual Disabilities and Their Experience of Harassment, Abuse and Related Crime in the Community*. London: Lemos and Crane.

Groce, N., Izutsu, T., Reier, S., Rinehart, W. and Temple, B. (2009) *Promoting Sexual and Reproductive Health for Persons with Disabilities*. WHO/UNFPA Guidance Note. Geneva: World Health Organization and United Nations Population Fund.

Hague, G., Thiara, R. and Mullender, A. (2011) 'Disabled women, domestic violence and social care: The risk of isolation, vulnerability and neglect.' *British Journal of Social Work 41*, 148–165.

Hague, G., Thiara, R.K., Magowan, P. and Mullender, A. (2008) *Making the Links: Disabled Women and Domestic Violence. Full Report*. Bristol: Women's Aid.

Hassouneh-Phillips, D. and McNeff, E. (2005) '"I thought I was less worthy": Low sexual and body esteem and increased vulnerability to intimate partner abuse in women with physical disabilities.' *Sexuality and Disability 23*, 227–240.

Hester, M. (2013) 'Who does what to whom? Gender and domestic violence perpetrators in English police records.' *European Journal of Criminology 10*, 5, 623–637.

Home Office (2010) *Forced Marriage and Learning Disabilities: Multi-Agency Practice Guidelines*. London.

Kelly, L., Regan, L. and Burton, S. (1991) *An Exploratory Study of the Prevalence of Sexual Abuse in a Sample of 16–21 Year Olds*. London: Child and Woman Abuse Studies Unit.

Khalifeh, H., Moran, P., Borschmann, R., Dean, K., Hart, C., Hogg, J., *et al.* (2015) 'Domestic and sexual violence against patients with severe mental illness.' *Psychological Medicine 45*, 4, 875–886.

Landman R. (2014) '"A counterfeit friendship": Mate crime and people with learning disabilities.' *Journal of Adult Protection 16*, 355–366.

LGA (Local Government Association) and ADASS (Association of Directors of Adult Social Services) (2015) *Adult Safeguarding and Domestic Abuse: A Guide to Support Practitioners and Managers* (Second edition). London: LGA.

Martin, S., Ray, N., Sotres-Alvarez, D., Kupper, L., *et al.* (2006) 'Physical violence and sexual assault on women with disabilities.' *Violence Against Women 12*, 9, 823–837.

McCarthy, M. (2017) '"What kind of abuse is him spitting in my food?" Reflections on the similarities between disability hate crime, so-called "mate" crime and domestic violence against women with intellectual disabilities.' *Disability & Society 32*, 4, 595–600.

McCarthy, M. (2019) '"All I wanted was a happy life": The struggles of women with learning disabilities to raise their children whilst also experiencing domestic violence.' *Journal of Gender-Based Violence 3*, 1, 101–117.

McCarthy, M., Hunt, S. and Milne-Skillman, K. (2017) '"I know it was every week, but I can't be sure if it was every day": Domestic violence and women with learning disabilities.' *Journal of Applied Research in Intellectual Disability 30*, 2, 269–282.

McCarthy, M., Bates, C., Triantafyllopoulou, P., Hunt, S. and Milne Skillman, K. (2019) '"Put bluntly, they are targeted by the worst creeps society has to offer": Police and professionals' views and actions relating to domestic violence and women with intellectual disabilities.' *Journal of Applied Research in Intellectual Disabilities 32*, 1, 71–81.

Mohamed, K. and Shefer, T. (2015) 'Gendering disability and disabling gender: Critical reflections on intersections of gender and disability.' *Agenda 29*, 2, 2–13.

Myhill, A. and Kelly, L. (2019) 'Counting with understanding? What is at stake in debates on researching domestic violence.' *Criminology and Criminal Justice*, 1–17. doi:10.1177/1748895819863098.

Nixon, J. (2009) 'Domestic violence and women with disabilities: Locating the issue on the periphery of social movements.' *Disability & Society 24*, 1, 77–89.

Nosek, M., Howland, C. and Hughes, R. (2001) 'The investigation of abuse and women with disabilities: Going beyond assumption.' *Violence Against Women 7*, 477–499.

Oliver, M. (1996) *Understanding Disability: From Theory to Practice*. London: Macmillan.

ONS (Office for National Statistics) (2018a) *Domestic Abuse: Findings from the Crime Survey for England and Wales: Year Ending March 2018*. November. London: ONS.

ONS (2018b) *Sexual Offences in England and Wales: Year Ending March 2017*. London: ONS.

Pestka, K. and Wendt, S. (2014) 'Belonging: Women's living with intellectual disabilities and experiences of domestic violence.' *Disability & Society 29*, 1031–1045.

PHE (Public Health England) (2015) *Disability and Domestic Abuse: Risk, Impacts and Response.* London: PHE.

Radford, J., Harne, L. and Trotter, J. (2006) 'Disabled women and domestic violence as violent crime in practice.' *Journal of the British Association of Social Welfare 18*, 4, 233–246.

SafeLives (2017) *Disabled Survivors Too: Disabled People and Domestic Abuse.* London: SafeLives.

Sait, W., Lorenzo, T., Steyn, M. and van Zyl, M. (2009) 'Nurturing the Sexuality of Disabled Girls: The Challenges of Parenting for Mothers.' In M. Steyn and M. van Zyl (eds) *The Prize and the Price: Shaping Sexualities in South Africa* (pp.192–219). Cape Town: HSRC Press.

Shah, S., Tsitsou, L. and Woodin, S. (2016) 'Hidden voices: Disabled women's experiences of violence and support over the life course.' *Violence Against Women 22*, 10, 1189–1210.

Shakespeare, T. (2014) *Disability Rights and Wrongs Revisited* (Second edition). Abingdon: Routledge.

Shakespeare, T. and Watson, N. (1997) 'Defending the social model.' *Disability & Society 12*, 2, 293–300.

Sisters of Frida (2020) *The Impact of COVID-19 on Disabled Women from Sisters of Frida.* London: Sisters of Frida.

Sobsey, D., Randall, W. and Parrila, R.K. (1997) 'Gender differences in abused children with and without disabilities.' *Child Abuse & Neglect 21*, 707–720.

Stay Safe East (2016, 2020a) *Disability and Domestic Abuse Risk Assessment.* Developed in partnership with disabled survivors. London: Stay Safe East. Available at: www.staysafe-east.org.uk

Stay Safe East (2020b) *Impact of Covid-19 on People with Protected Characteristics.* Policy Response – Equality Impact of Covid-19. London: Stay Safe East.

Sullivan, P. and Knutson, J. (2000) 'Maltreatment and disabilities: A population based epidemiological study.' *Child Abuse & Neglect 24*, 1257–1273.

Swain, J., Finkelstein, V., French, S. and Oliver, M. (eds) (2004) *Disabling Barriers – Enabling Environments.* London: Sage.

Taggart, L., McMillan, R. and Lawson, A. (2008) 'Women with and without intellectual disability and psychiatric disorders: An examination of the literature.' *Journal of Intellectual Disabilities 12*, 191–211.

Taggart, L., McMillan, R. and Lawson, A. (2009) 'Listening to women with intellectual disabilities and mental health problems: A focus on risk and resilient factors.' *Journal of Intellectual Disabilities 13*, 321–340.

Thiara, R.K., Hague, G. and Mullender, A. (2011) 'Losing out on both counts: Disabled women and domestic violence.' *Disability & Society 26*, 6, 757–771.

Thiara, R.K., Hague, G., Bashall, R., Ellis, B. and Mullender, A. (2012) *Disabled Women and Domestic Violence: Responding to the Experiences of Survivors.* London: Jessica Kingsley Publishers.

Trevillion, K. (2012) 'Experiences of domestic violence and mental disorders: A systematic review and meta-analysis.' *PLOS One 12*, 7.

Vernon, A. and Swain, J. (2002) 'Theorising Divisions and Hierarchies: Towards Commonality or Diversity?' In C. Barnes and M. Oliver (eds) *Disability Studies Today* (pp.77–97). Bristol: Policy Press.

Walter-Brice, A., Cox, R., Priest, H. and Thompson, F. (2012) 'What do women with learning disabilities say about their experiences of domestic abuse within the context of their intimate partner relationships?' *Disability & Society 27*, 4, 503–517.

WHO (World Health Organization) (2013) *Global and Regional Estimates of Violence Against Women: Prevalence and Health Effects of Intimate Partner Violence and Non-Partner Sexual Violence.* Geneva: WHO.

Chapter 8

Working with Perpetrators of Domestic Violence

Chris Newman

Introduction

Specialist services and methods of working to change the behaviour of perpetrators[1] of domestic abuse developed in the USA and Canada in the 1970s and somewhat later in the UK, Europe, Australia and New Zealand. The roots of this work lie diversely in the realms of therapy, the criminal justice system, feminist multi-agency working and the 'men's movement', pro-feminist and otherwise. Since the early days, work with perpetrators of domestic violence and abuse (DVA) has spread worldwide and covers all aspects of the work against violence, from primary prevention through to early intervention, protection responses, justice and rehabilitation. It is beyond the scope of this brief chapter to cover the full variety of this work. The focus instead will be on current research and practice on working with perpetrators in the multi-agency context in high-income countries such as the UK, USA, New Zealand and Australia, across the spectrum of protection/intervention responses.

Since the mid-1990s, I have been developing and delivering domestic abuse prevention programmes (DAPPs) in community and criminal justice settings and making formal assessments of risk and capacity to change in families where DVA is a child protection concern. This work has, of course, been alongside many creative and dedicated

---

1 In my view, 'perpetrator' is an unsatisfactory label for a range of reasons; it is rather pejorative and has an 'othering' connotation – we would never use this label when working with our clients. However, in its literal meaning of someone who has committed a harmful action, it is the most convenient shorthand available for a person who uses or has used violence and abuse in their intimate relationships.

colleagues; indeed my friend and colleague Kate Iwi and I have been thinking together about this subject for so long it is hard to know where her voice ends and mine begins. This chapter will focus primarily on areas of work I have been involved in, from 'front-line' assessment and intervention with adult perpetrators of violence, to more system-level initiatives where I and my colleagues have been engaged as consultants or programme developers.

Tensions and controversies have been present from the start about what the primary aim of the work is and how this is best achieved. Practitioners have engaged creatively with questions such as:

- Is the primary aim of the work to change violent men, or to keep women safe?

- To what extent should we offer collaborative engagement and support to perpetrators of violence and coercive control? Would that occlude the victim's experience? What is the boundary between support and collusion? How does this all fit with the wider societal aim of holding offenders accountable for their behaviour?

- Is the work done with perpetrators best thought of as educational or 'therapeutic'? Is there a danger of 'psychologizing' abusive behaviour rather than framing it as functional behaviour, a way of bullying and controlling a partner so your needs come first?

These themes will inevitably emerge in the discussion of various areas of practice in this chapter. I will first describe some innovative developments in the criminal justice system and multi-agency network, which seek to harness these tensions creatively – by pressuring perpetrators to change their behaviour while also seeking to engage with them in a process of change. I then consider the fact that the violent men we work with are very often fathers (or are very likely to become fathers). As we will see, this means that the harm caused by violent men's behaviour extends to the children who are involved in their lives through current or past relationships, and are therefore potentially exposed to and shaped by their father's behaviour. However, we also find that being a father can sometimes be a powerful motivator for change. I then look in more detail at child protection and safeguarding issues in relation to perpetrators of domestic abuse. Next I focus on practical advice about what we can do to increase the likelihood of engagement and to foster motivation to change in this difficult client group. The last section of the chapter turns to a discussion of cases where violence and abuse in relationships is used by women, and in LGBTQI (lesbian, gay, bisexual, transgender, queer (or questioning) and intersex) relationships.

A note on gender

Violence in intimate relationships takes many forms, and can be inflicted by men on women, by women on men, within same-sex relationships, and may include collusion or direct abuse from other family members. Surveys that ask whether people have suffered *any* form of physical violence in intimate relationships tend to show that women are only slightly more likely to report suffering violence than men. However, when surveys ask about the *impact* of the violence, it tends to be women who report more severe violence, who are more likely to be injured and more likely to live their lives in fear of their partners (Hester 2009; Johnson 2008). Even if women start out using violence in a relationship, men's greater physical strength often ends up shifting the power balance over time:

> I didn't call it domestic violence because I used to hit him too – I felt we were on even ground. But then it started to shift. Over time he became more aggressive. I would end up backing down and he wouldn't. Then I started to feel like I was getting bullied, I was avoiding saying things because I was scared of getting hurt. (Quoted in Iwi and Newman 2011, p.12)

This means that when agencies are set up to work with perpetrators of DVA, it tends to be largely men who walk through the door. However, we strongly believe that all forms of abuse in intimate relationships are unacceptable and avoidable, whoever is the perpetrator, and the practice suggestions included here can be readily adapted to whoever is the primary perpetrator of abuse in the relationship.

What do we know about domestic violence and abuse perpetration across the lifespan?

We know that experiences of interpersonal violence and abuse occur across the lifecourse, they often co-occur and are interrelated.

Violence between siblings: Violent behaviour within the family is common. Surveys indicate that violent sibling acts occur in approximately 85–96 per cent of families and are almost universal in younger children (Kolko, Kazdin and Day 1996). In the UK, a household survey of 6126 children, parents and young adults into children's experiences of all forms of interpersonal violence found the prevalence of sibling violence at some stage during childhood to be between 24 per cent (children under the age of 11) and 32 per cent (children aged 11–17). Sibling violence tends to be more common in younger age groups and tapers off in mid-adolescence, with the highest rates of violence in the previous year being for younger children (24 per cent victimized by a sibling in the last 12 months). Severe forms of sibling violence can persist into adult life (Radford *et al.* 2013). As Duncan (1999, pp.881–882) points out, 'whether 30% or 96% of children are victimized by siblings, it is evident that this is a prevalent source of violence in a child's life.' Sibling violence tends to be normalized as 'rough play' (for example, boys will be boys), and some argue that this has some developmental function in learning one's own strength and how to limit aggression (Caspi 2012). Caspi argues persuasively that *the very acts deemed to be abusive in parent–child, partner and stranger interactions are often considered ordinary behaviour among siblings.* He advises that professionals should routinely enquire about sibling violence, taking into account age-appropriateness, frequency, duration and degree of victimization. It is particularly important to understand levels of fear – for instance, by asking whether a child is or has been afraid to be alone with a sibling.

When children are violent to their parents or carers: While the problem of sibling violence is still under-recognized, there has been increasing recognition and development of intervention models for the parallel problem of children and young people who are violent and controlling towards their parents where there is often a history of the child and parent (usually the mother) living with DVA (this issue is addressed in detail in Chapter 9).

Violence in young people's intimate relationships: It is known that the age group that experiences the highest prevalence of violence in their intimate relationships is young women aged 16–19 (ONS 2015). DVA perpetration and victimization begins early – in a sample of 13- to 17-year-olds surveyed by the NSPCC (Barter *et al.* 2009), a quarter

(25 per cent) of girls and 18 per cent of boys in the study reported having experienced some form of physical violence from an intimate partner (although the same researchers also found that girls with partners two years or more older than them were much more likely to suffer abuse).

In common with other crime and violence perpetration, younger men, especially those under 30 years of age, commit DVA at far higher rates than their older counterparts and are more likely to reoffend (Hanson and Wallace-Capretta 2004; Hotaling and Sugarman 1986). The frequency and severity of physical assaults tend to diminish with ageing, although this may not apply to those individuals who exhibit anti-social or psychopathic personality traits, since these characteristics tend to endure across the lifespan (Hare and Neumann 2005). It may be that psychological and emotional abuse replaces physical violence as the abuser gets older, but there is little research evidence on this (Barnish 2004) (see Chapter 3 in this volume).

Abuse in older people's relationships: DVA also occurs in older people's relationships, and working with perpetrators in the post-retirement age group is under-developed and compounded by the personal care needs that often fall on partners (see Chapter 5).

Interventions with adult perpetrators of domestic abuse

Reflective question
The underlying question behind all our endeavours is what changes does our society need to make if we are to ensure that all our children grow up with the resources, ethical framework and emotional capacity to manage intimate relationships respectfully?

Society is still a long way from making the structural changes necessary to ensure that all our children grow up with the resources, ethical framework and emotional capacity to manage intimate relationships respectfully. Until those changes are made, we are faced with dealing with the fall-out from this systemic failure. One of the themes of this chapter is that responses to this problem will require effective ways of working with perpetrators of DVA – by targeting those causing most harm, preventing recidivism in 'first offenders', and also by finding ways to engage often reluctant and resentful perpetrators into a process of change. Since the early 1990s there has been a significant growth and transformation in intervention/direct work with perpetrators of DVA, where the aim is to help participants (the majority of whom are men) to stop using control and violence in their intimate relationships. DAPPs started with pioneering experiments in the voluntary sector, setting up group work interventions with men and parallel services for their (ex-)partners. After some initial (and quite understandable) scepticism there was a gradual acceptance from the women's sector that this model of work was a responsible contribution to efforts to make victims safer (Phillips, Kelly and Westmarland 2013). Over time, nationwide perpetrator programmes were also set up within probation services. From the start, workers in the sector have emphasized that any treatment or educational work with perpetrators of DVA should be seen as one element in a coordinated community response to the problem. It is a mark of progress that the concept of a coordinated multi-agency approach to DVA is now widely accepted as best practice. Practitioners working directly with perpetrators in DAPPs have been involved in a continual process of trying to understand 'what works' in engaging with a client group that is very often mandated to attend and reluctant to engage.

Regarding evidence about what works in terms of 'treatment' methods and approaches, there was little to draw on in the early stages, and even now there is little consensus in the research literature about whether one 'treatment' modality or another is the most effective. Work in the UK started with adaptations of the coordinated community response to DVA developed by the Duluth programme in the early 1980s, including groupwork interventions that used a pro-feminist, psycho-educational approach. Programmes in the UK now offer a range of interventions based on more than one perspective, often blending both pro-feminist and individual/psychological conceptualizations (see Hester and Newman 2020 for a discussion of how these approaches can be creatively combined). The accreditation standard developed by Respect[2] does not prescribe a particular model of work; rather, it seeks to ascertain that any programme is operating

---

2   Respect's aim is to advance best practice on work with perpetrators, male victims and young people who use violence and abuse in their close relationships, for services across the domestic abuse sector and more broadly. They offer training to front-line workers, accreditation of services to supporting perpetrators to change and a helplines for professionals, men who are worried about their own behaviour as well as male victims. See www.respect.uk.net

in a responsible way, with victims' safety being the primary concern, and that they use a coherent model of work that practitioners understand and apply consistently.

A research study based on findings from 12 Respect-accredited DAPPs in the UK has found encouraging results for men completing perpetrator programmes in the UK, particularly in reductions in the most overt forms of violence and abuse (Westmarland, Kelly and Chalder Mills 2010). Importantly, this study did not focus solely on measuring changes in the more overt forms of violence and abuse. Other measures of success were included – respectful relationships; expanded space for action; decreased isolation; enhanced parenting; and understanding the impact of domestic violence. The researchers found reductions in all these areas too, 'though not to the extent that was seen for the physical and sexual violence, and in many cases not to the extent that women might have hoped for' (Westmarland and Kelly 2015).

Perhaps the most important factor in the development of this area of work has been a culture of transparent and accountable experimentation within the field. Phillips *et al.* (2013) describe this process in their review of the development of perpetrator programmes in the UK. They noted that programme developers wanted to find ways of working that drew on victims' experiences of what it was actually like to live with a perpetrator of abuse, and the range and complexity of the abusive behaviour they faced. Alongside this, practitioners also used the hours spent in group rooms and interviews to understand from the inside what it is like to be someone who uses abuse, helping to gain some insight into the unrealistic expectations, attitudes, habits of thinking and patterns of emotional responding that enable a person to behave abusively to a partner. All programme developers they interviewed spoke about a process of adapting ways of working and programme content through listening and being responsive to the men in the groups, drawing on a wide range of approaches and experiences.

> You are creating an atmosphere where men can genuinely explore their beliefs and their fears and their insecurities. They can try out new ways of thinking. They can speak about them and see what the response of their peers is, challenge comes for other men much more significantly than it does from the workers. (Phillips *et al.* 2013, p.11)

Responding to different levels of risk

Given the high volume of DVA cases, all services face the problem of 'triage'. If there are more than a million calls to the police each year related to DVA (ONS 2018), there is a need to target valuable resources where they will be most effective in protecting vulnerable adults and children. Police and criminal justice systems make great efforts to enforce existing laws, protect victims and to disrupt perpetrator behaviour. Considerable progress has been made in developing cooperation between different parts of the system via multi-agency risk assessment conferences (MARACs), and the criminal justice system is developing new ways of assessing risk or harm so it can target increasingly scarce resources to cases where severe harm is imminent (see below). Limited resources and the high reoffending rates in the most harmful offenders means that law enforcement and punishment of perpetrator behaviour are unlikely to be successful in reducing the problem on their own. This has been recognized, and some innovative projects have started to harness a multi-agency approach to coordinate a 'carrot and stick' (or more formally 'support and disrupt') approach to working with serial perpetrators.

'Support and disruption' with serial perpetrators

Disruption in the context of crime prevention focuses on disrupting the offender's networks, lifestyle and routines (Kirby and Penna 2010). Recent innovations in DVA prevention have taken a multi-agency approach to combine disruption with intensive case work potential to address the offender's needs and help them achieve a level of stability in their lives, up to the point where they become more amenable to behaviour change work. Support and disruption methods can be used independently or alongside each other depending on the perpetrator's engagement and capacity to avoid reoffending.

Examples of projects using the 'support and disrupt' approach
The Drive project

The Drive project is a new response to DVA that aims to disrupt and change the behaviour of high-risk, complex needs perpetrators. The project was jointly developed by Respect, SafeLives and Social

Finance. The intervention lasts 10 months and is comprised of 'direct' one-to-one work with service users; 'indirect' work carried out at a multi-agency level primarily to share information, manage risk and disrupt perpetration; and one-to-one support from an independent domestic violence advisor (IDVA) for the linked victims/survivors. The case managers in the project coordinate the 'support and disrupt' approach to working with service users. Their supportive options include: assisting clients to meet basic needs (for example, around housing or substance misuse treatment and family support); doing motivational and safety work with clients individually; and referring them to therapeutic interventions to change behaviour. If this support is not taken up, case managers can coordinate criminal justice responses to drive perpetrators to change their behaviour.

A three-year evaluation study gives rise for optimism (Hester *et al.* 2020). The number of Drive service users using various types of violent or abusive behaviour reduced substantially. For example, high-risk physical abuse reduced by 82 per cent, sexual abuse reduced by 88 per cent, harassment and stalking behaviours reduced by 75 per cent and jealous and controlling behaviours reduced by 73 per cent. The study also followed a control group of survivors supported by an IDVA but without the Drive approach to partners. While there was a reduction in risk for both the Drive and IDVA only groups, there was a stronger reduction for Drive-associated victims/survivors. IDVAs assessed risk as 'permanently eliminated' at the point of case closure in almost three times as many cases for victims/survivors in the Drive-associated group (11 per cent) compared to those in the control group (4 per cent). One of the hopes from this pilot was that case managers would be able to engage with and guide offenders towards behaviour change programmes. However, in the first year, only one of the 30 perpetrators in the pilot group was suitable for a domestic violence perpetrator programme (DVPP) at the end of Drive support. Renewed focus was therefore placed on developing and delivering behaviour change programmes that can be delivered on an individual basis for this high-harm complex needs cohort, with a strong focus on motivational work and understanding barriers to engagement. The evaluation indicates that this was successful, and reports that workers developed considerable skill in balancing compulsion with an approach that emphasized collaborative working and the service user's choice to engage.

The effectiveness of a combination of 'pull and push' factors was also evident in the finding that the aspiration to 'be a better father' was a powerful motivation for engagement and change, while the presence of child protection proceedings functioned alongside this as an effective 'lever' or 'push factor' (Hester *et al.* 2020, p.42).

Table 8.1 Examples of 'support or disrupt' interventions within the Drive project

Preventing inappropriate step-down in a child protection case	*Increasing victim safety through behavioural change work*
Drive raised concerns at a child protection meeting about a service user continuing to perpetrate emotional harm towards his child. As a result, a multi-agency agreement was reached to extend child protection registration (at a time when the social worker was supporting deregistration)	Drive worked with a service user in prison and after release to explore topics including building empathy and healthy life choices. The service user has been alcohol free since leaving prison, and built healthy relationships with his two children from a previous relationship; the adult victim reports no longer feeling afraid of him
Disrupting the perpetrator's behaviour to prevent the eviction of the victim	*Disrupting abuse through the courts*
A perpetrator was controlling the victim from prison by hoarding goods in her garden and then complaining to the local authority about the state of the property. Drive worked with the police probation support services and housing to arrange a clearance, resulting in the threat of eviction being removed. Due to the time-consuming nature of the intervention, the Probation Service said this would not have been carried out without Drive	Drive supported the IDVA and victim to secure a non-molestation order via civil proceedings, after criminal proceedings released a high-risk violent and controlling perpetrator without bail conditions. This was followed by Drive advising on and supporting the gathering and submission of evidence required to secure a coercive control conviction. This was all indirect activity, and no contact was made with the perpetrator

Multi-agency tasking and coordination (MATAC)

Another approach targeting serial perpetrators is MATAC developed by the Northumbria Police. The MATAC approach also recognizes that many of the perpetrators who cause most harm and pose the highest risk often have complex needs. As a result their lives are chaotic and they may be difficult to engage in educational or supportive interventions. MATAC uses a range of methods to offer practical support, and to motivate offenders to attend behaviour change programmes.

As with the Drive project, if the offer of support is not accepted or is unsuccessful, the level of protection offered to victims is increased, as is the pressure to change on the perpetrator using disruption and enforcement techniques. The MATAC Domestic Abuse Toolkit provides a variety of strategies to manage perpetrators, dependent on their level of engagement in the project and their specific issues and needs. For perpetrators who engage, the toolkit's 'therapeutic pathway' is used, offering access to a DAPP, substance misuse services, mental health services, housing-related support and additional services if necessary. Perpetrators who do not engage are subject to 'prevention, diversion, disruption and enforcement' via the toolkit's 'criminal justice pathway'. This comprises a range of actions by the police and external agencies, including raising the profile of the perpetrator among neighbourhood police teams and at team briefings, circulating a photograph of the perpetrator, identifying any wider criminality with a view to arrest for this, maximizing opportunities to gather intelligence, undertaking vehicle stop and search, and allocating intelligence gathering to a designated officer. Police can also use Domestic Violence Protection Notices or Orders and criminal sanctions.

Compulsion and/or engagement with 'first offenders'

The Caution Against Relationship Abuse (CARA) (Strang *et al.* 2017) initiative arose from a recognition that DVA offences deemed to be low severity often resulted in no more than a caution for the offender, and additionally, a significant proportion of DVA cases fail to proceed due to victims' reluctance to testify. However, the point at which an individual has been arrested and has admitted the offence (a necessary prerequisite for a caution to be issued) may provide a window of opportunity for early and rapid intervention to prevent the escalation of frequency and severity of abuse over time. To this end, the CARA project tested the use of conditional cautions as a means of leveraging change in this group. The condition attached to the caution was attendance on two day-long workshops, using awareness-raising techniques plus exploration of the consequences of abusive behaviour to enable healthier ways of relating and to identify further sources of support where appropriate. The domestic abuse awareness-raising course was designed and delivered by the Hampton Trust, a Respect-accredited DVPP. Findings from a randomized controlled trial of this initiative indicate that those receiving the conditional caution and attending the course caused significantly less harm to their partners than those who did not (the control sample). Attendees were 46 per cent less likely to reoffend than controls, and 81 per cent of victims whose (ex-)partner attended the course reported an improvement in behaviour post attendance in comparison to 44 per cent in the control sample (Strang *et al.* 2017).

A common factor in all these programmes is the idea that if we are ever to reduce the number and severity of incidents of DVA, we need to do more to reduce it at its source. To quote from a Drive project briefing in 2017:

> We must get to the root of the problem: to expect the victim and their children to uproot and change their whole lives while the perpetrator remains unchallenged, unchanged and able to commit further offences (with new or ex-partners) is hugely problematic. From a moral and rational perspective, we must commit to holding perpetrators to account.

That said, it is important to be clear about what we mean by 'holding perpetrators to account'. I would argue that behaviour change is most likely to be sustainable if this includes the perpetrators themselves becoming more accountable, that is, more aware of the harm they have caused and more willing to change. While this is a desirable aim, it is another matter to find effective ways to motivate, persuade, support or pressure those causing the harm to change. Many of the people we work with, particularly those at the high harm/high needs end of the spectrum, are hostile to what they see as interference or oppression from professionals and are also experiencing multiple difficulties themselves. The extent of co-occurring problems in the initial cohort involved with the Drive project for high-risk perpetrators demonstrates this point, as Table 8.2 highlights (Hester *et al.* 2017).

Table 8.2 Complex needs and offending in the initial Drive pilot cohort

Substance misuse	64.7%
Alcohol misuse	62.5%
Mental health difficulties	68.4%
Housing	82.4%
Non-domestic abuse offences	92.9%
Previous domestic abuse offences	93.3%

Engaging with perpetrators of domestic violence and abuse as fathers

Child protection services and the family courts also face the problem of 'triage'. It is simply impossible for all cases involving DVA that come to the attention of agencies to be dealt with in a child protection framework. Furthermore, assessment in this arena has added complexities. As well as the risk of imminent harm, practitioners also have to take into account the potential for harm to children over the longer term from living with domestic abuse, and from the impacts of that abuse on parenting capacity. Some research has shown large variations between areas and socioeconomic groups in thresholds for intervention (Bywaters *et al.* 2015).

System-generated risk and unintended consequences

Alongside worries about system overload, a further unintended consequence of the increase in awareness of the risks to children posed by DVA is that non-abusive mothers often become the focus of professionals' efforts to safeguard children. This is largely because abusive fathers are difficult for professionals to engage with and less likely than mothers to accept that they need to be involved in the change process (Scourfield 2014; Thomson-Walsh *et al.* 2018). In the absence of any work with the perpetrator (most often the father), the onus falls on the victim to undergo assessment and ultimately to change. As a result, she is the one social workers and other professionals feel frustrated with and are sometimes blaming towards. She becomes the problem and can be seen as 'failing to protect' the children – often from fathers whose history would make us as professionals fear for our physical safety (see below for some guidelines on counteracting this tendency). Encouragingly, some local authorities in the UK have been seeking to address this problem directly, most notably via the adoption of the 'Safe and Together' approach in Edinburgh and some London boroughs.[3] Safe and Together is a system-level initiative that seeks to improve practice and to counter this gravitational tendency to focus change-making efforts on the mother. Professionals are encouraged to focus on DVA as a parenting choice by the perpetrator, who should therefore be targeted as the primary cause of family disruption. To this end,

---

3   https://safeandtogetherinstitute.com

there is also a strong focus on increasing practitioner skill in 'father-inclusive' ways of working while at the same time avoiding dangerous practices, such as attempting to promote father involvement without assessment for safety or the quality of a father's parenting (Mandel and Rankin 2018).

Focusing on the direct source of risk

This problem in child protection practice has been identified by researchers and practitioners for some time, and repeated calls have been made to focus efforts towards behaviour change back on the direct source of risk, the perpetrator (Iwi and Newman 2015; Scourfield 2006, 2014). However, despite the predominance of this issue in their caseload, child protection social workers (CPSWs) can today complete their training without any learning about how to work with DVA perpetrators. Others, such as family support workers, find themselves largely in the same boat. Over the years, my colleague Kate Iwi and I have trained hundreds of social workers in assessing and engaging with perpetrators. A turning point in our thinking came when a group of social workers told us that they had never had a father disclose DVA in interviews with them.

We started to ask ourselves why this was the case, when our experience was quite different – in both assessment and treatment settings it is our experience that people do disclose abuse, sometimes very severe abuse, and in settings where they are taking a risk that this disclosure could result in negative consequences for them. Some of this related to the role of the social worker, and the point in the process of involvement with a family at which the meetings take place. Initial interviews are often difficult and feel unproductive, as parents are often fearful of social workers and may believe that the best way of getting them to just go away is to deny any problems. Social workers face a particularly difficult challenge, as they are often expected to assess risk in the early stages of a case, and they may be the first professional to attempt to confront perpetrators about the effects of their behaviour on child/ren. Additionally, a mostly female workforce faces particular difficulties when expected (usually alone) to interview men who may have both problematic attitudes to women and a propensity for violence. This means that there are understandable fears about early intervention with fathers who are violent in the home. They may be seen as dangerous to professionals and there may also be a fear of making the situation worse and putting the children at greater risk if they are antagonized. There are often considerable difficulties in even making contact with male perpetrators, let alone getting them to attend appointments. Since mothers still tend to undertake the bulk of childcare in the home, it is usually easier to locate them.

However, despite all of this, the benefits of skilling front-line workers to do this work remain compelling: first, it is essential to persist in engaging with perpetrators if we are to prevent the spotlight of child protection investigation from focusing predominantly on the mother's imperfections rather than the direct source of risk, and if we are to take into account the harm caused to parenting by DVA. Second, any risks involved in this effort are likely to be reduced if front-line professionals can get practical, skills-based training for engaging with perpetrators. While DVPPs are not available across the country, the expertise that has developed in these programmes about how to assess and engage with perpetrators of DVA (which is consistent with skills and knowledge developed in other areas of work with clients with complex needs) could be much more widely disseminated.

A tendency we noticed in our social work students was that they were unclear about the purpose of a given interview or section of an interview. In particular, they tended to mix up 'finding out' and intervention, and so inadvertently decreased their chances of getting a clear account of the perpetrator's behaviour. Effective assessment depends to a large extent on getting a detailed behavioural account of what happened in any given incident, and the chances of getting this are greatly increased if workers can maintain the curious, neutral stance we recommend below. If we move too quickly into making judgements about the behaviour, suggesting alternatives, questioning the client's motives or asking him about the effect of his behaviour, we are likely to derail the client from making any disclosure. Again, maintaining a neutral stance is, in our view, the best way of creating a space in which people can talk about their harmful behaviour. Practice tips 1 and 2 might provide a better idea about how these different approaches feel and the client–worker relationships they foster.

Practice tip 1: Separate finding out from intervention

There are two distinct steps to working with perpetrators. It will help you a great deal to delineate these in your own mind as clearly as possible:

1. Finding out what has happened and assessing risk.

2. Intervention: Assessing suitability for intervention and then working for change alongside the person you are working with.

If you try to mix step 2 into step 1, you may well find that you fail on both fronts. For example, if you are just hearing about the build-up to an abusive incident and you start asking, 'What do you think that was like for your partner and children?', you may make your client defensive, which means they are likely to retreat from any openness they might have had in their account of the incident.

We advise you to go easy on yourself and on them; set out in your first session or two simply to get an account of what has been happening. Towards the end of one of these sessions you might neutrally summarize and reflect back some of the abuse and violence they have told you about here and there during the session. Trust that telling another person even a bit of what you have done and then hearing it reflected back, without any blame, judgement or justifications, is an intervention in and of itself.

Adapted from Iwi and Newman (2015)

We also realized in our training work that the difficulties social workers were facing were related more to the interviewing style and the 'stance' they took in the interview, rather than ignorance of certain techniques or not being clever enough 'interrogators' (Iwi and Newman 2015; see also Scourfield 2014). Research by Forrester, Westlake and Glynn (2012) has found similar tendencies in social work trainees (see Forrester *et al.* 2012 for a summary). In one study, 40 social workers who attended a course on motivational interviewing were found to have very confrontational communication styles. In a separate study, Forrester *et al.* (2012) taped interviews between social workers and an actor playing a client in a child protection situation. They found varied levels of skill. While all social workers successfully raised concerns, some did so empathically, but the majority were highly confrontational. The confrontational approaches tended to create high levels of resistance from the actors playing clients.

Engaging with perpetrators of domestic violence and abuse

Our work over the last 25 years in domestic violence assessment and intervention has taught us that a subset of the people we work with are very emotionally and psychologically vulnerable, and many have experienced abuse and violence in the past. Unfortunately, these experiences and vulnerabilities make them more likely to be emotionally dysregulated, unpredictable, self-centred and extremely dangerous. Nevertheless, like the rest of us, perpetrators of DVA carry with them a confusing mix of beliefs, expectations and values, some of which drive them towards negative behaviour, but some of which are positive and potentially protective. As such, we would argue that all except the most disturbed offenders have at least the seeds of values and motivations that can be harnessed towards change. The wish to play a positive role in their child's life can be one of the most powerful of these. So what can we do to increase the likelihood of engagement and to uncover and fan into life any embers of motivation in this client group?

Iwi and Newman (2015) have written a handbook based on these principles for front-line practitioners who aren't specialist perpetrator workers, focusing on what is most effective, easiest to learn and realistically applicable in the context of early intervention. The aim is to help practitioners to build a working alliance while tackling denial and minimization, assess risk, do some preparation work for a full perpetrator programme and to make the most effective possible interventions to decrease the risk in the meantime (see Practice tips 1 and 2).

Stance

When working with those who we think have behaved abusively, there is a tension between colluding with them on the one hand, and becoming accusatory or even persecutory on the other – often in an over-zealous attempt to avoid collusion. It is important that we make professional judgements about our client's abusive behaviour. It is also human that we will make personal judgements and have emotional reactions about some of the things we hear. However, it is also important to form an alliance with our clients towards change. If the person you are working with starts to feel judged and criticized, or picks up on your reactions to their behaviour, they are likely to become defensive. The conflict will then end up being between you and him; you will do all the urging to change while he sits back and gets more and more entrenched and invested in staying put. On the other hand, if you find yourself avoiding the difficult challenges, overemphasizing your relationship and becoming essentially client-centred, your client will happily use the time with you to get support without working significantly on their violence and abuse at all.

We recommend that you put your feelings and reactions aside in the session unless you are sure they are conducive to change. Be curious and interested and share that interest with your client; invite them to question their own behaviour as far as possible, but be calm and non-conflictual. Somewhere between the collusive and the accusatory stance lies a more neutral position, which is generally more constructive, especially in the early stages. The stance you take will change during the course of your contact with a client. Earlier in the process of change, you may need to veer towards the left-hand side of the table in Practice tip 2 and work in a less challenging and more non-directive way; later on it may become possible to be more direct in challenging. The same tension can also manifest within any given session, and one of the 'micro-skills' that develops in this work is the capacity to tune into this tension and vary the interviewing style accordingly (see Practice tips 2 and 3).

Practice tip 2: Maintaining a neutral, curious stance, especially in the early stages

Collusive stance	Earlier in process of change or resistant in interview	← → Neutral, useful stance	Later in process of change or receptive in interview	Accusatory stance
You are like mates		You form an alliance with the side of them that wants to change		You are like enemies

There is little challenge or conflict	You work to get them ready for challenge	You make gentle but persistent invitations to them to challenge themselves	You can challenge them directly and effectively	There is a high level of challenge and judgement
You sit alongside them to look at others' wrong behaviour	You work on their behaviours that harm themselves	You sit alongside them to look at their abusive behaviour	You work on their behaviours that harm others	You confront them with their wrongdoing
You empathize with them only as a victim of others	You empathize with them as a victim, sometimes for attunement and modelling	You empathize when they feel things that could motivate them to stop their abuse	You use their victim experience to help them empathize with others	You don't empathize at all

Practice tip 3

Focusing on the direct source of risk in domestic abuse child protection cases, try to ensure that:

- The perpetrator has been interviewed.
- Reports describe the pattern of control and abuse.
- Reports take the impact of DVA on the victim's parenting into account.
- Reports describe the victim's efforts to promote the safety and wellbeing of the children.
- There is no victim blaming language such as 'failure to protect'.
- Danger statements should be very clearly about the perpetrator – the protection plan and any mandation to

> programmes should mainly speak about the perpetrator
> rather than the victim.
>
> *Developed by Kate Iwi, Positive Change*
> *programme, Tower Hamlets, London*

Intervention approaches in other relationship contexts

The early experience of developing work with male perpetrators is likely to be useful in developing work with abuse in other relationship contexts, that is, starting with and understanding victims' experiences in their social and political context, but also seeking to understand the ways in which power is misused in the detail of their lives. This understanding can then inform a collaborative enquiry with individual perpetrators about the assumptions and expectations that lead them to believe that violence is acceptable or gives them permission to bully an intimate partner. A cognitive behavioural therapy (CBT) based approach can be helpful here, enquiring about specific incidents of abuse and the thoughts and emotions that accompanied the actions, then 'drilling down' to identify what must have been the underlying thinking and driving beliefs for their behaviour. Since this approach starts with the behaviour and does not make any assumptions about what is driving the behaviour, it can be useful for working with violence in any context – men's violence to women partners, women's violence to men partners and for those who are abusive in same-sex relationships.

Work with women who use violence in relationships

There is a lot of controversy in the research literature about the prevalence of female-to-male DVA. This seems to arise from the fact that while surveys in the general population indicate that men and women use some forms of violence in relationships at roughly equal rates, this does not fit with the experience of those working in front-line agencies such as the police, probation and children's services, where there is a significant majority of male perpetrators. (For a good summary of the research and an attempt at synthesizing some of the controversies in this area, see Johnson 2008.) It should be noted that whatever their motives, women who act aggressively towards their partner put themselves at significantly increased risk of suffering injury themselves. A woman's use of violence has been identified as the biggest single predictor of her future victimization (Stith *et al.* 2004). Further, Feld and Straus (1989) found that women who employed severe violence (kicking, biting, threatening with a weapon, etc.) against their non-violent spouse or partner were up to seven times more likely than women who did not to suffer severe victimization from their partner in the ensuing year.

When thinking about interventions with women using violence in relationships, any pre-programme assessment should seek to gain a detailed understanding of behavioural patterns and power dynamics. My experience of supervision with a range of agencies in the UK indicates that it may take some time after treatment has started to gain sufficient understanding of both partners' behaviour and the context in which female violence is taking place, to enable a properly tailored intervention plan (see Practice tip 4).

Practice tip 4: Assessment and intervention with women using violence and abuse in their relationship

On a case-by-case basis, enquire in detail about *patterns* of violent, abusive, threatening and controlling behaviour. Find out about:

- Frequency.

- Severity.

- Impact.

- The level of *coercive control* – the pattern of other controlling behaviours in the relationship, and the extent to which one partner lives in fear of the other.

These guidelines are, of course, applicable to any case of DVA.

Violence in LGBTQI couples

Prevalence studies indicate that LGBTQI (lesbian, gay, bisexual, transgender, queer and intersex) people are subjected to DVA at least as frequently, if not more frequently, than heterosexual people, with transgender participants reporting significantly higher rates than cisgender peers (Woulfe and Goodman 2018). In the UK an estimated

2.0 per cent of the population identified themselves as lesbian, gay or bisexual in 2018 (ONS 2018), and in the same year SafeLives IDVAs reported that a similar percentage of their cases identified as lesbian, gay or bisexual (SafeLives n.d.).

Of course, similar prevalence rates do not mean that the patterns of abuse and control experienced by victims are the same. LGBTQI people continue to experience specific forms of discrimination and stigma that can be manipulated and leveraged by a controlling intimate partner. Woulfe and Goodman (2018) have identified a range of such tactics of 'identity abuse':

- *Threatening to disclose a partner's LGBTQI status or 'out' them without their consent.* Doing so can expose the individual to harassment, threaten their employment or housing security, and limit their access to networks that may not be LGBTQI-affirming.

- *Undermining, attacking or denying a partner's identity as an LGBTQI person.* Using tactics such as accusing the participant of being straight, questioning their authenticity (for example, you're not a 'real' lesbian), or telling them they were not 'good enough' at their chosen gender identity.

- *Using homophobic or transphobic language.* Use of slurs or derogatory language regarding the target's sexual orientation or gender identity.

- *Isolating survivors from the LGBTQI community.* When isolation is used against LGBTQI survivors, the result may be even more damaging than for heterosexual and cisgender survivors. Many LGBTQI couples share a single community, and these communities of support or 'families of choice' often play a central role in providing social support for LGBTQI people who have experienced rejection from their families of origin.

These researchers found that trans and non-monosexual subgroups experience the highest levels of risk of identify abuse, which they speculate is linked to the higher levels of stigma they experience, and therefore the greater leveraging power of this form of abuse.

There is a more general lesson here for working with DVA, and specifically for work with perpetrators. It has long been recognized that

DVA consists of a range of tactics that people use to control those close to them. While all relationships feature power dynamics and all partners seek to influence their partners in some way or another, the capacity to abuse depends on the exertion of a credible threat that one partner will suffer some form of harm if they do not comply with the wishes of the other. The 'domains of control' that this threat is exercised in and the forms that abuse will take in any given relationship depend on the particular social and relationship context (Dutton and Goodman 2005). This means we need to enquire about the specific social, situational and relationship vulnerabilities that are being exploited by the perpetrator, and seek to understand how oppression and inequality in all their forms shape the choices and experience of the victim.

Practice tip 5: Making an assessment where the pattern of violence is unclear or contested by the partners

These guidelines apply to any assessment of relationship violence. However, where the pattern of violence is unclear or contested by the partners (such as in allegations of two-way violence and/ or violence in same-sex and LGBTQI (lesbian, gay, bisexual, transgender, queer (or questioning) and intersex) relationships), it is particularly important to avoid prior assumptions in the approach to an assessment. At the same time we need to be very wary about falling into simplistic formulations such as 'they are just as bad as each other'.

The first step to assessing effectively and responding appropriately, especially with children's welfare in mind, is to get as much detail as possible of the pattern of violence and abuse in the relationship.

The most useful way to do this is to enquire in detail with both partners (always in separate interviews) about the specific patterns of abuse in this and previous relationships. This means, on a case-by-case basis, looking in detail at overall patterns of violence and abuse, but also unpacking the dynamics of specific incidents, to get as much information as possible with each partner about:

- The frequency and severity of the full range of behaviours that fit within the definition of domestic abuse and coercive control.

- Whether there are patterns of behaviour as opposed to isolated incidents – incidents of abuse that may not look severe in isolation will give rise to greater concerns if they fit within a wider pattern of abuse and domination.

- Who is physically stronger and who has the greater capacity for violence and to induce fear. Who is afraid of whom? In what ways can one partner pose a credible threat to the other (whether that be threat of violence or any other way in which one person can cause the other fear or limit their freedom)?

- What the overall impact of the abuse has been on each partner.

- Whether one partner feels controlled in their day-to-day life (do they limit what they say, what they do, where they go, who they see, what they wear because of pressure or threat by the other partner?); what effect it would have on the child to live in a home where this type of abuse is going on.

Once you have broached the topic of DVA in the interview and got some sense of the trajectory of the relationship, it is useful to ask each partner to independently fill out 'Behaviour inventories' that ask about the frequency of specific abusive behaviours, such as those set out in Iwi and Newman (2015), which provide a very helpful aid to this kind of assessment.

References

Barnish, M. (2004) *Domestic Violence: A Literature Review*. London: HM Inspectorate of Probation.
Barter, C., McCarry, M., Berridge, D. and Evans, K. (2009) *Partner Exploitation and Violence in Teenage Intimate Relationships*. London: NSPCC.
Bywaters, P., Brady, G., Sparks, T., Bos, E., *et al.* (2015) 'Exploring inequities in child welfare and child protection services: Explaining the "inverse intervention law"'. *Children and Youth Services Review 57*, 98–105. doi:10.1016/j.childyouth.2015.07.017.
Caspi, J. (2012) *Sibling Aggression: Assessment and Treatment*. New York: Springer.
Duncan, R.D. (1999) 'Peer and sibling aggression: An investigation of intra- and extra-familial bullying.' *Journal of Interpersonal Violence 14*, 8, 871–886. doi:10.1177/088626099014008005.
Dutton, M. and Goodman, L. (2005) 'Coercion in intimate partner violence: Toward a new conceptualization.' *Sex Roles 52*, 743–756. doi:10.1007/s11199-005-4196-6.

Feld, S.L. and Straus, M.A. (1989) 'Escalation and desistance of wife assault in marriage.' *Criminology 27*, 1.

Forrester, D., Westlake, D. and Glynn, G. (2012) 'Parental resistance and social worker skills: Towards a theory of motivational social work.' *Child & Family Social Work 17*, 118–129.

Hanson, R.K. and Wallace-Capretta, S. (2004) 'Predictors of criminal recidivism among male batterers.' *Psychology, Crime & Law 10*, 4, 413–427.

Hare, R.D. and Neumann, C.S. (2005) 'Structural models of psychopathy.' *Current Psychiatry Reports 7*, 57–64.

Hester, M. (2009) 'Who does what to whom? Gender and domestic violence perpetrators.' *European Journal of Criminology 10*. doi:10.1177/1477370813479078.

Hester, M. and Newman, C. (2020) 'Considering "Treatment" and Gender in Programmes for Intimate Partner Violence Perpetrators.' In L. Gottzén, M. Bjørnholt and F. Boonzaier (eds) *Men, Masculinities and Intimate Partner Violence* (Chapter 10). Abingdon: Taylor & Francis.

Hester, M., Eisenstadt, N., Jones, C., and Morgan, K. (2017) *Evaluation of the Drive Project – A Pilot to Address High-risk Perpetrators of Domestic Abuse. Year 1 Feasibility Study.* Bristol: University of Bristol Drive Evaluation Team, Centre for Gender & Violence Research, University of Bristol.

Hester, M., Eisenstadt, N., Ortega-Avila, A., Morgan, K., Walker, S.J. and Bell, J. (2020) *Evaluation of the Drive Project – A Three-Year Pilot to Address High-Risk, High-Harm Perpetrators of Domestic Abuse.* Bristol: University of Bristol Drive Evaluation Team, Centre for Gender & Violence Research, University of Bristol.

Hotaling, G.T. and Sugarman, D.B. (1986) 'An analysis of risk markers in husband to wife violence: The current state of knowledge.' *Violence & Victims 1*, 2, 101–124.

Iwi, K. and Newman, C. (2011) *Picking up the Pieces after Domestic Violence: A Practical Resource for Supporting Parenting Skills.* London: Jessica Kingsley Publishers.

Iwi, K. and Newman, C. (2015) *Engaging with Perpetrators of Domestic Violence: Practical Techniques for Early Intervention.* London: Jessica Kingsley Publishers.

Johnson, M.P. (2008) *A Typology of Domestic Violence.* London: North Eastern University Press.

Kirby, S. and Penna, S. (2010) 'Policing Mobile Criminality: Towards a Situational Crime Prevention Approach to Organised Crime.' In K. Bullock, R.V. Clarke and N. Tilley (eds) *Situational Prevention of Organised Crime* (pp.193–212). Collumpton: Willan Publishing.

Kolko, D., Kazdin, A. and Day, B. (1996) 'Children's perspectives in the assessment of family violence.' *Child Maltreatment 1*, 2, 156–167.

Mandel, D. and Rankin, H. (2018) *Working with Men as Parents: Becoming Father-Inclusive to Improve Child Welfare Outcomes in Domestic Violence Cases.* Columbus, OH: Family and Youth Law Center, Capital University Law School.

ONS (Office for National Statistics) (2018) *Sexual Orientation, UK: 2018.* Bulletin. Available at: www.ons.gov.uk/peoplepopulationandcommunity/culturalidentity/sexuality/bulletins/sexualidentityuk/2018

ONS (2020) Domestic abuse victim characteristics, England and Wales: year ending March 2020. Available at: https://www.ons.gov.uk/peoplepopulationandcommunity/crimeandjustice/articles/domesticabusevictim characteristicsenglandandwales/yearendingmarch2020#age

Phillips, R., Kelly, L. and Westmarland, N. (2013) *Domestic Violence Perpetrator Programmes: An Historical Overview.* London and Durham: London Metropolitan University and Durham University.

Radford, L., Corral, S., Bradley, C. and Fisher, H. (2013) 'The prevalence and impact of child maltreatment and other types of victimization in the UK: Findings from a population survey of caregivers, children and young people and young adults.' *Child Abuse & Neglect 37*, 10, 801–813. Available at: http://dx.doi.org/10.1016/j.chiabu.2013.02.004

Safe Lives Insights Briefing (no date) *Safe Young Lives: Young People and Domestic Abuse.* Available at: https://safelives.org.uk/node/1112

Scourfield, J. (2006) 'The challenge of engaging fathers in the child protection process.' Special Issue on Gender and Child Welfare. *Critical Social Policy 26*, 2, 440–449.

Scourfield, J. (2014) 'Improving work with fathers to prevent child maltreatment.' *Child Abuse and Neglect 38*, 6, 974–981.

Stith, S.M., Smith, D.B., Penn, C.E., Ward, D.B. and Tritt, D. (2004) 'Intimate partner physical abuse perpetration and victimization risk factors: A meta-analytic review.' *Aggression and Violent Behaviour 10*, 1.

Strang, H., Sherman, L., Ariel, B., Chilton, S., *et al.* (2017) 'Reducing the harm of intimate Partner Violence: Randomized Controlled Trial of the Hampshire Constabulary CARA Experiment.' *Cambridge Journal of Evidence-Based Policing 1*, 160–173. doi:10.1007/s41887-017-0007-x.

Thompson-Walsh, C.A., Scott, K.L., Dyson, A. and Lishak, V. (2018) 'Are we in this together? Post-separation co-parenting of fathers with and without a history of domestic violence.' *Child Abuse Review 27*, 2, 137–149.

Westmarland, N. and Kelly, L. (2015) 'Leopards can't change their spots but domestic violence programmes do change lives.' 'Thought Leadership', Durham University, 14 January. Available at: www.dur.ac.uk/research/news/thoughtleadership/?itemno=23339

Westmarland, N., Kelly, L. and Chalder-Mills, J. (2010) *Domestic Violence Perpetrator Programmes: What Counts as Success?* London: Respect.

Woulfe, J. and Goodman, L. (2018) 'Identity abuse as a tactic of violence in LGBTQ communities: Initial validation of the identity abuse measure.' *Journal of Interpersonal Violence.* doi:10.1177/0886260518760018.

Chapter 9

Adolescent-to-Parent Violence and Abuse

Victoria Baker

Introduction

Adolescent-to-parent violence and abuse (APVA) was first identified by Harbin and Madden in 1979 who, drawing parallels from the domestic violence and abuse (DVA) research at the time, used the term 'battered parents syndrome' (Harbin and Madden 1979) to refer to physical violence from children to parents. Definitions have since broadened to include a range of non-physical abusive behaviours such as verbal, financial and psychological aggression, with the presentation and causes of abuse varying from family to family. What is now seen as abuse can cover fairly infrequent acts, to a more regular pattern of behaviour drawn out over a number of years and typically used to gain power and control over a parent. Both male and female adolescents can be 'perpetrators', but this is a gendered phenomenon, with mothers the more likely victims. However, mothers and fathers, sons and daughters can all be involved and, in this chapter, the complex dynamics of APVA will be explored. It is characterized by secrecy and shame, affecting not just adolescents and parents, but also entire families.

Support for families experiencing APVA is scarce, with few well-evaluated programmes to date. Services that are available have limited accessibility, with families subject to a service 'postcode lottery'. As we shall explore throughout the course of this chapter, parent abuse can be particularly hard to address, as both the presentation of abuse and its underlying causes vary according to individual and family circumstances, history and context. For practitioners this can mean uncertainty about the most appropriate course of action. To a certain extent, research is behind practice in understanding what works in tackling APVA. The research literature, although increasing in its coverage of APVA, has developed within the framework of the adult domestic violence research literature, and is still a long way off from providing a clear and cohesive account of its antecedents and the support and interventions that can be used to address it. The lack of a clear and coherent policy framework within which to place and address parent abuse in the UK means that support for families can often be patchy and inconsistent.

This chapter is designed to provide an overview of APVA for practitioners likely to come into contact with it, to highlight what is known about its nature, extent and consequences, the current evidence on best practice, and where to obtain further information or original source material. Interwoven throughout the chapter are policy and practice points to help guide practitioners' thinking on the subject, with a range of additional resources provided as further reading. It is beyond the scope of this chapter to be either a comprehensive account of all research in this area, or a 'how to' for parent abuse. As we shall discuss throughout this chapter, the varying nature of parent abuse and its causes makes this an impossible task. However, this chapter is a good place for practitioners to start their journey of understanding this complex social problem.

What is adolescent-to-parent violence and abuse?

APVA refers to a pattern of harmful physical, verbal, emotional/ psychological, economic and, in a few cases, sexually harassing/abusive behaviour that is used intentionally by adolescents to exert power and control over their parents:

> He'll scream and shout at me, awful abuse, absolutely awful abuse, he'll throw things at me, he'll punch holes in doors, he'll threaten to hit me, and this'll be all in front of my three little ones. (Mother, quoted in Holt 2009, p.4)

As highlighted by the quote above, it nearly always involves a constellation of overlapping forms of abuse and, in many cases, can also involve siblings. A number of other terms are also used to refer to the issue, including 'child-to-parent violence', 'battered parents syndrome', 'parent assault', 'parent-directed aggression' and 'parent abuse'. It involves a subversion of the typical power hierarchy within the parent–child relationship and is characterized by parental shame, minimization, secrecy, societal stigma and blame. Parents experiencing this problem can be biological parents, but also step-parents, adoptive and foster parents, or other caregivers with whom the child lives. In fact, recent research has suggested that adoptive families may be disproportionately affected (Thorley and Coates 2017). While the term 'adolescent' is used here, children instigating abuse can be younger, although most commonly fall between the ages of 11 to 18. It is the most under-researched and invisible form of family abuse in the UK, with only recent recognition of it as a social problem in the form of the Home Office document *Information Guide: Adolescent to Parent Violence and Abuse (APVA)* (Home Office 2015).

In the UK there is no legal definition of parent abuse, with variation in the terminology used and a lack of any official language to record cases. Variation in terminology and definitions is problematic for a number of reasons. As Holt (2013) argues, not only is it problematic for researchers attempting to measure prevalence and draw comparisons across studies, but it is also problematic in terms of parents' and children's 'ability and readiness to articulate their experiences and seek help and support' (Holt 2013, p.3). It impacts on the ways in which practitioners, commissioners and policy-makers are conceptualizing and responding to the issue – for example, whether it is dealt with as a case of child delinquency, crime or welfare. As we shall see, parent abuse does not readily fit into any of these frameworks, being its own distinct social problem requiring a range of distinct and adaptive solutions.

The term 'abuse' (rather than 'aggression' or simply 'violence') is used here to highlight the harm that is caused and the fact that behaviour is not limited to physical violence alone. One of the challenging aspects of parent abuse is that it defies the typical view of a powerful abuser and vulnerable victim. It is important to say here that parent abuse should not be confused with acts of self-defence, one-off incidents of aggression borne out of extreme stress, or aggression that may be due to developmental or neurological conditions such as autism or global developmental delay (Gallagher 2008). Although such aggression may be harmful to parents, it is not 'abusive' in the sense that aggressive or violent behaviour is not necessarily a pattern of intentionally harmful behaviour used to gain power and control over parents. Furthermore, such behaviour may actually be protective in nature, acting to reduce abuse experienced by adolescents themselves or by other family members.

The following are descriptions of the various categories of abuse, taken from a range of reports by parents, practitioners and, in some cases, adolescents themselves.

Physical abuse includes, but is not limited to, pushing, punching, kicking, pinning, pulling hair and twisting skin, throwing, biting, hitting with objects and, in some cases trapping in the home. It can also include less common but more severe forms of violence such as the use of weapons (such as knives), strangling, scalding, poisoning and threats to life involving arson and suffocation. Physical abuse typically represents an escalation of abuse, with forms such as verbal and emotional preceding it. As highlighted by the two quotations below, physical abuse can result in physical pain and injury (both short and long term), as well as having an impact on parents' emotional wellbeing:

> …[he] actually grabbed a dog leash and whacked it across my knuckles, he cut my knuckle open. Just…little things like that. (Mother, quoted in Howard and Rottem 2008, p.37)

> We started fightin' and then it ended up me throwin' things at her and it smashin' near her and then she was getting' hurt and…she got badly hurt…so that's why she phoned the police. (14-year-old female describing physical violence towards her mother, quoted in Baker 2021)

Verbal abuse includes, but is not limited to, shouting, swearing, name-calling and verbal threats. Verbal abuse is used to intimidate, challenge, frustrate, demean and undermine a parent's sense of self (Cottrell 2001). In many cases, verbal abuse is part of emotional and psychological abuse, involving threats, mind games and attacks on a parent's identity. Non-verbal communication such as refusing to speak ('the silent treatment'), scoffing, sniggering and laughing in a parent's face can also be used as a way of rejecting, punishing and undermining. Verbal abuse is a destructive form of communication (Eckstein 2004) that can be very detrimental to parents and the parent–child relationship. It can be a precursor to more serious forms of abuse, such as physical violence, and is often the first form of abuse to be experienced (Holt 2013). The form that the abuse takes has also been reported by some mothers to mimic that of previous partners who were also abusive (Howard and Rottem 2008).

Like...I yell at her a lot...I don't wanna push her or anything out of the way, so I just shout at her to move. (17-year-old female describing verbal abuse towards her mother, quoted in Baker 2021)

Erm, like I call her a rat an' that sometimes. (15-year-old male describing verbal abuse towards his mother, quoted in Baker 2021)

Psychological/emotional abuse includes, but is not limited to, undermining and humiliation, the use of threats to incite fear and intimidation, withholding affection to emotionally hurt, coercion to manipulate and gain control, playing 'mind games' to frustrate, intimidate and punish. Parents cite emotional and psychological abuse as being the most damaging form, and many say it made them feel like they were going 'crazy' (Cottrell 2001; Edenborough *et al.* 2008; Howard and Rottem 2008).

As with other forms of abuse, psychological and emotional abuse can also be verbal, and/or physical – for example, the abuse of space by following parents around the house and preventing them from leaving. Psychological and emotional abuse can be 'obstructive' (Stewart, Burns and Leonard 2007), involving the erosion of a parent's social support, blocking opportunities for social interaction or damaging relationships by telling lies or abusing extended family or friends.

I would just follow her around the house...not doing anything, I would literally just...that's another tactic I used to do...it wouldn't be violent, it wouldn't be anything, I'd literally just...follow her...around the house. If she went to the toilet, I'd go into the toilet with her...she sat down, I'd sit down right next to her. 'Cos I knew it...I knew it annoyed her. (18-year-old female, quoted in Baker 2021)

Psychological and emotional abuse often reflects directly the nature of the parent–child relationship (Holt 2013). For example, it can include direct attacks on a parent's identity as an effective caregiver. It can involve threats to 'go to social services' or the police to report abuse (which may or may not have happened) (Cottrell 2001; Cottrell and Monk 2004; Eckstein 2004), or threats to leave the family home. There is often a self-destructive nature that is very specific to the manipulation of the parent–child bond, such as threats to harm themselves or their life chances through reckless or dangerous behaviour (Calvete *et al.* 2014).

I was like, 'I'll file reports on you 'cos you...you hit me', even though she didn't. And I'd go to the levels of getting my friends to hit me…to make bruises…like, on my arms. (18-year-old female, quoted in Baker 2021)

Although some of these acts may seem like 'typical' teenage behaviour, what separates these acts out as 'abuse' is their repeated nature, and their use to gain power and control over parents and the household (Cottrell 2001; Holt 2013). Parents have reported the repeated nature of these acts as being at the heart of the harm caused by abuse (Holt 2013), contributing to emotional hurt and a sense of 'walking on egg shells'.

Economic abuse includes, but is not limited to, the destruction of property in the home or the property itself, including punching or kicking holes in walls, breaking doors and windows and smashing household objects (Condry and Miles 2014; Cottrell 2001; Howard and Rottem 2008). It can also include the destruction of parents' personal items such as objects that hold sentimental value, as well as the theft of goods and money.

Erm, because, I was feelin' violent, I was rippin' me curtains down. (14-year-old female, quoted in Baker 2021)

The destruction of property can have a psychological impact, causing fear of future physical violence (Cottrell 2001).

Money can also be extorted from parents, often through manipulation around the potential for harm to the child if debts (particularly drug debts) are not paid. Indirect economic effects can also be seen if the abuse undermines a parent's ability to maintain employment (due to time needed away from work or inability to work effectively); puts tenancies at risk (due to property damage) (Hunter, Nixon and Parr 2010); or results in legal penalties for parents from the adolescent's anti-social and criminal behaviour (Cottrell 2001; Holt 2009, 2013).

…she nearly got fired loads of times because of me because…of me truanting and school demanding that she came and got me…from the police station and stuff like that. I nearly got her fired from her job and then we'd have been…probably made homeless 'cos she had no job an' stuff. (18-year-old female, quoted in Baker 2021)

Economic abuse, as with verbal abuse, appears early on in the parent abuse dynamic and has been found to be a fairly common form of abuse (Holt 2013; Howard and Rottem 2008). As Holt (2013) points out, the specific nature of the parent–child relationship and the legal and financial responsibilities the parent has for the child act as a lever for manipulation within the context of parent abuse.

> He literally broke so many of my things. Yeah, taunting me, thinking it was all a game to him. 'What am I going to break next?' and he would break them. (Mother, quoted in Howard and Rottem 2008, p.39)

Sexual abuse includes, but is not limited to, sexual assault and the use of sexualized behaviour and language to intimidate and demean. Adolescent-to-parent sexual abuse is relatively rare in the research literature, although it is likely to be the most under-reported of all the forms of abuse due to the nature of the parent–child relationship. Research with mothers has identified adolescents coercing mothers into sexual behaviour with friends as a means to humiliate and degrade them (Howard and Rottem 2008), and the use of sexually explicit and degrading language.

> …the most derogatory language, it's just disgusting, but to a point where it just became so normal that that's how they would talk to me every day. They'd be like that from the minute you wake up to the time they go to bed. The derogatory things that come out of my boys' mouths is a major concern…not just calling me 'slut' and 'whore' and things like that, really disgusting things that they've told me to do with my friend Amanda because they hate her…they've gone and told me to do sexual things. (Mother, quoted in Howard and Rottem 2008, p.38)

Consequences of abuse for families

APVA can have harmful consequences for parents, siblings, other family members living in the home, as well as for the adolescents instigating abuse. Evidence for the harm that parent abuse causes comes primarily from interviews and focus groups with parents, but also from practitioners working with families.

Parents

Harmful effects for parents can include minor and major physical injuries (including long-term injuries), emotional distress and trauma including feelings of guilt and shame, mental health difficulties such as anxiety and depression, the physical symptoms of stress, destruction to property and the home, financial and legal difficulties, and impacts on social supports and personal freedoms. It can also damage parents' identity as parents, and undermine their confidence and capacity to parent effectively. Further, for the parent, their relationship with the abusive child can be damaged, both in the short and longer term, with other family relationships also strained or damaged. This is particularly relevant for adoptive parents, where APVA has been highlighted as a significant factor in adoption breakdowns (Selwyn and Meakings 2016). For many parents the impact of emotional abuse exceeds that of the physical symptoms of abuse, remaining long after the abuse itself has stopped.

> The physical could hurt you more, but the emotional is going to last the longest. You can get over a bruise. (Parent, quoted in Eckstein 2004, p.375)

> …I can hear her crying after every one of them. After every fight, she'd cry. (18-year-old female, quoted in Baker 2021)

> …it's ruined my relationship between me and my mum. (14-year-old female, quoted in Baker 2021)

Siblings

Siblings can also feel the impact of APVA, either directly via physical or verbal abuse from abusive brothers or sisters, or indirectly by witnessing abuse or receiving less attention from parents whose capacity is taken up with trying to manage the relationship with the abusive child. In some cases this can result in siblings mirroring the abuse they witness. They can also experience trauma through the loss of the sibling relationship, especially in cases where children are removed from the family home.

For families, the consequences of abuse can be short-lived such as cuts and grazes, or can be longer term, such as with the separation of children from the family home and the impact on family relationships. Parents may also feel the 'double stigma' (Holt 2011) attached to parenting a problematic child and experiencing domestic violence.

The consequences and impacts are not uniform across all families, but will be specific to the interactions between the individual characteristics of parents and their children, as well as the family context (including history) within which the abuse takes place. As with all forms of family abuse, the continual cycle of abuse and its extended nature compounds the negative impacts felt, and the secretive nature of abuse helps to maintain this cycle.

Adolescents

For adolescents instigating the abuse, they can feel emotional distress in the form of guilt, isolation within the home, difficulties around self-esteem and damaged family relationships. They can experience injuries or harm from punching and kicking doors, walls and windows, and from being restrained, from placing themselves in danger, from risky behaviour around sex and drug misuse, running away from home and self-harm. There can be legal implications for their behaviour, which places them at risk of criminalization and reduced life chances through a lack of engagement with education. Adolescents instigating abuse may also be experiencing mental health issues and problems with schooling and peers, which can be both outcomes of and risk factors for abuse. Lastly, as APVA has been identified as a significant factor in adoption breakdown, it has implications in terms of their emotional wellbeing as a result of inconsistent care arrangements.

Adolescents may also be experiencing trauma from their own experiences of abuse or from exposure to domestic violence between parents. It is important to understand that within the context of APVA, parents and their children can be both victims and perpetrators of abuse.

> And I think obviously, you are gonna feel like, I felt like I wasn't good enough and I was not good enough for anyone because I was violent and stuff, so obviously I took the overdose. (17-year-old female, quoted in Baker 2021)

The onset of abuse

Parents often report that abuse develops gradually over time, starting with verbal forms and escalating into physical abuse and psychological manipulation and control. For some families, however, abusive behaviour can be experienced from children early on, with more gene-ralized patterns of aggression. The most common age for the onset of abuse is around 12 to 14 (Cottrell 2001; Haw 2010; Holt 2013), with

15 being the peak age and 18 representing the age at which behaviours tend to significantly decline (Holt 2013). Daughters instigating abuse tend to be reported as younger than their male counterparts. Although the typical age for the onset of abuse is between 12 to 14, parents have reported abuse as early as five years, sometimes reflecting a broader pattern of early onset aggression, which is often not reported to support agencies until adolescence, when the behaviour has become unmanageable for parents. For the purposes of this chapter, APVA relates to children aged between 11 and 18, reflecting the developmental stage of adolescence rather than earlier childhood or later young adulthood. Parents experiencing abuse typically fall between the ages of 41 and 50 (Holt 2013), reflective of parents caring for teenage children.

But when does 'normal' teenage behaviour become 'abuse'? Practitioners, parents and researchers often comment that the line between what is 'typical' teenage behaviour (such as challenge, defiance and moodiness) and what is 'abusive' behaviour is difficult to draw, and that this difficulty contributes to the silence around the issue. In her work with families in Canada, Barbara Cottrell draws a useful distinction, explaining that 'There is a difference, however, between resistance and aggression, between separating from a parent and trying to take control of a parent, between "normal" teenage behaviour and "parent abuse"' (Cottrell 2001, p.3). In this case it is the use of threats, force and manipulation that is the key difference between 'typical' teenage behaviour and that which is abusive.

Denial about when children's behaviour becomes abusive contributes to the secrecy around this hidden form of family violence, with many parents minimizing the abuse they experience. As with all forms of family abuse, there is significant self-blame, shame and guilt, with a reluctance on the part of parents to seek help due to the fear of either being separated from their child or criminalizing them. As we shall explore later, the lack of appropriate support options for parents and the judgement and blame experienced from agencies when parents do seek help all contribute to the stigma and shame around this issue.

Identifying parent abuse

Indicators of APVA may be observed in the adolescent, the parent being victimized or in siblings. As with other types of violence, some of the indicators are not specific to APVA and may be signs of other troubles and adversities in the adolescent's life.

Identifying parent abuse: What to look out for when working with families

- Parent abuse can present in a variety of different ways and there is no one 'type' of family it affects more than others.

- However, parents struggling to set boundaries for fear of their child's reaction is a good indicator of the dynamic taking place.

- More subtle indicators of abuse can be a decrease in school attendance or a decrease in parents' attendance at work. Young people regularly going missing from home may also be an indicator of the issue.

- Sometimes siblings starting to misbehave or displaying evidence of harm (either emotional or physical) can indicate parent abuse is present.

- Parent abuse is a hidden harm – parents often do not want to talk about the violence and abuse as they are worried they may be judged for their parenting or family situation. This often means parents are not forthcoming about the abuse.

- Parents and young people may have other vulnerabilities, such as mental health, developmental or physical health needs that could be shaping the development and maintenance of abuse.

- Parents with physical or mental health needs are more vulnerable to this type of abuse occurring.

- Young people with neurodevelopmental disorders such as autistic spectrum conditions (ASCs) or attention deficit hyperactivity disorder (ADHD) may have difficulties in regulating their emotions, understanding the perspectives of others, and communicating their thoughts and feelings. They are also more likely to feel overwhelmed by environmental stimulus.

How common is it? Prevalence and incidence

APVA has been appearing with increasing regularity on practitioners' caseloads:

[Practitioners attending the courses] say that they get so many calls every day about child to parent violence. And loads of social workers are reporting that's the big issue that they're working on. (Practitioner-trainer, quoted in Condry and Miles 2012, p.161)

However, prevalence estimates for APVA still vary widely in the research literature, in relation to the type of abuse measured (for example, physical, verbal, psychological or financial), the sample that estimates are taken from (for example, clinical or general population) and the research methods used (for example, randomly sampled population surveys or prevalence in clinical case files). Along with the hidden nature of APVA, this means that establishing reliable prevalence estimates can be particularly difficult, with any estimates most likely significantly under-reporting the extent of the problem. Across the various types of research, rates of physical violence towards parents have been identified as being between 3 and 29 per cent, with lower rates reflecting more serious violence and higher rates reflecting the high-risk samples from which they are taken.

In the UK, data on lifetime prevalence comes from a study of university students (Browne and Hamilton 1998) in which 14.5 per cent self-reported violence towards parents and 3.8 per cent more serious violence over their lifetime. Data on yearly prevalence comes from an analysis of Metropolitan Police reports between 2009 and 2010 (Condry and Miles 2014), where 1892 cases of APVA involving 13- to 19-year-olds were identified within the Greater London area. Incidents included physical violence, threats of violence, sexual assault, robbery and criminal damage to the home. An analysis of calls received by the parent support helpline 'Parentline' between 2007 and 2008 (Parentline Plus 2008) identified 2000 cases of child-to-parent physical violence in the UK, which then nearly doubled over the following two years (Parentline Plus 2010). Non-physical aggression from children to their parents was identified in 22,537 cases, indicating that the issue is not just one of physical violence alone. This, along with practitioners reporting increasing numbers of parent abuse cases on their caseloads (Holt and Retford 2013; Nixon 2012), makes this a prevalent social problem requiring attention.

More reliable estimates of APVA come from the USA and Canada in the form of large population studies using random samples – a method that reduces self-selection bias and increases the chance that results are representative of the wider populations from which they are drawn. Although the majority of these surveys are over 40 years old, data collected indicates estimates of between 6.5 and 10.8 per cent for 11- to 18-year-olds admitting to 'hitting' parents at least once over the previous one to three years (Peek, Fischer and Kidwell 1985). Once 'trivial' incidents were removed from the sample and the recall period reduced to 12 months, rates reduced to around 5 per cent, with even fewer (around 1 per cent) resulting in injury (Agnew and Huguley 1989). Reports from parents in another USA-based population survey – the *National Family Violence Survey* (1975) – identified rates of 20.2 per cent physical violence towards mothers and 14 per cent towards fathers, when asking parents whether they had been 'hit' by their child over the previous 12 months (Ulman and Straus 2003). Lastly, a Canadian-based study combining both parent and child reports – The *Quebec Longitudinal Study of Kindergarten Children* (1986–1996) – found that physical aggression was reported in 13.8 per cent of cases towards mothers and 11 per cent towards fathers, with verbal aggression being higher – reported in 64 per cent of cases towards mothers and 56 per cent towards fathers (Pagani *et al.* 2004, 2009).

However, as such questions tend to be embedded within larger national surveys on broader subjects such as crime, childhood and youth or broader violence, often the information collected is not specific to APVA, excludes certain age groups or genders, or has very surface-level information on physical aggression alone. Although community studies do provide greater detail on non-physical forms of parent abuse, they are typically based on non-random community samples and as such should be viewed with caution.

Who is involved? Victims and perpetrators
Gender
APVA can involve both sons and daughters abusing mothers and fathers. However, to a large extent, the research methods and populations studied determine the profile of victims and perpetrators. For example, studies drawing on crime reports, clinical case files and evaluations of community-based support programmes tend to identify a profile

of mothers being abused by their teenage sons, with epidemiological surveys presenting a less gendered picture of mothers and fathers abused by both sons and daughters. On balance, mothers do appear to be the primary targets of abuse (Gallagher 2008; Holt 2013; Ibabe, Jaureguizar and Bentler 2013), possibly due to their role as primary caregiver, the fact they are more likely to be setting boundaries and spending time with adolescents than fathers (Agnew and Huguley 1989; Ulman and Straus 2003), but also potentially because of 'hyper masculinity' in sons and the lower status of women in society (Wilcox 2012). Although criminal justice reports show a greater proportion of sons perpetrating violence to mothers, there is some evidence pointing to a narrowing of this gap (Strom *et al.* 2014). A number of studies, however, found gender was related to the type of abuse used, with sons more likely to use physical violence and daughters more likely to use psychological violence. Some studies have found daughters more frequently using weapons than sons (Charles 1986), although data are taken from clinical and court cases, and so are not necessarily reflective of the general population.

Ethnicity, religion, social class and family structure

There is no conclusive evidence to suggest that the prevalence of APVA varies according to ethnicity, religion, social class and family structure. However, a number of studies found fewer cases in families holding strong religious beliefs (Elliott *et al.* 2011; Paulson, Coombs and Landsverk 1990; Peek *et al.* 1985). It is also important to recognize that although there is little conclusive evidence in relation to ethnicity and family income, experiences of ethnicity and social class are important in understanding the family context for abuse, in addition to issues such as help-seeking behaviour and the way support services are experienced by families (Holt 2013).

Why does parent abuse happen?

No one theory or combination of theories is adequate to explain all cases of APVA that arise. Existing theories can broadly be categorized into individual (child) level, family level and societal level explanations, with interactions within and between all levels. Although it is beyond the scope of this chapter to explore all of these theories of parent abuse, those with the strongest evidence base are detailed below.

Individual (child) level explanations

Gender: The gender of both the child and parent has a bearing on the development of parent abuse, with sons reported as the most likely instigators of abuse and mothers the most likely victims. Some adolescents speaking in interviews have said that the closeness of the mother–child bond made it more likely they would lash out and express their feelings to mothers than they would fathers, with fathers more likely to be feared (Cottrell 2001). An upward trend in female adolescent violence has been mirrored by an increase in cases of girls' violence to mothers (Cottrell 2001; Holt 2013). This may reflect changes in identification and reporting practices and/or changes in girls' behaviour. One explanation is that it may be a reaction against gender socialization and the perception that 'girls are timid, passive and fearful' (Cottrell 2001, p.20), and girls' anger towards mothers perceived to be weak for living with violent partners, thereby exposing themselves and their children to domestic violence.

Adolescence: As adolescence is a developmental stage characterized by developing agency and personal autonomy, the onset of adolescence has been highlighted as an important factor in the development of parent abuse. Biological and social changes – for example, changes in mood, physical size and social demands and expectations – experienced by young people can provide the context for greater challenge and conflict, for example when parents attempt to curtail personal freedoms and autonomy. The developmental context within which parent abuse takes place therefore – as a period where greater personal autonomy is sought but where adult responsibilities are yet to take effect – is important to take into consideration when understanding the various dynamics that play out at the individual, family and societal levels.

Mental health and behavioural disorders: Mental health and behavioural difficulties such as depression, conduct disorder, obsessive compulsive disorder, oppositional defiant disorder, ADHD, and in some cases schizophrenia and bipolar disorder have all been linked to parent abuse and given as potential explanatory factors (for a review, see Simmons *et al.* 2018). However, often the supporting research is clinical in nature, dealing with populations who are more likely to experience such disorders and cases that are at the more extreme end of the spectrum of abuse. Further, research is often a snapshot in time, meaning there is no ability to assess whether such mental health conditions or behavioural disorders are causing, or are caused by, the parent abuse dynamic. It is also possible that those diagnosed with some form of disorder may be more likely to be reported.

Where mental health problems and parent abuse are co-occurring, parents have the difficult task of attempting to address the needs of the child in relation to both, and in some cases parents have reported the mental health needs of the child as obscuring the need to address the abuse the parents are being exposed to (Cottrell 2001).

Self-esteem and 'mattering': Poor self-esteem, as a result of not feeling heard and feeling that you do not 'matter' in the family home, has been identified as a potential explanation of abuse. Elliott and colleagues (2011) argue that children who do not feel they matter can lash out violently in response to the shame and frustration they feel within the context of the home.

Stress: Stress theories have also been used as explanations of parent abuse, with pressures around school and peer groups cited as stress factors that can result in violent outbursts at home (Cottrell 2001). Such outbursts can (as with family abuse) be a coping mechanism used by adolescents to establish control in a situation where they feel they have none.

Substances and risky behaviour: Factors such as adolescent substance misuse can impact the parent abuse dynamic in a number of ways. First, it can alter the young person's mood, making them more irritable and likely to engage in aggressive communication with parents; second, parents' knowledge that the young person is misusing substances can result in harsher parenting, the limiting of freedoms and greater stress in the parent–child relationship; and third, it can result in a lack of engagement by the young person in school or work (Cottrell 2001), which can place further strain on the relationship as well as stress on the young person. Lastly, interviews with parents have highlighted that their children can become more demanding when they are misusing substances, with some demanding money to buy drugs or alcohol, and getting abusive when these demands are refused (Cottrell 2001).

Parent abuse can also take place within a context of wider adolescent violence and criminality including theft, destruction of property and assault. However, such behaviours, although contributing to the parent abuse dynamic, could also be reactions to other factors such as domestic violence or other environmental stressors.

It is important that individual child level factors are understood within the contexts in which they have developed, thus avoiding overly simplified or overly deterministic explanations of parent abuse that problematize children or frame them as 'deviant'. Individual factors relating to the child often arise in response to family and societal level factors – for example, mental health or behavioural problems as a result of the trauma of child abuse or domestic violence. Thus they may be experiencing and displaying symptoms which, although contributing to the parent abuse dynamic, could actually be the result of factors within the home environment.

Family level explanations

Family abuse: Other forms of family abuse, such as domestic violence and abuse (DVA) between parents as well as direct abuse experienced by the child, can be risk factors for the development of APVA (Hunter *et al.* 2010). Witnessing DVA between parents can affect adolescents in a number of ways, but one consequence can be in the development of abusive behaviour, either towards parents or later intimate partners (Laporte *et al.* 2011). Although some adolescent aggression within the context of interparental violence and abuse can be defensive in nature – that is, in protection of a parent – outside of this, adolescents can take on the role of abuser, particularly in cases where mothers have left a DVA relationship and are acting as the single parent for the child (mostly sons). This can be due to a number of reasons such as social learning and identification with the abusive parent, or frustration and anger at the break-up of the family unit. It is important to say here that although there may be an intergenerational element to parent abuse (as with other forms of family abuse), not all children experiencing DVA in the home go on to become victims or victimizers; in fact, the majority go on to live lives free from abuse (Holt 2013; Wilcox 2012). However, for some who have been abused or have witnessed abuse, violence and aggression can be a form of gaining control in a context where adolescents feel they have none (Brezina 1999; Cottrell 2001).

Parenting: The ways in which parenting is practised is the dominant explanation used in relation to parent abuse (Holt 2013), with theories around the quality of attachment and parenting styles being the most commonly cited. A number of studies have found that adolescents who do not feel close to or accepted by their parents are more likely to instigate parent abuse. With respect to parenting style, links to permissive (lacking rules and boundaries), authoritarian (overly punitive and controlling) and inconsistent parenting have been identified. However, it is important to remember that such parenting can be in response to parent abuse and the helplessness that leads from it, or in response to other stress factors such as DVA. In terms of the latter, some parents (usually mothers) can be more vulnerable to abusive behaviour from their children due to the guilt and self-blame surrounding historic partner abuse. Such feelings can result in an overly indulgent parenting style where the parent is trying to 'make up' for the previous traumas inflicted on the child (Wilcox 2012).

It is important when responding to cases of parent abuse that we move away from the dominant discourse of the 'parenting deficit' and 'problem families' that can serve to blame parents (particularly mothers) for the abuse that they are experiencing. This can serve only to increase the harm that abuse causes in the short and longer term.

Family structure: Changes in family structure can also contribute to changes in the parent–child dynamic, with parents (most often mothers) becoming the target of the adolescent's frustration and hurt around the loss of a parent (Cottrell 2001). This can be particularly acute when previous parental relationships involved violence and abuse, where the child may reproduce those behaviours or may be manipulated to punish the non-abusing parent.

Family stress: Family stressors such as money difficulties, divorce, housing and work can all contribute to strained parent–child interactions, with adolescents sometimes 'acting out' in order to gain attention or communicate they are distressed in some way (Cottrell 2001).

Family interaction and communication: Negative communication habits within the family have also been identified as possible contributors to parent abuse. For example, a focus on the abuse and the child as 'the problem' serves to place the abuse at the centre of family life to the detriment of all other areas, which may actually feed the abuse dynamic.

Further, problematizing the child can result in other family members ignoring their own role and can result in the child feeling labelled, potentially then living up to that label due to frustration and shame. Adolescent aggression can also be a way of communicating when rules of behaviour within the home are overly strict and when adolescents have no forum to voice rational challenge. Aggression by the young person can then result in patterns of coercive communication within the home, where parents can end up giving into demands to prevent further aggressive episodes (Eckstein 2004). However, such coercive communication habits only serve to further entrench the parent abuse dynamic.

Societal level explanations

In terms of societal level explanations of parent abuse, these are focused mainly around gender inequalities, norms supporting violence against women and socialization, particularly the development of 'hyper masculinity' in adolescent boys and attitudes justifying violence by men. Men's continued dominance over women in society sends a message to young people that the violence and dominance of women is normal and acceptable, and in certain circumstances, this can take the form of parent abuse, particularly towards mothers. Also acting at the societal level is the normalization of violence through the media, which often has a gendered aspect of men being violent towards women. Media depictions of violence can serve to desensitize young people to violence and glamorize its use. However, there are few studies that explore the potential societal level factors involved in the development of parent abuse, and greater research is needed in this area to draw firmer conclusions.

Some limitations of the evidence

One of the key issues in understanding the causes or 'etiology' of parent abuse is that the majority of research looks only at a snapshot of parent abuse cases at one point in time. This is known as cross-sectional research and limits the extent to which we can say with confidence which factors are likely 'predictors' of parent abuse. This means that quite often research may identify factors such as poor mental health, substance misuse or parental stress and anxiety as being present in those young people and parents experiencing the abuse dynamic, but it is not clear to what extent these factors caused or were a result of the abuse. For example, poor parent mental health could be both a cause of and a result of parent abuse. Without longitudinal research, the extent to which we can establish the causal path is fairly limited.

Parent abuse policy and practice in the UK

Despite being recognized as a serious social problem, both internationally and in the UK, there is a distinct policy 'silence' around the subject of APVA (Condry and Miles 2012; Holt and Retford 2013; Hunter *et al.* 2010), with very little guidance for practitioners on how to address the issue and indeed, which agencies should be responsible for addressing it. This has resulted in a situation where responses to parent abuse in the UK are inconsistent, with availability of programmes varying greatly from area to area. Interviews with practitioners from across youth offending, child protection, victim support, health, domestic violence support and the police have highlighted that there is inconsistency in how different agencies understand and talk about parent abuse, and that the way agencies frame parents and young people as 'troublesome' leads to parents feeling ashamed and blamed and less likely to report abuse when it does occur.

> Until you came up with the term 'parent abuse' I must admit I really didn't think of it like that. (CYP-Marat Practitioner, quoted in Holt and Retford 2013, p.3)

When parents do reach out for help, the range of statutory agencies and voluntary and community services often fail to respond appropriately (Holt 2009; Hunter *et al.* 2010; Parentline Plus 2010). Parents often report that their concerns are not being taken seriously (particularly by the police), or that they are blamed for the abuse they are experiencing.

But why is there such a policy silence? Unfortunately, the ambiguity and secrecy that surrounds the issue has limited both its recognition and visibility in policy and also its exploration within research. APVA inverts the typical power dynamics in the home. Practitioners have highlighted how the nature of the parent–child relationship complicates and limits the service responses they can provide, particularly in cases where parents and children are both victims and perpetrators of abuse. Currently in the UK there is no legal definition of APVA, and although it shares similarities with DVA, it does not sit neatly under the current UK definition that emphasizes violence and abuse only between those aged 16 and over – unhelpful for addressing parent abuse that often begins in early adolescence. Child protection policies have until recently predominantly viewed children as victims of violence from adults. While peer-to-peer abuse is increasingly recognized, violence by children and adolescents has traditionally been the preserve of youth justice and community safety policies (Firmin 2019), with definitions of youth offending being limited to public spaces rather than the home, and with parents viewed as being responsible for youth violence rather than as potential victims of it. Policy responses, such as the issuing of Parenting Orders (typically to mothers), has served only to further victimize parents for the abuse they are subjected to, rather than providing the support they so badly require.

Encouragingly, in 2015 the Home Office released a practitioner guide entitled *Information Guide: Adolescent to Parent Violence and Abuse (APVA)* (Home Office 2015) in an attempt to provide practitioners from a range of agencies with a better understanding of the issues and how to respond. This covers key areas such as assessment and signposting to suitable agencies and services that can provide further support. Importantly, the document also raises the profile of parent abuse, and marks its first recognition as a serious social problem requiring attention. The guide is a first step in developing parent abuse policy and practice in the UK, but more specific agency-level guidance is needed on how to recognize and address cases when they do arise, and the most appropriate referral pathways to be used to ensure families receive the right support at the right time.

Parent abuse interventions

It is beyond the scope of this chapter to detail all approaches to supporting families experiencing parent abuse. This section highlights some of the better-evidenced programmes currently being used in the UK, with a summary of the broader types of practice approaches highlighted in the research literature.

Currently there are few well-evaluated programmes that are designed to address parent abuse specifically. The programmes that exist draw on a range of different theories about APVA, and most are adaptations of work with children with behavioural and family problems. Some are multi-level in focus, addressing issues for the individual child, family and other relationships. Some combine evidence-based strategies for behavioural problems in children such as cognitive behavioural therapy (CBT), with family communication and skills building, or anger management, conflict resolution and strengthening parenting relationships after DVA. They tend to use a combination of group work and one-to-one work, with peer support for parents being a key component. Common to the programmes is work with both parents and young people responsible for the abuse, providing a non-judgemental environment that recognizes and makes visible the issue of parent abuse, while teaching the skills and techniques to improve communication and family relationships. While Table 9.1 is not exhaustive, getting in touch with your local youth offending service, child protection agency or domestic violence support organization can often be a good way of finding out if there are any services local to your area.

Table 9.1 APVA services and programmes in the UK

Service/ programme	Type of intervention	Further information
Break4Change (various locations)	Group; parent and young person; solution-focused, restorative, skills-based, non-violent resistance	Email: Break4Change@riseuk.org.uk
Non-Violent Resistance (NVR) (various locations)	Group; parent and carer; empowerment, relationship-focused, parent behaviour, whole family, conflict management, self-care	Email: enquiries@nvrpc.org.uk Website: https://nvrpc.org.uk
Respect Young People's Programme (RYPP) (various locations)	Group and individual; parent and young person; CBT, anger management, conflict resolution skills, narrative therapy, systemic, NVR, solution-focused, arts-based	Tel: 0203 559 6650 Email: info@respect.uk.net Website: www.respect.uk.net
Step-Up (various locations)	Group; parent, young person and whole family; skills-based, restorative, cognitive behavioural, Duluth model	Website: www.kingcounty.gov/courts/superior-court/juvenile/step-up.aspx Local websites of various youth offending services across the UK

Service/ programme	Type of intervention	Further information
Who's in Charge? (various locations)	Group; parent and carer; skills-based, empowerment, solution-focused, behaviour management, therapeutic, knowledge-based	Email: info@whosincharge. co.uk Website: www.whosincharge. co.uk
Yuva (Domestic Violence Intervention Programme, DVIP) (London boroughs)	Individual and group; parent and young person; behaviour management training, skills-based, parent and young person empowerment, cognitive behavioural, attachment-focused, systemic	Tel: 020 87418020/07501 722609 Email: dvip.yuva@ richmondfellowship.org.uk Website: https://dvip.org/for-young-people
Family Based Solutions (formerly PAARS) (Enfield)	Group and individual; whole-family approach; solution-focused, peer support	Email: admin@ familybasedsolutions.org.uk Website: https:// familybasedsolutions.org.uk/ paars
Family Lives (previously Parentline)	Online/telephone; families; emotional support, information, advice, forums	Tel: 0808 800 2222 Email: askus@familylives.org. uk Website: www.familylives.org. uk
Children 1st Parentline (Scotland)	Online/telephone; families; emotional support, information, advice, forums	Tel: 0800 028 2233 Email: parentlinescotland@ children1st.org.uk Website: www.children1st. org.uk/help-for-families/ parentline-scotland
Capa First Response CIC	Online; parents, carers, young people and professionals; live web chats, webinars, one-to-one support	Email: info@capauk.org Website: www.capauk.org
PAC-UK	Individual and group; adoptive parents; NVR; therapeutic support	Website: www.pac-uk.org/our-services/cpv

Working with adolescent-to-parent violence and abuse

APVA sits between many policy areas and the responsibilities of practitioners fall across child and adult safeguarding. All practitioners working with children, adolescents and parents need to be alert to the possible indicators of APVA, have an understanding of what they can do in their roles, know who else should be involved and where to go to for further help and advice, and work together with others. Training on APVA needs to be incorporated into training on DVA and child and adult safeguarding. Although the research evidence on best practice is still slim, there is considerable practice-based knowledge that can guide future work. The practice points below draw on the author's research and work with APVA practitioners.

Assessing parent abuse cases

Assessment needs to cover the different risks and contexts for APVA and:

- Identify whether any violence from an adolescent is primarily defensive, in response to victimization by a parent.

- Address some of the other surrounding issues such as education problems, housing and finance and DVA between parents.

Assessment should reflect an ecological and systemic understanding of the issue, considering factors and contexts at the individual, family, school/community and wider societal/cultural levels:

- Individual factors such as trauma and loss, mental health difficulties, substance misuse, and neurodevelopmental disorders.

- Family factors such as quality of communication, domestic violence and abuse, child abuse, financial stresses and strains, approaches to parenting, power dynamics and access to social supports.

- Community factors such as peer violence, bullying and difficulties with school.

- Societal and cultural factors relating to gender, ethnicity, religion and disability.

Once assessment has taken place, the first step is for the family to acknowledge that the abuse is taking place and for the young person to take responsibility for the abuse (Cottrell 2001). It is important to stress, however, that there is no single approach for addressing parent abuse, and the process families go through may differ according to the context of abuse and surrounding difficulties that families may be experiencing concurrently. For practitioners, this means taking an approach that is flexible and adaptive, non-judgemental, and potentially draws on multiple approaches and practitioners with varying expertise in areas such as DVA, trauma, parenting, education and even bereavement.

Working with parent abuse cases
Taking the time to talk

- The most important thing for practitioners to do is to get parents and the family talking about what is going on, taking away the stigma of abuse and getting them to feel comfortable about accepting help.

- Listening to parents' experiences is vital.

- Spending time with families will enable you to build rapport and find out what is happening, the triggers for violence and abuse, how the family communicates with one another and what will work for them. This scoping and rapport-building period cannot be rushed.

Context is key

- Understanding the contexts within which the abuse is taking place is key to understanding *why* it may be taking place.

- Contexts will differ from family to family and may also change over time.

- The behaviour of the young person is the symptom – practitioners need to look behind the behaviour and ask young people what they are feeling and what may have happened to them.

- Rather than looking at what is 'wrong' with the young

person and problematizing them, consider what is going on for them.

Taking a whole-family approach

- Working with the whole family is vital, as the young person is more likely to adhere to family agreements and see the work through if the whole family is behind the process.

- Taking this approach means listening to and understanding the perspectives, experiences and feelings of all family members.

Empowering parents

- Many parents will feel disempowered as a result of the abuse, and will need reminding that they are part of the solution.

- Parents often feel tremendous guilt and feel like it is their fault that the abuse is happening. This is particularly the case in those families with histories of DVA. Working with parents around these feelings of guilt forms a key aspect of support.

Having a flexible approach

- Being flexible in delivery rather than prescriptive is vital. This means tailoring the content of programmes to the needs of families but also understanding that families are often experiencing multiple difficulties. Flexibility may also mean meeting families at times that suit them or meeting the young person at school if they feel more comfortable there. Flexibility is particularly relevant for young people with additional needs such as autism or ADHD where perspective-taking, communication and cognitive abilities may be delayed or impaired.

- Flexibility also means being patient and understanding that families will not always be in a position where they can engage with the support being provided.

The importance of multi-agency working

- Multi-agency working is an important part of supporting families experiencing parent abuse. For example, making schools aware may prevent parents from being penalized for their child's non-attendance and can mean they are able to play a more active role in supporting young people experiencing the issue – for example, by giving them a safe space to sit after they have completed a support session.

- Quite often families will already be in contact with a number of other agencies such as children's social care or youth offending. Talking to other agencies will mean less duplication and fewer contradictory messages for families receiving support.

- However, multi-agency working can sometimes mean having to persuade parents to give their permission for you to speak with other agencies, something that many parents may be nervous of, particularly when involving children's social care. Reassuring parents that sharing with other agencies is to ensure they receive the best support possible is vital.

Final thoughts and further resources

There is still much to learn about APVA. Although research into the issue is multi-disciplinary in nature, including studies from across psychology, criminology, family studies, counselling, child development, sociology and social policy, there are still a number of limitations and gaps in the literature that need to be addressed. One such gap is in the absence of the young person's voice. Although APVA involves both parents and their adolescent children, research is focused almost solely on the experiences of parents and practitioners. If we are to understand and address parent abuse more effectively, the experiences of young people must also be taken into account.

On the following page there are some links to further resources.

Websites

Holes in the Wall is a blog run by professional social worker Helen Bonnick for parents, practitioners and academics, providing updates on research, policy and practice in the area of parent abuse: http://holesinthewall.co.uk

Responding to Child to Parent Violence (RCPV), a pan-European project is a website hosting research and resources relating to the multi-agency research project led by the University of Brighton and funded by the European Union's Daphne III programme. Through the website you can access resources and manuals for practitioners: www.rcpv.eu

Adolescent to Parent Violence is a website developed from the Economic and Social Research Council (ESRC)-funded research project 'Investigating Adolescent Violence towards Parents' led by Dr Rachel Condry at the University of Oxford. The site hosts findings from the project and draws together knowledge and experience of parent abuse from research, policy and practice: www.law.ox.ac.uk/content/adolescent-parent-violence

The SEND VCB Project is a website run by writer, speaker and trainer Yvonne Newbold, hosting resources for parents and practitioners who are dealing with violent and challenging behaviour in children with an additional need: https://yvonnenewbold.com

Online documents

Home Office (2015) *Information Guide: Adolescent to Parent Violence and Abuse (APVA)*. Available at: https://assets.publishing.service.gov.uk/government/uploads/system/uploads/attachment_data/file/732573/APVA.pdf

Dedicated practice books

Bonnick, H. (2019) *Child to Parent Violence and Abuse: A Practitioner's Guide to Working with Families*. Shoreham-by-Sea: Pavilion Publishing and Media.

Holt, A. (2016) *Working with Adolescent Violence and Abuse towards Parents: Approaches and Contexts for Intervention*. Abingdon and New York: Routledge.

Acknowledgments

Particular thanks go to the young people interviewed as part of the thesis project 'Exploring adolescent violence and abuse towards parents: The experiences and perceptions of young people', whose voices are represented within this chapter. Thanks also go to the practitioners and staff of the Respect Young People's Programme (RYPP), whose insights have been key in developing the practice points within this chapter.

References

Agnew, R. and Huguley, S. (1989) 'Adolescent violence toward parents.' *Journal of Marriage and Family 51*, 3, 699–711.

Baker, V. (2021) 'Exploring adolescent violence and abuse towards parents: The experiences and perspectives of young people.' Unpublished doctoral thesis, University of Central Lancashire (UCLan).

Brezina, T. (1999) 'Teenage violence toward parents as an adaptation to family strain: Evidence from a national survey of male adolescents.' *Youth & Society 30*, 4, 416–444.

Browne, K.D. and Hamilton, C.E. (1998) 'Physical violence between young adults and their parents: Associations with a history of child maltreatment.' *Journal of Family Violence 13*, 1, 59–79.

Calvete, E., Orue, I., Gonzalez, Z., Padilla, P., *et al.* (2014) 'Child-to-parent violence in adolescents: The perspectives of the parents, children, and professionals in a sample of Spanish focus group participants.' *Journal of Family Violence 29*, 3, 343–352.

Charles, A.V. (1986) 'Physically abused parents.' *Journal of Family Violence 1*, 4, 343–355.

Condry, R. and Miles, C. (2012) 'Adolescent to parent violence and youth justice in England and Wales.' *Social Policy & Society 11*, 2, 241–250.

Condry, R. and Miles, C. (2014) 'Adolescent to parent violence: Framing and mapping a hidden problem.' *Criminology and Criminal Justice 14*, 3, 257–275.

Cottrell, B. (2001) *Parent Abuse: The Abuse of Parents by Their Teenage Children*. Ottawa: Family Violence Prevention Unit, Health Canada.

Cottrell, B. and Monk, P. (2004) 'Adolescent-to-parent abuse: A qualitative overview of common themes.' *Journal of Family Issues 25*, 8, 1072–1095.

Eckstein, N.J. (2004) 'Emergent issues in families experiencing adolescent-to-parent abuse.' *Western Journal of Communication 68*, 4, 365–388.

Edenborough, M., Jackson, D., Mannix, J. and Wilkes, L.M. (2008) 'Living in the red zone: The experience of child-to-mother violence.' *Child & Family Social Work 13*, 4, 464–473.

Elliott, G., Cunningham, S., Colangelo, M. and Gelles, R. (2011) 'Perceived mattering to the family and physical violence within the family by adolescents.' *Journal of Family Issues 32*, 8, 1007–1029.

Firmin, C. (2019) 'Contextual Safeguarding: Theorising the Contexts of Child Protection and Peer Abuse.' In J. Pearce (ed) *Child Sexual Exploitation: Why Theory Matters* (pp.63–86). Bristol: Policy Press.

Gallagher, E. (2008) *Children's Violence to Parents: A Critical Literature Review*. Melbourne, VIC: Monash University. Available at: www.eddiegallagher.com.au

Harbin, H.T. and Madden, D.J. (1979) 'Battered parents: A new syndrome.' *American Journal of Psychiatry 136*, 10, 1288–1291.

Haw, A. (2010) *Parenting Over Violence: Understanding and Empowering Mothers Affected by Adolescent Violence in the Home*. Perth, WA: The Patricia Giles Centre.

Holt, A. (2009) 'Parent abuse: Some reflections on the adequacy of a youth justice response.' *Internet Journal of Criminology*, 1–9.

Holt, A. (2011) 'The terrorist in my home: Teenagers' violence towards parents – Constructions of parent experiences in public online message boards.' *Child & Family Social Work 16*, 4, 454–463.

Holt, A. (2013) *Adolescent-to-parent Abuse: Current Understandings in Research, Policy and Practice.* Bristol and Chicago, IL: Policy Press.

Holt, A. and Retford, S. (2013) 'Practitioner accounts of responding to parent abuse – A case study in ad hoc delivery, perverse outcomes and a policy silence.' *Child & Family Social Work 18*, 3, 365–374.

Home Office (2015) *Information Guide: Adolescent to Parent Violence and Abuse (APVA).* UK Government. Available at: https://assets.publishing.service.gov.uk/government/uploads/system/uploads/attachment_data/file/732573/APVA.pdf

Howard, J. and Rottem, N. (2008) *It All Starts at Home: Male Adolescent Violence to Mothers: A Research Report.* St Kilda, VIC: Inner South Community Health Service.

Hunter, C., Nixon, J. and Parr, S. (2010) 'Mother abuse: A matter of youth justice, child welfare or domestic violence?' *Journal of Law and Society 37*, 2, 264–284.

Ibabe, I., Jaureguizar, J. and Bentler, P.M. (2013) 'Risk factors for child-to-parent violence.' *Journal of Family Violence 28*, 5, 523–534.

Laporte, L., Jiang, D., Pepler, D.J. and Chamberland, C. (2011) 'The relationship between adolescents' experience of family violence and dating violence.' *Youth and Society 43*, 1, 3–27.

Nixon, J. (2012) 'Practitioners' constructions of parent abuse.' *Social Policy & Society 11*, 2, 229–239.

Pagani, L.S., Tremblay, R.E., Nagin, D., Zoccolillo, M., Vitaro, F. and McDuff, P. (2004) 'Risk factor models for adolescent verbal and physical aggression toward mothers.' *International Journal of Behavioral Development 28*, 6, 528–537.

Pagani, L.S., Tremblay, R.E., Nagin, D., Zoccolillo, M., Vitaro, F. and McDuff, P. (2009) 'Risk factor models for adolescent verbal and physical aggression toward fathers.' *Journal of Family Violence 24*, 173–182.

Parentline Plus (2008) *Aggressive Behaviour in Children: Parents' Experiences and Needs.* Available at: https://app.pelorous.com/public/cms/209/432/256/392/Aggressive%20behaviour%20in%20children%202008.pdf?realName=4XFM9E.pdf

Parentline Plus (2010) *When Family Life Hurts: Family Experience of Aggression in Children.* Available at: www.familylives.org.uk/media_manager/public/209/Documents/Reports/When%20family%20life%20hurts%202010.pdf

Paulson, M.J., Coombs, R.H. and Landsverk, J. (1990) 'Youth who physically assault their parents.' *Journal of Family Violence 5*, 2, 121–133.

Peek, C.W., Fischer, J.L. and Kidwell, J.S. (1985) 'Teenage violence toward parents – A neglected dimension of family violence.' *Journal of Marriage and the Family 47*, 1051–1058.

Selwyn, J. and Meakings, S. (2016) 'Adolescent-to-parent violence in adoptive families.' *British Journal of Social Work 46*, 1224–1240.

Simmons, M., McEwan, T.E., Purcell, R. and Ogloff, J.R.P. (2018) 'Sixty years of child-to-parent abuse research: What we know and where to go.' *Aggression and Violent Behavior 38*, 31–52.

Stewart, M., Burns, A. and Leonard, R. (2007) 'Dark side of the mothering role: Abuse of mothers by adolescent and adult children.' *Sex Roles 56*, 3, 183–191.

Strom, K.J., Warner, T.D., Tichavsky, L. and Zahn, M.A. (2014) 'Policing juveniles: Domestic violence arrest policies, gender, and police response to child–parent violence.' *Crime and Delinquency 60*, 3, 427–450.

Thorley, W. and Coates, A. (2017) *Child-Parent Violence (CPV): An Exploratory Exercise.* Available at: www.academia.edu/30962152/Child_-Parent_Violence_CPV_an_exploratory_exercise

Ulman, A. and Straus, M.A. (2003) 'Violence by children against mothers in relation to violence between parents and corporal punishment by parents.' *Journal of Comparative Family Studies 34*, 41–60.

Wilcox, P. (2012) 'Is parent abuse a form of domestic violence?' *Social Policy & Society 11*, 2, 277–288.

Chapter 10

Concluding Thoughts

Ravi K. Thiara and Lorraine Radford

As importantly noted by Hutchison (2011, p.9), 'You could think of the life course as a path. But note that it is not a straight path; it is a path with both continuities and twists and turns.' This book emphasizes the importance of a lifecourse perspective, with its emphasis on multiple life stages, for understanding and addressing domestic violence and abuse (DVA) across diverse groups. This perspective enables us to understand how life experiences are connected and form a continuum across an entire lifetime and potentially across generations. A lifecourse perspective also helps to focus on the structural and cultural context over time, which crucially creates and shapes differentiated experiences of DVA. Notions of life events, critical periods, turning points, transitions, trajectories or pathways, cumulative effects over time and intergenerational issues are integral to a lifecourse perspective. It recognizes the influence of time, social location, interactions and culture in shaping individual experience of each life stage. An integral aspect of the lifecourse perspective is an understanding that humans are interdependent (through social support and control), and that culture and social institutions shape the pattern of individual lives and pathways (Hutchison 2011, p.10).

The contributors to this book highlight the entangled experiences of DVA across the lifecourse, which shape individual experiences in diverse ways. They bring focus to the challenges and new developments in addressing DVA. Crucially reminding us that DVA affects all groups, many of the chapters point to the complex and intersecting nature of DVA perpetrated and experienced in a multitude of contexts. They remind us that DVA is never a one-off but a pattern of coercive and controlling behaviour, deliberately enacted to ensure compliance, to subjugate and to terrorize. This understanding of the nuanced dynamics of DVA is enhanced further when we consider, alongside individual contexts, the broader structural dynamics within which it occurs. To this end, a number of the contributors underline the importance of an intersectional understanding of survivors' whole lives to take better account of DVA experiences, and the arising needs, as they are mediated through structural inequalities associated with race, gender, class, age, sexuality and disability. These crucially shape how DVA is experienced, perpetrated and responded to and the social–structural constraints that then need to be addressed to end DVA. As well as highlighting the role of context in concrete ways, contributors also point to the ambiguities that can arise when DVA is presented in non-specialist statutory settings. As noted by many, this can be shaped by the ways in which DVA presents, our dominant ideas about various groups and their needs, how safety and protection is defined and by the knowledge and insight of various practitioners.

This book is important in assisting practitioners to address the enduring gaps that remain in our responses to DVA, at both policy and practice levels. Not only do the chapters provide valuable up-to-date knowledge, but also promising practice to guide those with responsibility for protecting victims/survivors. Crucially they underline the importance of a connected multi-faceted and multi-sector approach. As noted across the chapters, key professionals from the police, social care and health are a crucial route to help and assistance for those experiencing DVA in different contexts and across the lifecourse. Indeed, the importance and efficacy of joined-up multi-agency approaches have been emphasized for some time (Harwin, Hague and Malos 1999; Hester and Westmarland 2005; Shepard and Pence 1999). Despite considerable developments in coordinated responses over the last two-and-a-half decades, tightening the system response continues to be a work in progress in many ways. Although services such as the police have improved the ways in which they address DVA, concern about this being 'not good enough', in the face of unacceptable attitudes towards survivors that often serve to marginalize their voice, remains (Myhill and Johnson 2016). As well as such continuing challenges in responses from single agencies, a number of the contributors point to the siloed nature of current responses from key services, and emphasize the urgent need to address this if the journeys and outcomes of many victims/survivors are to be enhanced. Moreover, the foregrounding of coercive control has both opened up spaces for a consideration of the coercion, power and control that marks DVA contexts, but it has also blurred lines for practitioners. Too many times victims/survivors still tell us that professionals did not get it right. This is certainly something to take heed of.

Throughout the book, the importance of a wide range of professionals strengthening their responses to both enduring and changing forms of DVA is urged. Recognizing the centrality of professional knowledge and insight to positive outcomes, recent years have seen an unprecedented development in guiding and supporting professionals to develop their responses to DVA in different settings. Numerous bodies, including the National Institute for Health and Care Excellence (NICE), have produced recommendations and guidance for a wide range of health, social care, police and education staff. Much of these emphasize training to recognize indicators of violence and abuse; to routinely and safely ask about DVA; to undertake risk assessment and safety planning; and to provide information about options (NICE 2014). Those who are not used to speaking about DVA face challenges in processing and giving name to their abuse experiences. This makes it all the more important for professionals to challenge abuse, even when confronted with sophisticated attempts to minimize and/or to justify it. While many professionals show great willingness to help victims of DVA, there continues to be a lack of confidence and understanding among many to have sensitive conversations and respond in helpful ways. The lack of confidence is an area that is identified by many professionals as inhibiting their ability to raise concerns with victims/survivors and to provide positive responses. While a great deal of emphasis has, importantly, been placed on training, it is also the case that training alone does not assure positive encounters for victims/survivors, who frequently place far greater value on being listened to in ways that are non-judgemental and non-blaming where they are made aware of their options and rights.

It is clear from the issues highlighted by the contributors that much more work remains to be done if we are to address the differentiated experiences and consequences of DVA in diverse contexts. Undoubtedly, training on DVA, intersectionality and lifecourse perspectives as well as trauma-informed skills can enable individuals to respond more sensitively to victims/survivors. A joined-up response that resists the reframing of DVA as 'something else' – so services like the police do not victim blame, courts do not force victims/survivors to protect themselves, and services do not turn children or perpetrators into different specialist issues – is also underlined. As many emphasize, beyond professional responses it is our systems that require change. Much more needs to be done to address the structural factors that act as drivers for DVA and indeed violence against women and girls (VAWG) more generally, so that more effort also goes into prevention efforts. Here we can learn from global efforts, such as INSPIRE strategies on violence against children (VAC) and RESPECT strategies on gender-based violence (GBV) (WHO 2016, 2019). Much has been said about policy processes and funding arrangements, which remain fragmented and have to address the connections between DVA and other issues in order to capture the totality of victims/survivors' lived realities, rather than treat them as separate entities. As already noted, even though siloed policy and practice responses endure, these are not helpful for victims/survivors. Instead, change in thinking is needed at the highest level, as DVA requires a more sophisticated response at multiple levels to challenge the established disconnected ways of working.

Specialist DVA-VAWG support services have historically carried a disproportionate responsibility for supporting victims/survivors and continue to be an essential lifeline, despite themselves being victims to wide-ranging cuts under austerity measures. While undergoing some change over the years, such interventions remain central to both protecting and rebuilding lives. The importance of treating the person as a whole and responding to the entirety of individual experiences, rather than a single presenting issue, is repeatedly emphasized by specialist services. Inevitably, as noted by contributors, gaps remain in providing such support and protection to some groups of survivors, who may require more bespoke responses. In order to address existing systemic exclusions, many in this book underscore the importance of specialist interventions that have been crafted in the form of holistic trauma-informed, gender-responsive services over decades of work with women and children. These are considered to better reflect an understanding of the totality of victim/survivor experiences. Not all victims/survivors can access the necessary legal and support provision themselves or indeed, receive positive responses. In the face of inadequate system responses to many, the importance of advocacy from specialist providers to help victims/survivors negotiate their routes through welfare and other support systems has been widely highlighted. As alluded to by a number of contributors, intersectional advocacy, alongside community-based support, as part of a wraparound holistic response is crucially important for those who face multiple disadvantage and constraints in receiving positive responses from support providers (Thiara and Roy 2020). Although austerity and wide-ranging cuts to the very services that are most needed at times of societal upheaval, including during the period of the COVID-19 pandemic, have created tremendous challenges, it is precisely now that greater resourcing is required for existing and innovative interventions to address the newer trajectories in DVA. An investment in addressing diverse perpetration without compromising support to women and children is a clear message of many in this book.

Contributors to the book provide much food for thought for a wide range of professionals. The importance of gender in the perpetration and victimization of DVA is a factor highlighted by many chapters in the book, and while it is now widely accepted that men are also subjected to DVA in different contexts, the preponderance of women as the most commonly victimized remains a fact. This is even more likely to be the case when we consider older and disabled women, for instance, both groups that report more frequent and severe DVA. The importance of a gendered understanding of DVA and gender-responsive interventions is critical to positive and appropriate help and support. Gender-neutral responses do no favours in addressing the gender disproportionality of DVA-VAWG. A recognition that when gender intersects with 'race'/ethnicity and other forms of marginality, this 'deepens' the impact of DVA since structural inequality plays an important role in both experiences of DVA and the options available to victims/survivors, is further urged. A greater recognition and understanding of these complex and intersecting factors would help in assisting those that fear seeking external help.

Addressing DVA requires us to consider inequality and marginality in society that creates the conditions for the continuum of DVA across the lifecourse. Power, control and domination within the relationship and power and oppression within society reproduce the conditions for the perpetuation of violence in victims/survivors' lives. It is this intersectional oppression that we are urged to tackle to address both societal oppression and marginalization and violence in intimate and family lives. Societal and professional framing of DVA as something other than a key form of VAW can be a considerable barrier to appropriate responses and a disservice to survivors. Some of the contributors note that when DVA is reframed as elder abuse or disability hate crime, for instance, with the accompanying notions of dependency, frailty and lack of capacity, this refocuses interventions that limit possibilities for empowerment (see Chapters 5 and 7). It is in these areas that this book and its contributors seek to expand our thinking and actions.

Victims/survivors experience complex and compounded traumas that have wide-reaching consequences for their sense of self and their place in the world. The importance of professional recognition of DVA as trauma-inducing, along with other forms of debility such as racism, disablism and homophobia, is repeatedly underlined. The all-encompassing consequences of DVA point to the need for wide-ranging support services that can offer not only immediate safety and protection and meet physical health needs, but also address the ongoing issues across the lifecourse, such as eroded sense of self and mental health and wellbeing. This is not a 'one size fits all' approach but a differentiated response that recognizes the specific needs and circumstances of diverse groups of DVA victims/survivors and indeed its perpetrators. The importance for practitioners to recognize commonalities and differences in victims/survivors' experiences, so that interventions and responses can be specifically shaped to their situations and lived realities, is repeatedly underscored. There is a rich history of innovative interventions and approaches in the UK that can be drawn from, which is highlighted across the different chapters.

This book importantly contributes to increasing knowledge about under-researched DVA group dimensions, and gives us much to consider. However, there is a further need for longitudinal studies that take greater cognizance of social context to increase our understanding of the true effects of DVA and its trajectories for diverse individuals and groups. We have to expand the time frame for considering effects and evaluating practice impact. As well as more research, however, we need to effectively use and apply the knowledge we have gained to develop new and strengthen existing interventions that seek to allay and address adverse consequences. Similarly, there is a need to close the silos across sectors. In particular, we have to address the under-investment in responding to children's experiences of DVA as an effective way to reduce adversity later in life. Over and above these facets, not only do we have to understand more deeply but to also challenge and change systems of multiple disadvantage and oppression that re/produce DVA and VAWG.

This book advocates for greater knowledge, understanding and sensitivity among practitioners when confronted with those who require their help and support for their experiences of DVA. It is doing this at a time when austerity and cuts to a raft of services have created increasing challenges in meeting needs in appropriate and relevant ways. The need for greater collaboration and partnership working is even more pressing during these difficult times. If we are to tackle the scourge of DVA, this has to be done by all of us, by working together to ensure that those who require help get it to transform their lives.

References

Harwin, N., Hague, G. and Malos, E. (eds) (1999) *The Multi-Agency Approach to Domestic Violence: New Opportunities, Old Challenges.* London: Whiting & Birch.

Hester, M. and Westmarland, N. (2005) *Tackling Domestic Violence: Effective Interventions and Approaches.* Home Office Research Study 290. London: Home Office Research, Development and Statistics Directorate.

Hutchison, E.D. (2011) *Dimensions of Human Behaviour: The Changing Life Course.* Los Angeles, CA: Sage.

Myhill, A. and Johnson, K. (2016) 'Police use of discretion in response to domestic violence.' *Criminology and Criminal Justice 16*, 1, 3–20.

NICE (National Institute for Health and Care Excellence) (2014) *Domestic Violence and Abuse: Multi-Agency Working.* London: NICE.

Shepard, M. and Pence, E. (eds) (1999) *Coordinating Community Responses to Domestic Violence: Lessons from Duluth and Beyond.* Thousand Oaks, CA: Sage.

Thiara, R. and Roy, S. (2020) *Reclaiming Voice: Minoritised Women and Sexual Violence. Key Findings.* London: Imkaan.

WHO (World Health Organization) (2016) *INSPIRE: Seven Strategies for Ending Violence Against Children.* Geneva: WHO.

WHO (2019) *RESPECT Women: Preventing Violence Against Women.* Geneva: WHO.

Contributor Profiles

Victoria Baker's research interests are in the fields of family violence and gender-based violence and harm. She is currently completing her PhD thesis on young people's experiences of adolescent-to-parent abuse at the University of Central Lancashire's Connect Centre for International Research on Violence and Harm. She also works in an associate capacity at the research charity Dartington Service Design Lab, carrying out applied research and service design across the public and third sectors to improve services and support for children and families.

Christine Barter, PhD, is a Professor of Interpersonal Violence Prevention and Co-Director of the Connect Centre for International Research on Interpersonal Violence and Harm, University of Central Lancashire. Her research has predominantly focused on children's and young people's experiences of abuse and violence. She has led on a range of national and international research projects, most recently on exploring young people's experiences and perceptions of abuse and harm in their intimate relationships. She publishes widely in national and international journals and sits on the editorial boards for *Child Abuse Review* and the *Journal of Gender-Based Violence*.

Ruth Bashall is Chief Executive of Stay Safe East, a user-led East-London advocacy organization that supports Deaf and disabled survivors of domestic and sexual violence, hate crime and other human rights abuses. Ruth has been an activist for human rights all her life, as a feminist, LGBTQI, anti-racist and community campaigner, and for the past 30 years as a disability rights advocate. Ruth has trained professionals and activists in the UK and France, including the police, disabled people's organizations and the violence against women and girls (VAWG) sector on disability, hate crime, human rights and on tackling violence against disabled women and girls. Ruth is co-author of *Disabled Women and Domestic Violence – Responding to the Experiences of Survivors* (2012).

Deidre Cartwright, BA, MSc, IDVA is an expert advisor and practitioner with 10 years' experience in the domestic abuse sector. As a qualified independent domestic violence advisor (IDVA), Deidre worked as an advocate for survivors of domestic abuse in East London and Bristol before becoming a Practice Advisor at SafeLives, where she led local authority areas to develop new and innovative approaches to coordinating multi-agency responses to child safeguarding and domestic abuse, particularly for young people experiencing intimate partner violence and abuse. She is now a Development Manager at Standing Together Against Domestic Violence, where she supports local authority areas to develop coordinated housing responses to families at risk of homelessness due to domestic abuse.

John Devaney is Centenary Chair of Social Work at the University of Edinburgh. He has nearly 20 years' experience in social work practice, and his research interests relate to child maltreatment, domestic violence and the impact of adversity across the lifecourse.

Amanda Elwen has worked in the domestic abuse field for 25 years. She is the Founder of The Emily Davison Centre, the first EVAWG Hub in the UK. She is currently the business manager for Paladin, the national stalking advocacy service, and is a Director and Founder of HARV Housing and HARV Domestic Abuse Services. Amanda also sits on the board at Women's Aid national. In 2006, Amanda set up one of the first specialist community-based domestic abuse support services for children and young people of all ages in the UK.

Sarah Fox is a Research Associate within the Substance Use and Associated Behaviours (SUAB) research group based in the Department of Sociology at Manchester Metropolitan University. She was awarded her doctorate in February 2019, which explored the journeys to support among women who experienced co-occurring substance use and domestic abuse victimization. She holds an MSc in Drug and Alcohol Studies from the University of Glasgow, an MSc in Applied Social

Research from Trinity College Dublin and a BA (Hons) in Humanities from Dublin City University. She has professional experience in research and social care including children's support, homelessness and women's services. She has worked as a researcher for a homeless organization, as a support worker in a children's charity, in a homeless organization and a domestic abuse service. Her research with SUAB focuses on women's experiences of substances, using qualitative methodologies, particularly narrative and creative methods.

Aisha K. Gill, PhD, FRSA, CBE, is Professor of Criminology at the University of Roehampton. Her main areas of interest and research focus on health and criminal justice responses to violence against black, minority ethnic and refugee women in the UK, Iraqi Kurdistan, India and Pakistan. She has been involved in addressing the problem of violence against women and girls, 'honour' crimes and forced marriage at the grassroots and activist level for the past 20 years. Her recent publications include articles on crimes related to the murder of women/ femicide, 'honour' killings, coercion and forced marriage, child sexual exploitation and sexual abuse in South Asian/Kurdish and Somali communities, female genital mutilation (FGM), sex-selective abortions, intersectionality and women who kill. In 2019, she was appointed Co-Chair of the End Violence Against Women (EVAW) Coalition.

Jennifer Holly has worked in the violence against women (VAW) sector for over 15 years as a front-line practitioner, mixed-methods researcher and trainer. Over the past decade she has acquired extensive knowledge of developing and delivering services to women affected by experiences of violence and abuse, substance use and mental distress. She is a champion for the creation of services that are trauma-informed and gender-responsive. Her focus is on enabling whole organizational change that supports front-line professionals to implement new practice. Jennifer holds an MSc in Gender and Social Policy from the London School of Economics and a Postgraduate Diploma in Psychology from the University of Derby. She is a qualified trainer.

Elizabeth Martin, PhD, is a Lecturer in Queen's University, Belfast. Her PhD was focused on older women and domestic abuse, and her research interests include the impact of intimate partner violence across the lifecourse and giving a voice to marginalized communities.

262 Working with Domestic Violence and Abuse Across the Lifecourse

Chris Newman is a practice supervisor and consultant to organizations working with perpetrators of domestic violence. He worked as a research psychologist before moving on to specialize in risk assessment, violence prevention and parenting work with those who have used violence in the family.

Lorraine Radford, PhD, MA, is Emeritus Professor of Social Policy and Social Work at the University of Central Lancashire and Co-Founder of the Connect Centre for International Research on Interpersonal Violence and Harm. She has been involved in research, training and campaigning to prevent violence against women and children for over 30 years, working in partnership in the UK and internationally with other researchers, professionals and policy-makers in governmental and non-governmental organizations. Her research and publications include one of the first studies highlighting coercive control, mothering and abusive child contact (with Marianne Hester), the first UK-wide household survey of children's and young people's experiences of violence (while head of research at the NSPCC), and more recent work with UNICEF and Together for Girls on what works to prevent sexual violence against children and young people.

Nicky Stanley is Professor of Social Work at the University of Central Lancashire. She researches on domestic violence, child protection, parental mental health and young people's mental health. She has led numerous international and national research studies, and is involved in training practitioners and students. She has contributed to national guidelines and policy on domestic violence.

Ravi K. Thiara is Associate Professor in Sociology at the University of Warwick, and was previously Director of the Centre for the Study of Safety and Wellbeing (SWELL), which specialized in research on violence against women and children and on marginalized communities. Ravi is a highly experienced and respected researcher who has conducted extensive research at national and international levels. She has an expertise in gender violence and black and minoritized communities, and has carried out research for third sector organizations, the Home Office, numerous local authorities and children's charities. Exploring and theorizing the intersection of major social divisions is central to work on gendered violence. She has published widely and teaches on these issues.

Gurpreet Virdee is a black feminist activist with a strong commitment to challenging and redressing the injustices and inequalities faced by women and girls. Gurpreet has spent the last 25 years working within specialist black and minority-led organizations supporting women and girls who have experienced violence and abuse. Over the last decade, Gurpreet has played a pivotal role in responding to the impact of austerity on the survival and sustainability of violence against women and girls (VAWG) organizations in London through the development of partnerships and consortia, campaigning and lobbying. Gurpreet is currently Co-Director at the Women and Girls Network and a trustee at the End Violence Against Women and Girls (EVAW) Coalition and Race on the Agenda.

Subject Index

Author Index

CPI Antony Rowe
Eastbourne, UK
December 10, 2024